# DARE

## TO BE

# DIFFERENT !
## By
# DAYLE
## SCHEAR
## PSYCHIC

**If you are interested in ordering any future books by Dayle Schear,**
Write to ESP & Me Inc., P. O. Box 172, Zephyr Cove, Nevada 89448, to get on our mailing list.
Soon to be released: **"The Psychic Within."** Read all about missing people, Psychic detective work and how ESP works.
To order more copies of "Dare To Be Different" see back page for order form.

Published by
ESP & Me Inc.,
P. O. Box 172,
Zephyr Cove, Nevada 89448

Book Design by Josie Herr

Library of Congress Cataloging-in-Publication Data
92-72619


SOFT COVER ISBN #0-9633064 - 2 -1
HARD COVER ISBN #0-9633064 - 9 - 9

Printed in the United States of America

July 1992

Best Wishes

Dale Selsa

I GAVE UP MY OLD LIFE
TO BECOME
THE PERSON I AM NOW!
I CHOSE TO BARE MY SOUL
FOR THE SAKE OF
HELPING OTHERS

# CAUTION!

While reading this book, please do not judge me! For I have judged myself. While writing this book, my whole life flashed before my eyes; lessons were learned, compassion was found. I chose to bare my soul for the sake of helping others. The person you will be reading about no longer exists. A new person has emerged.

This book is the culmination of my spiritual growth in the Islands of Hawaii. For without these experiences I wouldn't be the person I am now.

As a Psychic, I have a quest. That quest is to reach out and touch people, to give help to all of mankind. There were many lessons that I learned along the way. I always chose the path of knowledge and in that path I had to experience many things; but the most important lesson I learned—I had to change me first in order to help others.

I am not a saint or a guru, nor do I want to be treated as such. It's time to step down from the pedestal; it's time to let you look into my life. As you open the pages, read carefully, for each and every word that was written took me on a self-search journey. As I faced myself deep within the mirror, the flaws began to appear. One by one I conquered those fears, no matter how much pain and sorrow I put myself through.

I'm not proud of the person I used to be, but I'm pleased to say that person died a long time ago.

# PSYCHIC DAYLE SCHEAR

## TELEVISION APPEARANCES

**Hard Copy Magazine** (National Telecast
and Australian Telecast)
**New Year TV Special** (FUJI-TV Tokyo, Japan-National)
**Hour Magazine** CBS (National Telecast)
**The Late Show** FOX (National Telecast)
**AM San Francisco** KGO-ABC (Regular 1 Year)
**2 At Noon** KTVU (Oakland)
**ESP & You** One Hour Specials (KGMB-CBS, Hawaii, 7 Yrs)
**Your Future** One Hour Special (KGMB-CBS Hawaii)
**Hawaiian Moving Company** (KGMB-CBS Hawaii)
**Anchorage Live** (KIMO-ABC Alaska)
**Good Morning Alaska** (KIMO-ABC Alaska)
**ESP & You** One Hour Special (KIMO-ABC Alaska)
**KHON News** (NBC Hawaii)
**KITV News** (ABC Hawaii)
**Mystical Healing** (Cable 22, Hawaii)
**Daytime Show** (KOLO-ABC Reno)
**KOLO News** (ABC Reno)
**KHBC** (Hilo, Hawaii)
Numerous Telethons (Charities)

## NIGHT CLUBS

**Harrah's** (Lake Tahoe & Reno, Nevada)
**American Hawaii Cruise** (Cruise Ship)
**Holiday Inn** (Waikiki, Hawaii)
**23rd Step** (Hawaii)

## RADIO SHOWS

**21st Century Radio** (Syndicated Nationally);
**KGO, K101, KEST, KALX** (San Francisco);
**KSSK (K59), KGU, KULA, KKUA, KIKI, KCCN,
I-94, KISA, KMVI, KKON, KPUA, KAUI** (Hawaii);
**KOWL, KTHO, KPTL, KLKT,** (Lake Tahoe & Reno);
**KENI** (Alaska); **WWDB** (Philadelphia); **WCBM** (Baltimore)

## ARTICLES/OTHERS

**The Washington Times**
**Honolulu Advertiser**
**Honolulu Star Bulletin**
**Honolulu Magazine**
**Tahoe Tribune**
**Reno Gazettte**

# Acknowledgements

I wish to thank the following people for their encouragement, help, and support: My husband, Blythe; my teacher and mentor, Peter Hurkos, his wife Stephany and daughter Gloria; Doug Bushousen, who hired me for my first nightclub show at Harrah's; Barbara from Side Street Boutique, who supplied all my show clothes for Harrah's; John Parker for my first radio show; Duane Triplett, for my first television special; The whole staff at KGMB (CBS), Richard Grimm, Phil Arnone, Bob Turner, Laura Chee, Anita Brady, etc.; Mark Williams, my director; Michelle Honda and Jamie Oshiro, my asst. producers; Randy Brandt, "Hawaiian Moving Company," for my first television segment in Hawaii; Radio KSSK, Perry and Price; all the television and radio deejays and hosts I worked with, Mark Lennartz, Ken Hunter, Dave Lancaster, etc.; Doug Bruckner; "Hard Copy Magazine"; all the people who helped with my live shows and appearances; special thanks to Dr. Bob and Zoh Hieronimus, 21st Century Radio, Hieronimus & Co., for their endless help; Dr. Joe Dobler, chiropractor, who kept my back in shape while I wrote this book.

Special thanks to Bob, Gene, Gerry, Toni Y., Phil and Esther, Peg, Diane, Dana, Barbara, Alonzo, Jerry, Bernie, and all the players in this book and in my life, past, present and future.

I also wish to thank Mom and Dad, Mother and Father Arakawa, BJ & Fred, Laraine Yamamoto, Dr. Andrija Puharich, Mel Doerr, Beverly Lyons, Arthur Pacheco, Peggy Oshiro, Gloria Lundholm, Jon Young, David and Rachel Glyn, Jackie Newbre, Tom Marr, Phil Giriodi, Stan Souza, Karin Beals, Robert Dore, Chuck Uyeda, Margaret & Ron Aderman, Crissy Kengla, Dale Ogata, Aunt Molly, Donna Shankleton, Gerri Williams, Nita Valdez, Audrey Maider, Ron Bischke from "Hair Salon", Connie Yee, Bob Izabal, Media West.

**Special Thanks** to my editor, **Maybelle Boyd.** As a writer writes and creates special thoughts, feelings pour out from within the heart. Within these special moments a writer's thoughts are locked within the mind till they find their way to the paper without rhyme nor reason. I found on many given occasions I had virtually no one to turn to, to unlock my special feelings until I found Maybelle Boyd. Through her patience and understanding she taught me what it was like to be a writer. My thoughts flowed through her hands as she edited with kindness and understanding every word that I wrote. There are no words to thank someone who has given you so much, for without this very special editor this book would have never been written. The special gift that Maybelle has is always knowing what I was thinking and then being able to make my words sound beautiful and touching. Although there were times my grammar was not quite appropriate, I thank Maybelle for letting me be me. Thank you, Maybelle, for your countless hours, most of which came from your heart.

**Special Thanks** to **Marvin Kooken** of South Lake Tahoe Computer Base. Thanks, Marvin, for your countless hours of computer time, and especially for teaching me how a computer works. If it wasn't for your kindness and relentless hours of patience, this book would have never been handed to my editor, **Maybelle Boyd.**

**Special Thanks** to **Marion** and **Stanley** for always being there when I needed you the most.

**THANK YOU**

This Book Is Dedicated
To My Husband **Blythe Arakawa,**
To All The Wonderful People Of **Hawaii,**
And, Of Course, To Beautiful **Lake Tahoe.**

# DARE TO BE DIFFERENT

## TABLE OF CONTENTS

# TABLE OF CONTENTS

**THE END!**

Some people who appear in my book are presented as composite characters. In order to protect their privacy, the sequence of some events is modified accordingly. However, all the events are true.

# HARRAH'S LAKE TAHOE
## CHAPTER 1

### I GAVE IT ALL UP
### TO BECOME
### THE PERSON I AM NOW

As I look out my window, watching the snow fall ever so gently, time seems to stand still. While I sit here writing my book, I ponder the thought..... How can so many tiny changes alter a person's life so dramatically?

I started flashing back, back in time to try to find some meaning to my life. Where did it all begin?

**Was it all worth it?**

I flashed back to September, the year 1984. Although it seemed like any other day, this day was different. I began driving slowly as I entered the town of Lake Tahoe. The bright **NEON** lights of the casinos kept **Flashing** at me.

Within a mere moment my whole life would change. I was approaching...**MY FANTASY.** There it was, bigger than life! **"PSYCHIC DAYLE SCHEAR."** As I stared at the billboard high above Harrah's Hotel an Casino, the emotional feelings I had seeing my name up in lights for the first time were overwhelming. Although Tom Jones was the headliner, all I could see was my name blaring at me. **THIS WAS MY DEBUT.**

I knew then that fantasies could become a reality. I felt like I was watching one of my favorite old-time movies, "It Should Only Happen To You," starring Jack Lemmon and Judy Holliday. In the movie; Judy Holliday rented several billboards and placed her name on each billboard until she became famous. However, this wasn't a movie, this was real. Within hours I would be on the same stage where some of the greatest performers in history have performed.

I caught myself daydreaming. My thoughts began to fade; reality kicked in. I put the car in drive and went racing home. Fear came rushing over me. The shock of my name in lights was one thing, but performing was another.

## MY DEBUT

The whole day was a blur. Costumes were thrown at me. Make-up artists were practicing their new techniques. I was trying to remain composed thoughout this whole ordeal. The clock was racing. This was my test. If I were to make it, I would receive a signed contract. If I **BOMBED**, it would have been just an audition.

As I approached the hallway of Harrah's, there were two men who showed me to my dressing room. I peeked in rather shyly. The dressing room was enormous. I was overwhelmed.

There sat my co-host, Ken Hunter. "Come in, Dayle," he said. Ken and I go a long way back to my radio days. We aired a local radio show together on KOWL radio in Lake Tahoe for years.

It was approximately two hours before showtime; my nerves were at level nine. The tension was building. However, Ken remained calm.

## SHOW TIME

I was about to face that long walk down the stairs, through the kitchen, through the hallway, toward the stage. It felt like a **DEATH** walk to me.

The people were standing in line; soon the room would be filled to capacity. It seemed as though every local in town must have been there. The curtains were dropped. The lights were low.

Behind the curtain I sat. My feelings were mixed, my emotions were running amok. I wanted to run and hide. Yet this was my audition.

How did I get here anyway? The music started, "Eye in the Sky" by "The Alan Parson's Project." The chatter started to die. The music faded as the audience quieted. I glanced at Ken. There was a calmness about him. Suddenly, Ken turned to me with panic in his voice. "Well, Schear, this is another fine mess you have gotten us into," he said. "It's now or never, Lady. Let's give them one hell of a show."

The curtain rose slowly...

**AND NOW,
LADIES AND GENTLEMEN,
HARRAH'S STATELINE CABARET
IS PROUD
TO PRESENT IN OUR SHOWROOM**

# PSYCHIC
# DAYLE SCHEAR

**FIRST TIME EVER PSYCHIC APPEARS
AT HARRAH'S IN LAKE TAHOE.**

**FIRST TIME EVER PSYCHIC APPEARS
AT HARRAH'S IN RENO.**

**INTRODUCING
PSYCHIC DAYLE SCHEAR.**
*Reno Gazette November 1984*

**KRESKIN'S NOT IN TOWN, BUT
PSYCHIC DAYLE SCHEAR IS.**
*By Mel Scheilds*

**PSYCHIC DAYLE SCHEAR—SHE TRIES TO BE AS
ACCURATE AS POSSIBLE BECAUSE HER ADVICE
HAS AN INFLUENCE ON MANY PEOPLE.**
*Joanna Miller Tahoe Tribune*

**ASTOUNDING PSYCHIC AT
HARRAH'S  CABARET.**
*Gary Dalton Harrah's Press*

## Billboard at Harrah's

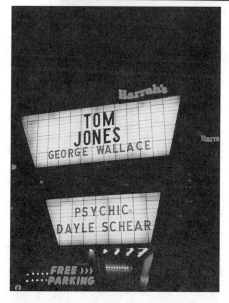

**PSYCHOMETRY** takes center stage at Harrah's Reno and Harrah's Tahoe as local Psychic Dayle Schear continues to astound audiences with her extrasensory gifts. Ms. Schear, scheduled for an indefinite run in the Reno Casino Cabaret on Tuesday nights and the Tahoe Stateline Cabaret on Monday, makes her predictions based on the "vibrations" she receives from a personal object given to her by an audience member. "Using an object I can see into past, present or future" she says. "The object provides the link."

# MY DESTINY
## CHAPTER 2

**August 27, 1984**

I believe that everything in life happens for a reason. There are no coincidences. When I first met Doug Bushousen, he was the head of Harrah's entertainment. We met through a private consultation that he had booked with me. After the consultation, Doug asked if there was anything he could do for me. I politely said, "No."

In August of 1984, I happened to run into Doug once again at the Stateline Post Office. Such a meeting is not at all uncommon in a small town of approximately 25,000 people. Doug invited me to his office to chit-chat for an hour or so. I accepted.

It was then an idea hit me. I wanted to bring to Doug's attention a group that I had been working closely with in Hawaii. The group was called "Bernadette and the Sunshine Company."

Bernadette is a very close friend of mine. She has a sensational voice. The whole point of my meeting with Doug was to try to book Bernadette at Harrah's in Lake Tahoe.

When I met with Doug, he asked me how my career was going. I explained to him that I had a radio show and a nightclub act at the Holiday Inn in Waikiki. I was the opening act for Bernadette. I pulled out a cassette tape that I brought along with me, and asked Doug if he would mind listening to it. He listened politely and seemed to enjoy Bernadette's voice.

I noticed Doug's eyes and face began to light up; he had the most unusual expression upon his face. Suddenly, he blurted out, "Dayle, how about an audition at Harrah's?"

"Audition for me?" I couldn't believe what I was hearing.

"Yes, you! If you do well, we'll consider hiring you for the whole winter."

I was perplexed. I had come into the office to pitch Bernie and here I was walking out of the office with a possible job. I didn't have a show put together, nor did I have a clue as to what I would do. I remember leaving the office dazed.

Later, fate took a turn again. Doug asked me what I would need in the way of a salary and was surprised when I said a thousand dollars per show. He thought, when he offered me the position, that since I was just starting out, I would do it for practically nothing. He offered me $350 a week to work on the off-nights, Monday and Tuesday. I knew it was too good to be true, but I also knew I would have to turn it down.

My pride was in the way. I remember telling Doug I made more money doing readings. I did not need the stress of a show for the same amount of money. I left and went home and cried. My big break was over even before it had begun.

Two days later Doug called me. "Okay, you win. I'll give you seven hundred fifty to start; and if you make it, you'll get your thousand dollars a show. You drive a hard bargain, Lady." He then added, "You have one week to put your show together for your audition."

I prayed a lot during that week. I began asking for the help of anyone at Harrah's. Much to my surprise, the second in charge of entertainment, Bob McLure, came to my aid.

Bob had a background in television and showroom. He was the one who devised my stage show for me. This was unheard of in the nightclub industry. Usually, you have an agent pitching for you and a show ready to go. Yet, I had neither. Deep in their hearts the people at Harrah's really wanted my show to work. Till this day I thank them for giving me the exposure and having enough faith in me to make that happen.

My next step was to get a co-host. I called one of my favorite deejays, Ken Hunter. I don't know how we did it, but we managed to put the show together within the allotted time.

Our show was a hit from October through December 31, 1984. We brought in record crowds for our time slot. We appeared on the off-nights, every Monday in Lake Tahoe and every Tuesday at Harrah's in Reno. Doug had us working in the middle of winter in Reno, mainly to draw the locals into the show. The one thing that stands out in my mind is that at least we never disappointed Doug. The locals were very supportive.

All things must end, however, and might I add we had a great ending. It was a wonderful three-month run. Against all odds we made it. Shortly after that, my need to appear in nightclubs dwindled.

I didn't feel I was helping mankind. I felt what I did in the nightclubs was too much of an act. That was not what I wanted out of life. I really wanted to help people.

Working at Harrah's taught me many new and different things about life. It taught me how to handle an audience. It taught me how to deal with skeptics and how to handle a rough crowd. It was one of the most unique experiences I could ever wish for. Mostly, I learned something very important about myself. I learned I was not happy just doing a show. It seemed so shallow.

In my business as a Psychic, the utmost importance is placed on the clients and in helping them to one's fullest extent. Almost nothing is withheld from the client in a reading.

On the other hand, I found out that when you work in nightclubs, you are simply entertaining and working the audience. You tend to just plain show off. That wasn't for me. My desire to help mankind was overwhelming; I realized I had to follow my quest. In that quest I was learning how to help myself.

I searched my soul to find out what I truly needed in this life. I remember wondering, every time I was on stage at Harrah's, how I could help someone. I began to ask myself, "What am I doing here? What is my purpose? **HOW LONG HAS IT BEEN SINCE I'VE BEEN HAPPY?**"

**I started flashing back, back in time. Back through my past. My thoughts were racing at an incredible speed. I flashed back to 1962, to when I first laid eyes on my husband. I remembered how poor and extremely happy we once were.**

# THE MARRYING YEARS
## CHAPTER 3

The year was 1962, just before the Vietnam war; John F. Kennedy was President. My family and I had just moved from West New York, New Jersey. Mom, Dad, and I were living in a suburb of Los Angeles called Baldwin Hills. In the 1960's Baldwin Hills in the Crenshaw district was renowned for several reasons. For one, its dam collapsed during the 1960's and made national headlines. For another, Baldwin Hills became one of L.A.'s first integrated areas. And a number of famous personalities came from the Crenshaw district, including Michael Landon, Marilyn McCoo, a long time friend in those days, and, of course, Bill Cosby.

Our family lived in the low-income housing section of this elite area. I attended Dorsey High, one of the roughest schools in L.A. I didn't have many friends since I was so new to the area.

However, I remember one neighbor and friend who changed my life. He was **Jerry Nisker**, an extremely handsome fellow with green eyes, jet-black hair, and a fantastic personality. Jerry had a desire to be connected with the police department or the military. He always drove around with a CB radio and camera in his two-tone '57 Chevy, in the event there might be a disaster on the road. If there were, he would take a picture of it to sell to the local newspaper.

One hot summer afternoon as I sat comfortably on my lawn enjoying the beautiful sunshine and studying for an upcoming exam, I noticed a very handsome young man in a green Austin Healey Sprite drive by. He stopped the car and looked in my direction. My neighbor Jerry seemed to know him and went over to speak to him. My eyes were glued to the car and the handsome fellow in it. I thought, "My god, my dream has come true."

My dream turned out to be Jerry's best friend, Bob. Jerry introduced us briefly to each other. After a shy "Hello," Bob asked me if I were new to the neighborhood. When he found out I was, he said, "Maybe we could get together sometime." The introduction was completed. Destiny played its hand and my whole life would be changed.

To describe Bob... he was a cross between George Hamilton and Tony Perkins. He stood about six feet tall. I was a tiny little thing: five-foot-two, ninety-eight pounds, blonde and SEXY.

That special day when I first laid eyes on Bob and when Jerry introduced us, I knew that I would marry him someday. It was an exclusive feeling, call it Psychic, or intuitive, whatever; I knew he was mine.

Bob was a sweet, kind, and very loving individual. We had everything in the world in common, including the fact that both our parents were off the wall (**crazy**). We came from the same ethnic background and our families were poor.

Bob's family, which included his brother Steve and sister Susan, as well as his parents, came from the Bronx in N.Y. Bob was his parents' prize possession, their only hope for a meal ticket out of the slums. They wanted him to marry wealthy, a rich debutante, someone I was not. But we were matched so perfectly for each other.

In the two years we went together, we never left each other's side; we virtually did everything together. We were two lost souls on this planet, trying to band together in the face of adversity.

The Vietnam conflict was just breaking out; times were uncertain. Bob wanted to choose a branch of military service before one chose him, so he joined the Navy. After six weeks in boot camp, he injured his right knee. Although the fighting was starting to escalate, he somehow managed to receive an honorable discharge from the Navy. But as the war in Vietnam escalated, we knew he might be drafted anyway. We were right; the Army tried to draft him. Bob appealed and won. We soon heard that some of our friends were coming home in coffins.

A few months before President Kennedy was assassinated, a law went into effect, for one year only, which exempted people from the draft if they were married, attending college full-time, or the sole support of their familes. Since Bob and I were planning to marry later that year anyway, we decided to move up our wedding date. By now, Vietnam was a full-scaled war. We married in June. I was 18 and he was 21.

I remember our wedding day well. We were married by a justice of the peace in L.A. I recall shaking all through the ceremony. We were too poor to afford a hotel room for our honeymoon, so we moved directly into our one-bedroom apartment.

The apartment was dingy and the blue plastic furnishings were falling apart. We could barely afford the rent of one hundred dollars a month. But it didn't matter at times, because I was so much in love with him.

In those days I worked as a telephone operator for Ma Bell and

Bob was a photographer for the Unimart store chain. For the most part, Bob and I were always struggling. There was a point when we both had lost our jobs, and we were ready to live with our parents. Times were tough; we couldn't afford to pay the rent much longer.

Now, you have to understand that our worst nightmare was yet to happen. We had vowed never to go back to our parents because their lifestyles were totally unacceptable to us. We both came from dysfunctional families. Our main goal in life was to feed ourselves on a regular basis, and to become self-supporting. As Scarlett O'Hara once said to Rhett Butler, "As God is my witness, I will never go hungry again."

We had this special love for each other; the bond was incredible. As the years passed, I wanted a child so badly. We tried to no avail to have children; Bob was sterile. It was heartbreaking. I wanted a child more than anything else in the world and thought of adoption. But as the years went by, we became the children to ourselves. That was the period in both our lives when we grew together at a rapid pace. Throughout our marriage we kept no secrets from each other; we were honest with each other.

I told Bob about my Psychic ability, that it was a genetic factor and ran within my family. On many occasions Bob found this ability difficult to understand. He was very logical; I was very emotional.

One day I saw my first deck of Tarot cards in a magic shop in Hollywood. I took them home, treating the cards as if they were some kind of treasure with hidden meanings. I started experimenting with the cards on my friends and family. Much to Bob's surprise and mine, almost everything I told anyone came true. That was the start of my recognizing the true extent of my Psychic ability.

I spoke of car wrecks, airplane crashes, all kinds of gruesome things. These events were unfolding right before my eyes. Bob started to take notice. Within a split moment, a flash of reality, the realization came upon him. Especially when I began predicting events about his family that would eventually come true. Maybe I wasn't making up these stories, so he thought. Maybe they weren't coincidences after all. As much as he didn't want to believe in my visions, they were too overwhelming not to believe them.

During our vacation in the Hawaiian Islands, Bob became a total believer. Our friends Sue and Jack joined us and off we went to the Reno airport. The vacation would turn out to be more of a nightmare for us.

The United Airlines flight from San Francisco to Honolulu was smooth; it was clear sailing all the way. But, when we landed in Honolulu, it happened to be Hawaii's rainy season. It poured. This was not the usual rain that anyone would have expected. It was the monsoons! It rained and rained. It rained so hard, we were confined to our rooms for ten long days. I must admit we had fun anyway; there were other things to do, although catching a little bit of sun wasn't one of them. Of course, on the day we were to leave the islands, the sun came out. It was time to go home. Then, the series of bizarre events began.

## SKEPTICS, BEWARE!

The four of us had an enjoyable flight back to San Francisco. The flight was beautiful and, as we arrived at the airport, we were all glad to be going home. Except for one thing; it was raining.

**HERE WE GO AGAIN!**

I was beginning to feel uneasy about the flight to Reno. I remember that Sue was picking up her daughter in San Francisco, and her ex-husband had made a special trip to the airport to deliver the little girl to us. We were just one hour away by plane from Reno.

We boarded a Pacific Southwest Airline plane. I sat down; buckled my seat belt. Suddenly, I turned and stared at Bob. I had a knowing sensation, and I reacted: **"GET ME OFF THIS PLANE NOW! THIS PLANE IS NOT SAFE. WE'RE NOT GOING TO MAKE IT TO RENO."** Everyone turned to stare at me now. I guess I was creating a scene.

Bob said to me, "Don't be silly. It's just your fear of flying." Then he shouted, *"Stop with the Psychic mumbo-jumbo!* Sit down and buckle up again."

I did not leave the plane. I wanted to make a point—I think. Maybe I was crazy; maybe not. The plane took off. It was a scene out of "Casablanca." The turbulence was incredible; the rain, horrendous. Out of the corner of my eye I saw Bob reaching for his barf bag.

Then, five minutes from Reno, the unexpected happened! Lightning struck the plane. The cabin lights went out. We were flying through the storm on one engine.

I heard the pilot's voice over the loudspeaker. He spoke firmly, but I could sense that he was as shaken up as everyone else. "Sorry, folks. We're not going to make it to Reno. We have severe engine damage. Even though we're just five minutes out of Reno, we are advised not to land. The control tower has advised me that we do not have ample mechanics in Reno at this time. We will be turning the plane around and heading back to the San Francisco airport."

The flight attendant sat beside me for just a moment. "I guess we should have believed in what you said when you boarded the plane," she said. "Are you Psychic or something?" When I replied, "Yes," she grabbed her cross and asked,"Are we going to make it?"

I paused to gather my thoughts before answering her. I glanced across the aisle at Sue's little girl sleeping so peacefully. Visions of her future flashed before me. I turned back to the flight attendant and reassured her,"We'll make it. Don't worry." The one thing that always rings true is that if you can see a person's future, **THEN THERE IS ONE.** I knew we would all be safe.

And land we did, safely. We finally made it. Ambulances surrounded the plane. I remember the pilot saying at this point, "We will only be an hour or so. If you would like to re-board, please remain seated."

"I don't think so," I muttered to myself.

Bob left the plane first at record speed. I said sarcastically, "Why are you rushing now, Dummy? The plane landed safely." He gave me a strange look.

Bob was determined to make it back to Tahoe that same night. I pleaded with him to stay just one more night in San Francisco. I knew if we started off fresh the next morning, everything would be fine.

For some strange reason, Bob decided that we should rent a car and try our luck. **HERE WE GO AGAIN. I WAS MARRIED TO A MAN WHO WAS TRYING TO KILL ME!** To say that Bob was determined to make it to Tahoe is a gross understatement.

As I look back on that day, I think I must have been crazy to get into the car with a **MANIAC.** There was a blizzard on the way to Tahoe. After already spending a total of nine hours in the air and in delays, we were now facing treacherous conditions on the road. We inched our way to Tahoe through the blizzard, our eyes peeled to the road, trying to see through all that snow. What normally would have been a four-hour drive to reach home took us twenty-four hours. We were so, so lucky. I was convinced God must have greater plans for me.

**NOT EVEN PSA WOULD FLY AGAIN THAT NIGHT. ONLY BOB, DAYLE, SUE, JACK, AND CHILD WERE TRAVELING THE ROAD OF THE TWILIGHT ZONE.**

We finally made it to Tahoe, only to realize that we had no luggage. Our bags had been left on the plane to Reno. So off we went to Reno early the next morning. Not even a good night's sleep was to be had.

By now you may be wondering why I stayed married to a man like that. I didn't know; I wondered myself. Yet, shortly after our wild and crazy life-shaking trip, Bob never again questioned my Psychic ability.

To be able to turn a **SKEPTIC** like Bob into a total believer is a feat in itself. It always happens that way, you know. People don't want to believe in anything that they can't feel, see, or touch. We tend to live in our own worlds. It seems to me that innovators throughout history were all deemed crazy at one time or another: people like the Wright Brothers, Edison, and the men who landed on the moon.

Just because we do not understand something doesn't mean it can't exist. It means we have to be knowledgeable and try to learn more about the subject. Just maybe there is more out there than we can imagine, more than meets the eye.

The epitome of stupidity is the person who speaks unkindly of a subject that he knows nothing about.

Extra-sensory perception, ESP, is one of those subjects. We need to study the field to understand why it works, not how it works. We need to study the emotional impact behind ESP. Only then will we gain the proper knowledge of something that is so precious. When we learn "there is nothing to fear but fear itself," that knowledge alone just may open doors to many new and wonderful things in the future.

**There comes a time when a person has to try to understand what he fears the most. At least, that is what Bob found out. It was mind-boggling for him and at times he couldn't put his finger on it. Yet, I proved to him repeatedly, through hundreds of clients and friends, that ESP is real. I must admit that Bob did try to understand how it works and why it works. He knew that it was something he could not ignore!**

# FRIDAY THE 13TH
## CHAPTER 4

Bob and I were happily married for fifteen years. Early in the 1960's, I recall it was the second year of our marriage, something happened that **DEVASTATED ME** and changed my whole life. The day was **FRIDAY THE 13TH.**

I will never forget that day. It was early in the morning, my car refused to start and I was forced to ride the bus to work. That afternoon I got fired from my part-time job. My choices were limited in the job market, and the day grew ever so long. Time passed slowly on the long bus ride home.

Once home, I tried my car again. It started. I was happy that something had gone right that day. As I prepared to leave to pick up Bob at his workplace, the phone rang.

Toni Gold was on the line. She spoke with extreme urgency. "Dayle, please come to my house right away. Something terrible has happened. I can't talk about this on the phone." I immediately got in my car and drove directly to her apartment.

Toni was my best friend. We attended junior high and senior high school together, played together, and enjoyed a close friendship for many years.

When I arrived at Toni's apartment, she had tears in her eyes. "What's wrong?" I asked. I thought someone had died.

I was shocked by her answer. She blurted out, "Dayle, your

husband violated me sexually!" I didn't hear another word she said; her voice faded as I thought back over the day's events. It really was **FRIDAY THE 13TH.** What more could happen? I felt numb all over. Then Toni's voice ricocheted me back to reality. "Well, what do you think about what I've told you?"

"I can't think right now," I said, keeping my voice as steady as I could. "I'll have to check with Bob and see what he has to say." I walked out of her apartment.

Toni was now shouting, "Well, aren't you going to get a divorce?" THE GIRL HAD A LOT OF CLASS.

My head began to spin as I walked to my car. I knew Toni wouldn't lie. On the other hand, I also knew Bob wouldn't do this to me. How was I going to handle it? I searched for the answer. Toni was accusing the man I loved. Our sex life was great. Why would he do this to me? This couldn't be happening. But maybe it could. After all, it was **FRIDAY THE 13TH.**

I drove to the Unimart where Bob worked and waited patiently until his shift in the camera department ended. He greeted me as if nothing was wrong. I informed Bob that I had just left Toni's apartment. I asked him straightforwardly, "Is it true what she told me about you?"

He seemed to know what I was referring to. "Not quite," he replied. He explained that Toni had called him about something that needed repair in her apartment. Could he fix it? When he arrived at her apartment, she met him in a see-through nightgown. Toni wanted him badly. Both were tempted; there seemed to be a mutual agreement between them.

Bob said he felt terrible about the incident. "It was awful. I made a mistake." He begged me to forgive him.

"Why did you do this to me?" I demanded an answer.

"Do you want the truth?"

"Yes!" I screamed.

"You were the only woman I've ever had sexually," he said. "I was curious what someone else would be like." Bob then assured me he would never do that again; he never wanted to hurt me. I would have to trust and believe him now.

My stomach began to churn. I believed marriage was forever. I cried, "You just don't do these things, **Especially with your wife's best friend!**" It hurt like hell. The pain went much deeper than anything I had ever experienced.

There wasn't enough screaming or crying in the world to make me feel any better at that moment. I decided then that nothing could ever be the same between us again. I would never trust him again. Once that trust was lost, so was our marriage.

I felt my whole world caving in on me. I told Bob, point-blank, I was leaving him. I packed some clothes and drove to my friend Linda's. I needed to talk to someone. Linda and I had gone to school together and she knew of Toni Gold.

When she heard what I had just been through, Linda ordered me to leave Bob permanently. She said I could move in with her and her family for a while if I wanted to. I listened to her every word. "Once a cheat, Dayle, always a cheat." I cried and cried.

I was crying when Linda's mother entered the room and asked what happened. I told her everything. She asked me, "Do you still love him?"

I sobbed, "Yes."

"Then go back to him and give him another chance," she said. "Everyone makes mistakes."

Linda's mom was right. I went home to Bob. It was the first time I ever saw him cry and beg me to stay. I still loved him and hoped I could trust him in the future.

I decided to stay. In the back of my mind I knew that somehow, someday, I would make him feel the pain I felt. I wanted him to understand the agony I was going through; it was not something one took lightly.

But I was anxious to deal with Toni now. I had just begun.

I stormed to her apartment and literally busted down the door. Toni and her husband were dining in the bedroom; they invited me in. I confronted Toni angrily. "Toni, I checked with the neighbors. There were no screams from your apartment. Why didn't you call the police if you felt violated?" Her answer was "I don't know."

I lashed into her for the terrible thing she did. Furthermore, I told her, I was not divorcing Bob. I would see this through. I warned her never to show her face around me again or a fate worse than death would come upon her. By now I was livid. I mustered all the Psychic powers within me:

**You, Toni Gold, are stricken from my memory, never to be seen again. I wish all the bad upon you for many lifetimes to come. Toni Gold, with God as my witness this surely will come to pass.**

She then had the audacity to ask, "But, Dayle, can't we still be friends?"

I cursed her all the way home.

Later that evening, I went back to Bob. For two long years I would have nightmares about his affair. I would wake up in the middle of the night, screaming with anguish. I was furious with Bob. **His one mistake brought us a lifetime of pain.** I often asked myself why I would not seek help to learn to forgive him. It seemed it just wasn't in my makcup.

I remembered when I was a child my mother loved my father so much; yet, he was a womanizer. The lonely nights my mother spent crying, her pain and suffering, were embedded in my mind. I never wanted to go through what she did. But now I was reliving all that pain. My mother always felt "marriage" was a sacred word and one should keep one's promise to God. I felt the same way. Life with Bob was now different.

**My thoughts drifted back in time to the greatest love of my life, well before Bob came along. They drifted back to The Entertainer and all the chances I had to cheat on Bob but never would because I was married.**

**BUT MAYBE, JUST MAYBE, NOW IT WAS MY TURN!**

# THE ENTERTAINER
## CHAPTER 5

**"YES, SHIRLEY MACLAINE, THERE IS ANOTHER GERRY"**

The story I am about to tell you is true. The names and dates have been changed to protect the innocent and, above all, to avoid harming, hurting, or embarrassing anyone.

The year was 1960, long before my husband Bob entered the picture. In a small town where my parents and I lived at one time, Lakewood, New Jersey, we had an electrical fire. Our house went up in flames and burned down to the ground. We were homeless. To make matters worse, Dad was now unemployed due to the fire. My aunt and uncle in West New York, New Jersey, were so kind to take us in and give us shelter.

There wasn't much for me to do in this strange new town. It was just another neighborhood for me. If I were to count all the places and schools I went to within a six-year period, they would add up to thirteen. Purely out of boredom, my favorite pastime was watching television.

One afternoon about four o'clock, after finishing my home-work, I turned on the television. My eyes began to focus. There was a man hosting a new game show. He was so handsome, I became mesmerized. I didn't know what it was about him that was so special, but I couldn't take my eyes off him. What more can I say!

## AT THAT MOMENT MY FIRST REAL CRUSH BEGAN!

Who was this man? I felt as if I were being pulled right into the TV set. I somehow already knew him and everything about him. *Deja vu*? I had to meet him; he was everything I wanted in a man. I had a sense about this person I was watching on TV. I knew in my heart that somehow, in some way, I would meet him.

## DESTINY BEGAN TO PLAY HER HAND!

I was attending high school and well on my way to being an honor student in drama. When my teacher noticed my love for the theater, she handed me some passes for the TV show "In The Heart Of It," filmed live in New York City. I was thrilled! I had never been to a live taping of a television show before. My assignment was to write a report for the class on the show's production.

I asked some of my friends if they would like to go with me into New York, but no one was interested. So off I went by bus through the Lincoln Tunnel to uptown New York by myself. I walked from the Port of Authority to West 52nd Street, where the tickets stated the show would be. As I passed the street numbers, to the right of me out of the corner of my eyes I saw in big bright lights.....

## "THE GERRY TURNER SHOW."

I stopped! Right in the middle of the block. That was him, the man I wanted to meet. Gerry Turner. I ran to the lobby of the studio and asked hopefully for a ticket to the show.

**FATE AGAIN PLAYED A ROLE IN MY LIFE**. Ticket in hand, I waited patiently in line for well over an hour. It didn't matter to me. I had to see him!

Suddenly, there he was, walking out of a restaurant on his way to his show. As he approached me, I became speechless. My knees buckled. I was well on my way to passing out. I remember I was the only person standing in line. I think Gerry took pity on me. He walked over slowly and I thought I would die! He said, "Hi, my name is Gerry Turner. What's your name?" I think I answered. He asked, "Why are you waiting in line so early? Would you like to come in and have a seat?" Would I!

## THIS WAS THE BEGINNING OF A BEAUTIFUL FRIENDSHIP.

I took notes while I watched the entire show. He was wonderful. Deep inside I knew now that I was meant to meet him.

Back in school, I reported my experiences to the class. I said to my teacher, "I hope you didn't mind that I chose to go to a different show. I found the Gerry Turner show to be far more interesting." She was glad that I had enjoyed myself and gave me an A-Plus on my report.

From then on, every day after school I took the long bus ride into New York to see Gerry in his show. As time went by, Gerry spoke to me more frequently. We became friends. I don't think he knew that I had a maddening crush on him. But maybe he did.

I dug around for any information I could find out about his personal life. I learned he was about 37 years old, had two children, and was in the process of getting a divorce. I also learned he was drinking quite heavily in those days. I found myself very attracted to him and I wanted to help him.

Six months later, Gerry and I had become quite close. To Gerry I was probably the daughter he never had. Gerry was my first real love in my mind. I was just a teenager entering the beginning stages of my sexuality.

I studied Gerry in every detail whenever we were together. We occasionally took long walks together through the city and held lengthy conversations. Gerry was always polite, and he never in any way behaved in an unkindly manner. He gave me a beautiful gift, a new name. He called me "Little One."

If ever I had any problems in my life, Gerry was always there. If I needed help with my schoolwork, Gerry was there. In contrast, my parents were never around or were always fighting. Besides, I didn't think they ever cared.

Gerry had a girlfriend, Tess, one of many to whom he introduced me. Somehow, it didn't bother me. I knew the relationship I had with him was different. He was a father and friend wrapped into one, someone who taught me right from wrong.

The difference of over twenty years in our ages never mattered to me. I was determined never to give up on this man; he was so very kind. I knew I had been born too late, but I could wait. Eventually time would be on my side. Gerry would wait for me to grow up. I just knew it.

Gerry's talent was unique, and he appeared on network television more frequently. I knew he would be mega-famous someday; he had all the signs of greatness.

One hot summer day, during a long walk in uptown New York, Gerry confessed his weakness for blondes. I was born a blonde, but over the years my hair had turned a dishwater light brown. So later that afternoon at home, I decided to lighten my hair with peroxide. Unfortunately, instead of blond, my hair turned orange. What a dilemma! PANIC! What was I going to do?

Just then my mother walked in. She about had a cow when she saw my orange hair. **"What did you do to your hair?"** she screeched. "Come here. I guess we'll have to bleach your hair out and make it blond." Within hours I had long, beautiful blond hair.

My new hair color was SEXY. I even looked older. I couldn't wait to show Gerry; I knew he would love it.

After school the next day, I headed to the television studio with a scarf covering my hair. I was too shy and embarrassed to face Gerry. After all, in those days if you bleached your hair, you were considered "fast and easy." In my case, it was accidental, almost!

For a brief moment I forgot all about my hair when I saw Gerry leave the restaurant and walk toward me. "Hi, Little One," he said. He stared into my eyes as he slowly pulled the scarf from my blond hair. "It's beautiful!" he exclaimed. "Your hair is beautiful. Don't EVER change it!"

I heard him mumble, "Someday, when you grow up... When you grow up... I just can't wait." I never knew then what he meant by that remark, but years later I found out.

In the two-and-a-half years we saw each other, he never touched me in a sexual way. I was always doing something unusual to attract his attention. The feeling I had for him grew deeper. It began to affect my schoolwork. I couldn't eat or sleep. I caught myself daydreaming on many occasions. I just wanted to be with him, no matter what the price.

I told a few close friends about Gerry. They were all very supportive of me. Vicky, who was an aspiring young actress, took a special interest in my case. She said, "Dayle, maybe you would look older if you smoked. Gerry might notice you more." Not a bad idea.

The next day in New York, we decided to test out this theory. Mind you, I had never picked up a cigarette before in my life. Vicky handed me a pack and said, "When you see Gerry, ask him to light your cigarette." I did just that.

Gerry played right into my hands. When he approached me I

took a cigarette from my purse and nervously put it between my lips. I was shaking. I asked Gerry for a light. He stared at me but said nothing as he lit my cigarette. I inhaled slowly, trying to look sophisticated. Then I started coughing uncontrollably.

I learned then that Gerry had a temper. He grabbed the cigarette from my mouth and threw it on the ground. He emptied my purse of all the cigarettes I had left. "If I ever catch you smoking around me again...!" He never finished his sentence, but walked away abruptly. He just kept shaking his head in disgust.

He must really care about me, I thought, or my smoking wouldn't have bothered him. Vicky, who was much older than I, said, "I guess you must be getting to him. He's beginning to show his true colors."

Gerry had one unusual trait. When he saw something he wanted, he would claim it for himself and never stop until he got it.

Later that evening, long after Gerry's show was over, Vicky and I went to Lindy's Restaurant. We had some extra money and wanted to try some of Lindy's "World Famous Cheesecake." Vicky and I both ordered cheesecake and a drink. (In the 1960's I carried a phony ID.)

Our conversation somehow led to my virginity and how it would be nice if Gerry was my "first." There was only one problem. I had little or no sex education, so I didn't understand what a virgin was. But I was game!

Vicky excused herself and went to the ladies' room. When she returned to our table, she said, "Dayle, you'll never guess who's at the bar. It's Gerry. He has two or three girls hanging all over him."

I didn't expect this. It was 10 p.m. and Gerry should have been home. Besides, after the lecture he gave me earlier today, I didn't want him to see me at all. I said to Vicky, "Let's get out of here." We paid our check and headed for the door. Gerry happened to turn at the bar and out of the corner of his eye he nailed me.

He flat out left the women at the bar and started toward me, shouting, "Hey, Little One... Little One. What are you doing out so late?" Gerry had one too many drinks. He walked up and put his arms around me. He wasn't about to let me go. This was too good to be true.

I realized I had a cigarette in my hand and I tried to hide it. But Gerry found it by accident while holding me. He began to scream at me. He yelled at me in the middle of this classy restaurant, "Didn't I tell you not to smoke!" He grabbed the cigarette from my hand, threw it down, and ground the lit cigarette into the red velvet carpet. He held me so tightly. He didn't want to let me go.

Gerry immediately forgot about my cigarette and began introducing me to everyone. "I want you to meet my girl," he said, as he held on to me for dear life. He was kissing me ever so gently. I knew the liquor was talking. Or maybe it wasn't.

Lucky for me, Gerry's friend Don was with him. He stepped in to help and managed to break Gerry's bear hug. As he escorted me away from Gerry, Don apologized for Gerry's behavior. "Please excuse Gerry tonight. He had a little too much to drink." Don asked me to forgive Gerry for making a scene and offered to pay for a cab so I could go home. His job was to protect Gerry and, besides, I was **jail bait**.

Vicky, however, wanted me to be with Gerry. We went to the ladies' room of a nearby hotel, and she dolled me up. The girl was preparing me for Gerry. **This would be the night! goodbye, virginity!**

We walked back to Lindy's just in time to see Gerry reluctantly getting into a cab with Don.

The door attendant asked me if my name was "Little One." When I replied "Yes," he said, "Gerry was looking all over for you. He wanted to take you home with him."

**OH!** There went my chance.

The next day, Friday, I decided to grab a quick bite to eat before Gerry's show went on. I stopped at a diner near the studio. I noticed Gerry walking outside the restaurant toward me. I picked up the menu and held it up high so Gerry couldn't see me. I hoped he would go away; I was still shy and embarrassed after that scene at Lindy's. When I pulled the menu down, there was Gerry staring at me through the plateglass window, making funny faces, smiling and waving to catch my attention. I felt so embarrassed I wanted to die.

As the years went by, Gerry appeared on several new television shows and seemed headed for fame. I sat back and watched him climb the ladder of success. In my heart I was very happy for him. Part of me wanted him all to myself, but the other part wished for his continued success. I envisioned this whole scenario as the "Lolita Syndrome," straight out of the movie "Lolita."

As Gerry and I grew closer, time raced on.

My feelings for Gerry grew deeper each day. At times I hurt so badly inside, it felt as though my heart would break. Why was I born too late?

No matter what your age, there is nothing like your first love. Nothing will ever compare. I never wanted anyone the way I wanted him. The funny thing was I didn't know why.

Even now, I don't know what possessed me to fall in love with him. Some friends say this was a past life relationship. Others say he reminded me of my dad, which was the farthest from the truth. I still don't know why.

Gerry was the only man for me. In the years that followed, I measured every man I met to him. I had put Gerry on a pedestal and the men I met had to match his standards. I must admit some came close, but no man could live up to my expectations. There was only one Gerry. I respected him, I believed in him, I idolized him.

Gerry was enjoying tremendous success on television. You could see his face on every game show. Now the time of change was near. My parents were finally getting wise to why I was spending so much time in New York. Even when they knew of my obsession with Gerry, they couldn't stop me. They figured I would grow out of it.

Gerry finally hit the jackpot. He landed his very own nationally syndicated TV game show. His best friend Don told me to save all of Gerry's autographs because they would be worth something someday. Within two years Gerry would be nationally famous.

While Gerry was achieving his fame, my parents decided to move to Los Angeles. They had good reasons: one, there was Gerry; two, my sister was giving birth. I refused to go, but I was still underage and had no choice in the matter. While my parents packed my bags, I slipped out to meet Gerry one last time.

I arrived at the studio just in time to catch him after the show. I congratulated him on his success, then started to cry. Gerry asked, "What's wrong, Baby?" I told him about my moving to L.A., that I would never see him again. I couldn't stop crying.

Gerry tried to calm me down. "L.A. is nice. You'll like it there," he said. "Don't be silly. We'll see each other again. Don't worry. Get those thoughts right out of your mind."

I knew in my heart that Gerry would become a huge success. He probably would forget me. What could I do? I kissed him goodbye as he wiped the tears from my eyes. That was the last time I would see Gerry Turner for what seemed like an eternity.

I cried all the way to Los Angeles. The first thing I did when we arrived there was to find a phone and call New York to see how Gerry was doing. My friend Vicky said he was fine and often asked about me.

A few years passed. I was attending a high school in Los Angeles and just beginning to date. Gerry had become the **BIGGEST** and **BRIGHTEST** star on television. There wasn't a movie magazine, TV guide, or newspaper around that didn't have his face plastered all over it. I couldn't read anything without seeing his face. But I was very happy for him.

I then reached one of the major turning points in my life; I call it "growing up." I learned of GERRY'S MARRIAGE TO TESS. Every paper carried the story. I read the paper slowly. Tears filled my eyes and spilled over onto my cheeks. The very tears that Gerry once wiped away were now reappearing. There are no words for what I felt. I had lost that precious dream within my heart. I knew I would never see him again. I had to face reality and keep reminding myself that it was really over. After three long years of loving Gerry, I had to go on with my life.

## IT WAS FINALLY OVER (?)

## DECISION TIME

The year was 1965, the month April. Within two months I was to marry Bob. My wounds from Gerry were almost healed. I was very honest with Bob and told him everything about Gerry and how I once felt. In my mind I accepted Gerry's marriage as final.

I felt secure with Bob. He was the first man, besides Gerry, that I could fall in love with. We were preparing for our wedding day when, suddenly, it happened again!

I passed by a newsstand and there he was, Gerry Turner, staring me right in the face. Haunted by his image, I had to purchase the magazine. It stated Gerry Turner would be making his debut in L.A. within two weeks. (Do you know, till this day I rarely buy magazines and rarely pass by newsstands. I think it's a phobia with me. I really don't want to know.)

When I informed Bob about Gerry's appearance in L.A., he not only encouraged me to go to the show, but also asked to go along so he could meet Gerry as well. In a sense, since Gerry was a big star now, I sometimes questioned whether Bob ever believed that I really knew him. I tried explaining to Bob the Gerry Turner that I knew was just a person. He was not the Gerry Turner that everyone else thought they knew.

I couldn't help but wonder if Gerry would remember me. Would he recall the little girl who sat waiting endlessly for him? The teenager who once cared? How would I feel after not seeing Gerry for so many years? More and more questions raced through my mind. I was scared. I didn't want those feelings from the past to resurface.

But as the saying goes, curiosity killed the cat. So, with Bob at my side, off I went to the Gerry Turner show.

We somehow managed to get backstage. I turned slowly as I caught a glimpse of Gerry talking with someone. I shouted, "Gerry! Gerry!" He turned around. He recognized me. "Little one, Little one. Is that you? Is that really you? I can't believe it. I just can't believe it!" My greatest fear was over. Gerry remembered me. He more than remembered me.

I couldn't hold back any longer and rushed into his arms. He picked me up and held me so tightly as he kissed me." Turn around," he said. "Let me look at you. I can't believe you've really grown up.

You see, I told you we'd see each other again."

For a moment I completely forgot about Bob; then, I remembered. I introduced Bob as my fiance and told Gerry we were going to be married soon. The look on Gerry's face! He was devastated. He felt hurt. I guess we both were experiencing the same feelings. Gerry was jealous. I remember those feelings when I found out Gerry was married. Now it was his turn, for I was about to be married.

After their introduction, Bob and Gerry did not seem to hit it off. I abruptly ended the conversation, excused myself, and sat Bob down in the audience. I then returned backstage to speak directly with Gerry. Gerry came toward me with anticipation. He definitely wanted to continue the conversation, as if Bob never existed.

For the first time Gerry teased me in a way he never had before. He kept telling me how much I had grown up. He couldn't believe it. He kept staring at me with his big blue eyes. As he held me tightly, he whispered, "Why do you want to get married so young?" He paused for a moment and looked straight into my eyes. "Little One, make it last. Don't make the same mistake I did." With tears in his eyes, he said goodbye. There was a sadness about him. I knew he was hurting inside. I also knew he wasn't too happy with his marriage.

Suddenly, the same feelings swept over me. OH GOD! Am I doing the right thing? Does a part of me still love Gerry? If I didn't leave right then, I would be in his dressing room with him, doing what I never got the chance to do, make love to him. Besides, this conversation was getting rather HOT!

Just before I left to take my seat, he asked if he could call me whenever he was in town. He said he would like very much to see me again. He wanted me to stay in touch this time, no matter what the cost. As I left Gerry, my heart SANK. I knew for the first time in my life that I could finally have him.

My marriage to Bob took place in spite of the feelings I had for Gerry.

**AS I PONDERED OVER THE PAST SITUATION OF FRIDAY THE 13TH, I REALIZED I HAD BEEN MARRIED ONLY TWO YEARS WHEN MY REAL SUFFERING BEGAN. I KEPT GOING OVER AND OVER IT IN MY MIND. WHY DID BOB HAVE TO CHEAT ON ME WITH TONI? WHY DID IT STILL HURT SO MUCH? EVEN NOW, TWENTY-TWO YEARS LATER, IT'S A HURT THAT CAN NEVER BE EXPLAINED. IT CUTS LIKE A KNIFE. IF THIS INCIDENT HAD NEVER HAPPENED, WOULD I STILL BE MARRIED TO BOB TODAY?**

**I KNEW IN MY HEART I COULD WIN GERRY'S AFFECTION. COULD I REALLY DO THIS TO MYSELF, ALL FOR THE SAKE OF GETTING EVEN?**

I wanted Bob to hurt like I did. I wanted him to feel the pain. Would it be worth it? I really struggled with this. It was not my nature to cheat.

Within a year and a half after Bob had his fling, I finally made up my mind. I was going to make love to Gerry. I had wanted this all along. **NOW IT WAS MY TURN TO BE HAPPY.**

I started to frequent Gerry's show whenever he was in town. Gerry and I talked just like old times. Now that I was married and so was he, Gerry's advances grew stronger and stronger. He asked me for my phone number; I gave him a friend's number where he could reach me. He asked permission to call. I didn't think much of it. I guess I felt he was just being kind and would never call.

As time moved onward, my relationship with Bob seemed to be

getting better. We were the best of friends. Actually, he was more like a brother. We did everything together, yet I kept my distance. A part of me warned, "Dayle, you know he'll cheat on you again. Beware of this and be careful."

Gerry finally got up his nerve to call. It was in the evening on one of his usual trips to L.A. Bob and I were living in a small downstairs apartment. Our best friend, Jerry Nisker, lived upstairs in the same building. Now remember, I had given Gerry the number of a friend where he could get in touch with me. The friend was Jerry Nisker.

On that special evening, I was out walking my dog when Jerry Nisker came running after me. He shouted, "Dayle! You just got a phone call from Gerry Turner. Was that really him on the phone? He gave me a number for you to call him back. Why is he calling you?" Before I could finish responding to his questions, he said, "I'll tell you what. Go make your phone call. Go upstairs and I'll take the dog and keep Bob busy. I'll tell him you're talking to a friend. Okay? Hurry now. Don't keep a man like Gerry Turner waiting."

I ran upstairs and dialed the number of the Beverly Wilshire Hotel. When the operator answered, I asked to speak with Gerry Turner. A moment went by, then Gerry answered.

"Hi! Who was that answering your phone, Dayle? Was it your butler?"

"Do I detect a little bit of jealousy here?" I asked in a teasing voice.

"No, Gerry, it was just a friend."

We talked on the phone for well over an hour. At that point, Gerry asked if I could come to the hotel to spend the rest of the evening with him.

I had been waiting for these very words almost all my life. I glanced at my watch; it was 11 p.m. I flashed on Bob being downstairs. What would I do with him? I also had to be at work early next morning. "I would love to," I said, "but it's getting late and I have to be at work in the morning early. Maybe another time soon."

Gerry paused. He seemed rather arrogant. "Please, Babe. I'm begging you. I just want to be with you tonight. I'll pick you up or I'll send a car for you. Just tell me where you live."

I didn't want to say "no," but I had to say, "I'm sorry, Gerry."

His voice had an edge to it. "What's the matter, Babe? Is it past your bedtime? Don't you know I can get anyone I want!"

"No, you can't, Gerry," I replied in anger. "You didn't get me tonight, did you?" I slammed the phone down.

I went downstairs to Bob and my dog. I thanked Jerry Nisker and he left our apartment politely. I proceeded to go to bed. As I was falling asleep, I was thinking, "Oh, well, I guess I blew my chance of a lifetime to be with Gerry. He'll never call me again. Gerry can get any girl he wants. He's rich, handsome, and famous."

Life went on. Six months later, Gerry and I somehow got connected again through the phone. He said, "Babe, I'll be in L.A. in February. Can we get together? I really miss you, and I'm giving you plenty of notice this time. OR, will it be past your bedtime?" I swear that man had a photographic memory. Even years later, he remembered everything we talked about.

This time I promised I would be there for him.

## DANA, MY FRIEND, I OWE IT ALL TO YOU!

Gerry was giving me ample time, at least two months, to prepare for his arrival in February. This time there would be no excuses. "This time, Babe, make sure you are available," he said. "I'll be staying at the Beverly Wilshire Hotel. I think we've waited long enough. Besides, I really want to be with you."

It was now time to consult Dana, my close friend since our junior high and high school days. Dana came from a very wealthy Italian family. She was simply beautiful, a shapely five-feet-seven with long black hair. We were buddies forever. I covered for her and she always covered for me. Dana worked in one of the oldest professions in the world; she was a HOOKER, A PROSTITUTE. I never held that against her. We grew up together and she was my friend. I made damn sure I would always be there for her when she needed me.

I told Dana everything about Gerry and me, and I made her aware he'd be arriving in town within two months. I let her know how worried and confused I was about the whole situation. This would be the first time I would cheat on Bob. As I confided in Dana, my feelings from the past were resurfacing. I still loved Bob, and I was still allowing Toni to eat away at me.

Since Bob was the only man I had sexually, I was very naive. Dana said, "Don't be scared. I'll tell you everything I know about pleasing a man." She proceeded to explain to me just what a man would love and need. "Boy, what an education!" I said to myself. In the days that followed, I became more confident.

Dana wanted me to contact Gerry one last time to firm up our date before he got here. I wanted to make SURE he still wanted me. I followed Dana's instructions to the tee.

I called Gerry at his office in New York. He was excited to hear from me. We talked on the phone for hours. The conversation was hot and heavy, downright sexual.

All at once, Gerry asked me in a sweet, seductive voice, "Little One, would you mind if I **kept** you?"

I replied, "I don't mind, if it makes you feel good."

He was silent for a moment. As I started to hang up the phone, he said, "See you soon, Babe." He couldn't wait.

I turned to Dana. "Gerry wants to keep me," I said. "What does that mean?"

Dana shrieked, **"He Wants You To Be His Mistress!"**

I couldn't believe it. "You're joking! Are you sure? How can I do that? I'm married!"

Dana answered me seriously. "Dayle, this is what you've always wanted. Now it's your turn, Girl; don't blow it, whatever you do. Let me tell you something. Sometimes, being a mistress is more important than being a wife. He obviously cares about you and wants you badly. That's a start anyway."

I had to think things over; this was too overwhelming. My mother always told me, "Be careful what you wish for; you just might get it." I thought about it, but the months of waiting and Dana's advice were beginning to get to me. I was determined to see Gerry now, more than ever.

That day in February finally arrived; our long-awaited moment. I had waited many long years for Gerry, and it seemed he had waited just as long for me. His words ring in my ears even now: "Little One, I can't wait for you to grow up." Well, now I was all grown up and more than ready for him.

**Just imagine this for one moment in time, if you will: you have waited almost an eternity for the love of your life, knowing somewhere in the future you will be together. My god, the build-up! As for me, hardly a moment went by when I didn't think of Gerry. In all those years, I wanted him with a passion burning in my heart into the depth of my soul. I wanted Gerry like no other woman ever wanted him or ever could have him.**

I had suppressed my desire all those years, thinking my marriage was forever. Then, Bob and Toni caused my feelings to surface. I wanted to love again.

It was February 24; the year was 1967. Gerry had arrived in town a few days earlier. When I called him at the Beverly Wilshire Hotel, he was happy to hear from me. He said he had to attend a few meetings but hoped we could get together that evening, although he wasn't sure because of his unpredictable schedule. He wanted me to keep trying to reach him at the hotel that evening; when we made contact, he would pick me up. I tried calling until 11 o'clock. Gerry was out. **Here we go again**, two ships passing in the night. I finally gave up for the evening.

Frustrated, I called Dana. She said, "Don't worry, you'll see him. I'd better come over bright and early in the morning for the final preparation."

The next morning the phone rang at 9:30, just after Bob left for work. Great timing. Gerry was on the line. "Sorry, Babe," he said. "I know I missed your call. I went out drinking with the boys after my meeting; the rest is history. I think I was trying to work up the nerve to see you. Would you like to come to the hotel this afternoon? I'll send a car for you, if you like."

I replied, "Don't worry, Gerry, I'll be there shortly." He then gave me his room number and directions on how to find his suite at the hotel

I immediately called Dana. "Dana!" I started screaming into the ringing phone, "Where are you?" By the time she answered, I was having a fit. My words came rushing out. "Gerry called and wants me to come to the hotel now! Hurry! Please hurry!"

I don't recall how fast Dana got to my house; she must have set a record. I was already dressed to the hilt, raring to go. My nerves were on edge. I didn't know if I could face what I always wanted.

Dana handed me a note and said, "Dayle, I wrote this for you. I want you to hand this to Gerry upon leaving the hotel."

The note said:

**"Gerry, I had a wonderful time. This was just an affair. That's all it was. Please don't take it for anything more than that. Dayle."**

I was shocked. "Give Gerry a note like this?" I had heavy reservations about it and argued the point. Dana explained she was looking at it from a woman's point of view, as well as a hooker's. She felt that no man should ever have the best of a woman. Being naive and stupid, I thought she knew what she was doing.

Off we went at record speed to the Beverly Wilshire Hotel. Dana was briefing me all the way. She dropped me off at the hotel and I told her I would call if I needed her. I followed Gerry's directions exactly and found his room without much effort.

I envisioned Gerry to be dressed like a star, somewhat right out of a movie. I envisioned him to be wearing a long, flowing robe and puffing on his pipe as he answered the door. I was dressed in your basic black; I looked great. I rang the doorbell of Room 457, Beverly Wilshire Hotel.

When Gerry opened the door, my vision of the romantic star faded in one hell of a hurry. He was unshaven and dressed in jeans. He wasn't even wearing a shirt. I was overdressed for the main event. Yet, it tickled me. Jeans and a sweatshirt were more my style. I rarely dress up unless I have to; in comfort is the way I choose to live. I could relate to Gerry.

Gerry showed me around the hotel suite and asked if I would like a drink. He was nervous as hell, extremely jumpy. He kept staring at me as though it were his first time. We were both uneasy, but I was gaining control of the situation.

It seems as though we talked for hours. We talked about our past.

For some reason he was very interested in me. I began to wonder, though, why he wasn't making any advances toward me. He could barely sit next to me without shaking.

Suddenly, he blurted out, "I love my wife." It sounded as if he were trying to convince himself.

I responded nonchalantly, "That's nice. I love my husband." Which meant: what are we both doing here?

He asked, **"Why do you want me?** Why are you so attracted to me?" He sounded very unsure of himself. I looked at him and I never responded. I was only 19.

I was thirsty and I went to get a glass of water from the kitchen. As I walked from the kitchen into the living room, Gerry was sitting on the couch. Much to my surprise, he had stripped all the way down to his underwear. I was shocked!

I sat down on the couch beside him. We gazed into each other's eyes; he pressed his hot, wet lips against mine. His warm hands fondled my breasts; he slowly touched me all over. He pressed his body against mine. I could feel the warmth of his desire. I put my arms around him and pulled him closer to me. I was burning inside; every inch of my body began to come alive. Our tongues met.

He began to undress me slowly; his hands were fondling every part of my body as we explored one another. In his thrust we landed on the floor. He held my hands behind my head as he devoured me. He started to penetrate me slowly when all of a sudden he jumped up. He stared at me as I was lying on the floor and said in anger, **"We're just not made for love."** He turned his head away for a moment and then looked back at me. **"Are you a virgin?"** he asked.

"Gerry, I'm married."

Gerry was feeling guilty about my youth. As guilt set in, I was a clear reminder we were twenty-two years apart. He was having second thoughts about making love to me. I was embarrassed; I wanted to leave. Suddenly, I wanted to get the hell out of this mess. I was infuriated, sexually frustrated; I started to get dressed.

I was fully clothed and ready to leave. I looked around and Gerry was gone. I walked into the bedroom, and there he was, lying on the bed naked, smoking a cigarette. He asked me to sit down beside him. He put the cigarette in the ashtray while he reached out for me with a desire from within. He pulled me close to him once again. He wrapped me in his arms and began kissing me ever so tenderly. He looked at me and said, **"DON'T LEAVE ME, BABE; I NEED YOU BADLY."** He looked me straight in the eye. **"I have to know, why do you want me?"**

I began to think at a very rapid pace as my heart was throbbing. I wanted to say, "Gerry, I've loved you from the moment I saw you. I wanted to be with you always. I wanted you, Gerry, because I loved you then, now, always and forever."

What came out of my mouth was ludicrous. I said, "I want you because the Bomb may go off at anytime and what the hell does it matter." It was the '60's. You know it made sense then. Gerry didn't let up. He kept asking me over and over again why I wanted him.

For some reason it didn't matter to him what I said. He reached for me; his lips touched my lips. He undressed me slowly once again. He pulled me closer to him. There was a gentleness about him now. We were both burning **HOT!** I had waited all these hours and now, finally, Gerry was making love to me. He made love to me like no man ever made love to me, in every which way, in every position known to mankind. He held my hands behind my head and wrapped my legs around him. As he penetrated me, it filled my burning body with ecstacy. I wanted him more. I wanted more and more of him. I couldn't hold back any longer; I started making love to him. I kissed him very passionately, slowly, from his neck down to his groin as I moved my body ever so gently on top of him. I could feel him penetrate me; I felt him deep inside of me. Now I was in rapture; we became one. I never had experienced anything like this before. Gerry held me tightly in his arms as if he never wanted me to leave. We made love for hours on end.

It was Gerry teaching me now! How to make love and how to be made love to. This truly was my very first time.

The sun was beginning to set. Neither one of us wanted to stop, but our time together was growing to a close.

I glanced at my watch; it was getting late. While Gerry showered, I got dressed. When he got out of the shower, I asked Gerry if he wanted to see me again. "Of course," he replied. "What a silly question! I have so much to teach you." He was exhausted. He said, "Babe, ordinarily, I would take you home; but you really drained me. Do you mind taking a cab home?"

I replied, "No, not at all," and began to scrounge around in my purse for the cabfare.

He noticed I had little or no money and said, "There's money on my dresser in the bedroom. Take whatever you want." At that point I got angry. I began to feel like a hooker. I knew he didn't mean it in that way, but it still bothered me. I took twenty dollars for cabfare. We held each other tightly as I kissed him goodbye.

He said, "I'll call you soon, Babe." He had that contented look about him.

As I was closing the door, I remembered Dana's letter, the one she wanted me to leave with Gerry. I did. But after I left the hotel room, I thought about it for a moment. I turned around and reopened the door, hoping to retrieve the letter before he read it. I told Gerry

I had forgotten something. It was too late! He was already reading Dana's letter.

The utter pain of it all! I knew leaving the letter was not right. Why couldn't I just take it back? The damage was done. I left in a cab and just made it home before Bob did.

Within a few days, Gerry returned to New York City.

Until this day I have always felt that if given just one chance in life to take back one of the more senseless things I have done, it would be the letter I gave to Gerry. Leaving the letter was insensitive and unkind on my part. How does one apologize to someone twenty years later for her stupidity! I always had the choice not to give Gerry the letter, but I felt then that Dana had much more experience than I had.

My apology to Gerry is twenty years too late. I don't know if this would have changed my destiny, but it doesn't matter. At least I can say to another human being, I'm sorry if I hurt you. I'm sorry, Gerry.

Gerry began drinking quite heavily. He called me periodically for about two years just to listen to my voice. Sometimes he would ask, "Are you sleeping with anyone?" We were both tormented. I still loved Gerry.

I wished the circumstances were different. I wished I could have told him my real feelings. I was just too shy and afraid of rejection. If things had worked out, we could have had a beautiful relationship.

I sat in on Gerry's show on several other occasions. We chatted briefly as if nothing ever happened. But the spark was still there for both of us.

About two years later his manager called to tell me Gerry was getting a divorce. He said Gerry wanted me to know how much he cared and respected me, that I was the only one he could trust.

His manager proceeded to tell me that Gerry wanted out of his marriage because he found out his wife had been cheating on him. Gerry's manager asked if I was still married to Bob, and how my marriage was going. I told him, "Fine." He stressed how much Gerry still cared about me and wanted me. He said if I ever needed anything or wanted anything, I shouldn't hesitate to call. The conversation ended.

After I heard about Gerry's divorce, I wondered if I could ever have a chance with him. But the letter was always there to haunt me. I don't know till this day if the letter even mattered to Gerry. It mattered to me. I was embarrassed, too embarrassed to face him again.

As the years went by, Bob and I lived a life of friendship and companionship. I eventually told Bob the truth about Gerry and me. Bob felt we were finally even and could start over again. In my heart I still loved Bob, but I felt the damage he and Toni did would never go away. Bob and I had a lot of good times together; still, I would hear tales of Gerry in passing.

Dana and I remained close friends. I told her everything that happened between Gerry and me, and she tried to analyze the situation. She felt Gerry cared too much, and that my age was a major factor. Dana always felt we would get together again. That almost rang true.

Dana was on her way to Las Vegas about a year after one of our many talks and ran smack into Gerry at the airport. He knew her as my friend and they talked while waiting for their planes. Gerry kept asking Dana questions about me. "How is Dayle? What is she doing now? Does she still smoke the same cigarettes?" He monopolized the conversation, talking only about me. When Dana came home, she couldn't wait to tell me all about Gerry and how right her feelings were.

She simply said, "Dayle, he cared."

Gerry remained in my heart and in my thoughts till 1974, when I moved to Lake Tahoe after my father's death.

**I've always thought to myself, you never really lose anything in life you don't want to. I knew my heart still belonged to Bob and I couldn't just leave him. Gerry always held a special space within my heart. And I knew somewhere in that space I would always love him.**

**Bob and I went on with our lives together. There were a lot of new changes to come.**

# TIDES OF CHANGE
## CHAPTER 6

Bob and I weathered the storm of Friday the 13th. We made it through the Gerry Turner years. Now we were about to approach a new existence, one of sadness and despair.

The year was 1974; I remember it well. Bob and I were managing an apartment building in Westwood, California. This was a nice retreat from poverty for us. Bob landed this job purely by accident. We had both been unemployed and just about to move in with our parents when the apartment manager of our building was suddenly fired. My survival instincts told me to discuss our taking over the apartment manager's position with the landlord of our building, and my salesmanship persuaded him to give us a chance.

So there we were with a roof over our heads, free rent and utilities. What more could I wish for. I was the new manager of The Westwood Apartments with thirty-six units all to myself. I was the Queen of Collecting Rents. The job was wonderful; it allowed Bob to work while I stayed home to supervise the building.

Bob found work as a sales representative for Diner's Club, a job he enjoyed. One of the benefits of the job was that we could eat at any restaurant in the L.A. area for free. We went from poverty to middle class overnight.

The times were grand; we didn't have a care in the world. For the first time we were saving money and could buy practically anything we wanted without scrimping and saving.

My dad lived a few blocks from us and I visited him regularly. I was very close to him. My dad was 70, ten years older than my mom. On one of my visits I began to sense something unusual, something I had never sensed before. I knew Dad had emphysema for a number of years, but there was something different about him now. I couldn't quite put my finger on it.

One day I woke up startled from a dream I had. In the dream my father was dead. That was a time marker in my mind. I've had such dreams before and they have always come to pass. I knew he didn't have long to live.

Dad recently had gone through an operation for prostate cancer, and the doctors had assured me he was doing well. However, when I went to the hospital to visit my dad, I could see the mist of death that surrounded him. I told Bob my dad was going to die. Bob kept reassuring me he'd be okay. Shortly thereafter, Dad was released from the hospital with a clean bill of health. He began to recover nicely.

But my vision of death kept pursuing me; in fact, it became an obsession. I recall going to priests, rabbis, anyone who would administer the last rites. I was told I was crazy; Dad was fine.

About three months later as I was driving my car, I heard the radio playing "Jim Croche, I have to say I love you in a song." This was a sign for me to follow. All my life the lyrics of music meant something to me. They were signs of things to come. There was always an inner meaning that I could grasp in times of need. I sometimes felt that if I happened to hear a song on the radio, I was meant to hear the song; a personal message might lie within the lyrics.

Jim Croche's song made that special impact upon me. I immediately phoned my dad. Little did I know he was back in the hospital for his emphysema. When Dad answered the phone from his hospital bed, I could hear that special feeling in his voice--the feeling of my knowing he wasn't going to make it. Dad asked me quite cheerfully to come to the hospital; he wanted to play one last game of gin rummy. I told him I loved him and would come by tomorrow. I knew I would never see him again.

Yet, I couldn't face going to the hospital to watch him die. So I had to say I loved him in a song, to quote Jim Croche. Within his lyrics would lie my answer. "I know it's rather late, I didn't mean to wake you, but there's something I still have to say. I guess it's too late; I have to say I love you in a song." The song I heard on the radio said it all! It expressed my inner feeling of knowing my father was going to die, and yet, I knew I couldn't be there with him.

The next day I told Bob to please take the phone off the hook. I didn't want to hear it ring and learn of my father's death. Bob did as I asked and we left the phone off the hook for several hours. I went into the den and sat down for a moment. As I relaxed and started to drift off, I felt something strange happening within me. Before I knew what it was, I began having an out-of-body experience. Suddenly, a part of me felt like I was dying. I sank into the chair and started crying.

My father had died the very moment I left my body. I glanced at the clock; it was 1 p.m. As Bob was putting the phone back on the hook, it began to ring. The hospital told him my father passed away at 12:55 p.m.

At the funeral I broke down like at no other time I can remember. It haunted me for several years.

**I flashed back, back in time to my youth, back to my dad, who was so special, and to my mom.**

## DAD, MOM, AND THE PAIN OF GROWING UP

I was born in Newark, New Jersey. It was an attractive little state, from what I recall. I was a tiny thing, always looking up at people. I had long, curly blond hair and big brown eyes. Most of the time I lived in a dream world. My grades were poor since I had attended at least thirteen different schools within the state of New Jersey, due to my father's occupation.

Dad's occupation was kept a secret from me for many a year. You see, he hid behind many fronts. He was a short-order cook and had at least three different types of restaurants. All of which either blew up or caught on fire.

Dad was almost six feet tall with big blue eyes; he had curly sandy-blond hair, just before he went bald. He was my idol; I was Daddy's Little Girl. It seemed he was always there for me as a child. Dad and I played all kinds of card games together. Might I add, **he cheated like hell**. At age six I knew how to play Knock Gin Rummy, bridge, and mahjongg. He taught me all the games of chance, including poker and dice.

At the age of nine I was a regular at the horse races. He would seat me at the bar while he placed his bets for the races. I saw the name "Ballentine Beer" so often I thought it was the name of a relative.

Dad had a great sense of humor and was always getting into some sort of mischievous deal. It wasn't till I was of legal age that I learned what my father really did for a living. He was in the **MAFIA.**

## CHILD OF THE MAFIA!

We traveled around New Jersey so much it seemed as if we were always moving or on the run. This was something I never quite understood. When I was young it meant nothing to me that men would come to our house, park their hats and guns, then proceed to play cards. I figured at one point that Dad might have been a police officer.

You see, my father was very poor when his parents came to this country. He supported his two brothers and sisters. Dad barely had a third-grade education and shined shoes for a living in New York. Although he lacked a skill or trade, he still had high hopes that he would amount to something.

In the early 1900's, in the era of prohibition, the Mob was BIG! And still is, for that matter. One of the leading gangsters whose shoes he shined recognized my dad's talent. The gangster handed Dad a tip of $100 and said, "If you come with us, there's more where that came from."

So Dad, being poor and barely able to read, joined the MAFIA. In those days, it was a group of neighborhood friends who had formed **Murder Incorporated**. Dad was suave, handsome, and always stylish. He knew everyone connected to the Mob.

Dad had met Mom at a dance. She was a speakeasy cabaret singer, and she was beautiful. When she met Dad, she fell madly in love with him. The favorite song she'd sing to him was "My Man I Love Him So." Mom did not know he was in the rackets until it was too late; she was already in love with him. Although her family had bred her well and told her not to get involved with any mobster, Dad was her man and she would stick by him "until death do us part." Their love affair spanned well over fifty years. But it was a love-hate relationship. She gradually began to find out a lot of what Dad did on the side. At times this drove her crazy; she had several nervous breakdowns, worrying about my father.

Their arguments and fights were unbearable to me. I often asked why they didn't get divorced. You see, my dad was a womanizer. He was always flirting with women and sometimes he'd disappear for days on end with some floozy. Mom, being tenacious, would hunt him down and have words with the other woman.

Then there was my sister, who changed her name to Terrie because her real name, Helene, was repulsive to her. Terrie spent eighteen normal years with my parents; they were much more settled then. Then Dad asked the Godfather for help with his finances. Shortly thereafter, Dad opened up his new restaurant.

We were still living in Newark, New Jersey. I remember very little about my sister; I barely knew her. We were almost twelve years apart. I do remember that Terrie sat me down one day and told me she was getting married. She would be leaving and I was not to cry. Cry? I couldn't wait! I would have the whole bedroom to myself and all the attention of my parents. Terrie moved to L.A. and we heard from her occasionally. Time marched on.

After nine years of stability, Mom, Dad, and I moved to Hillside then to Bloomfield, New Jersey. Dad had a luncheonette in Bloomfield, courtesy of the Godfather. Dad ran books and took bets behind his luncheonette.

Wrapped up in their own worlds, little did my parents know they were raising a Psychic child.

## PSYCHIC CHILD.

For some reason I can't remember a lot of what happened during my years in Bloomfield. I recall Mom having to remove me from school. Kids were making fun of me; I don't remember why. I think my Psychic ability was beginning to emerge again.

Growing up as a Psychic child was great. Everything I wished for seemed to come true. If I wanted anything badly enough, I got it, even though we were poor. I learned to use my power to protect myself. Most of the time if others in school hurt my feelings, I'd wish they'd fall off their bikes; and that would happen. Because my mother and father argued so much, I tended to space out as much as possible. I could not deal with their reality.

The personality of Psychics are all too similar. The Psychics I have met grew up in the same type of environment, one that caused them to revert into their shells. Many people always think a Psychic should know everything that goes on in another person's mind. This is so far from the truth, it's unbelievable. When you're growing up as a Psychic child, all you know is that you are different.

You are unlike all the rest of the children in the world. You understand that your thoughts are different. You tend to be more emotional than the next. You also realize that you sense things about people more so than do others in your age group. There are times you foresee disastrous situations involving your friends, but you're too frightened to tell them because you know they'll think you're crazy. Or worse, you might just lose a friend, which, for a Psychic child, is hard to come by. Try to imagine at any age walking up to your best friend and telling her that her brother is going to die in a car wreck. You know you are right and can't stop the event from happening. When you're Psychic, certain things sometimes are best left unsaid. But when you grow up all your life following your hunches, it becomes second nature, a way of life. For years I've blocked out much of my life in Bloomfield; but in my heart I feel I must have blurted out too many things and the teachers wanted me out of the school because I was odd.

Show me a Psychic with a screwed up past, abandonment, dysfunctional family, and abuse, and I'll show you a Psychic with potential every time. This is not something you can learn from books. The ability is either there or it isn't. Genetics play a very large part. My mother and grandmother were extremely Psychic. I inherited most of my Psychic ability from my mom. On many occasions she would dream of where my dad was with another woman, jump into a car and find him. She learned to read cards from my grandmother, who taught her everything she knew. Grandmother was uncanny. She came from Austria-Hungary and spoke five languages.

## LAKEWOOD, NEW JERSEY

Well, it was time to move on again. Dad got busted in Bloomfield for running books in his luncheonette, so off we went to Belville and finally to Lakewood, New Jersey.

Lakewood was my dream come true. It was heaven. I was about

12 years old and very happy there; I thought this place would be forever.

Dad purchased a luncheonette which was attached to a pharmacy. He was one hell of a chef. People lined up from miles around just to eat one of his Italian meatball sandwiches. Mom and Dad were getting to be very prosperous.

My parents went out every night; Mom was a nightclub entertainer and Dad was her manager. I recall waking up in the middle of the night, screaming because no one was there for me. There were times when they went on the road and left me with relatives for weeks on end. I knew my mom wasn't well at that time and Dad could no longer take care of me.

Living in Lakewood somehow made up for all the times of loneliness and abandonment. This special place was all mine. It was the first time in my life I remember feeling wonderful.

We had roots. We rented a real house for about a year, the first house I ever lived in. It was red brick, with a fireplace and a huge yard. Mom and Dad worked one mile away at the luncheonette. We were a normal family. Those were the days.

I remember being an adventurous child in Lakewood. One special day I went exploring on my bicycle. I had a boil on my foot that the doctor had threatened to lance if I didn't use my foot to walk. As a child, I was frightened by that; yet, it hurt too much to walk on my foot. Instead, I took off on my bicycle. Suddenly, I spotted a little puppy wandering the streets. I picked up the puppy and held her in my arms. I looked into her big brown sad-little-puppy eyes, held her ever so tightly, and named her Princess.

I found I could not carry her in my arms and ride a bike

simultaneously, so I walked the two miles home, holding Princess tightly. When I finally reached my dad's luncheonette, there were tears in my eyes. I asked Mom and Dad if I could keep Princess and they responded, "Yes, as long as you take good care of her."

Because of the instant love I had for this puppy, I had laid down the bike so I could hold her in my arms. If I hadn't loved Princess so much, I would have been hospitalized eventually for my boil. The two-mile walk caused the boil to miraculously heal itself. We all loved Princess with our hearts and souls. I finally had a friend.

Let me describe Lakewood in the pines, my special secret place. Lakewood in the sixties was a resort town where only the wealthy gathered. They came from all over New Jersey just to enjoy the beauty of this small, unique town. Time stood still in Lakewood: snowflakes falling with the silence no one can describe, Southern colonial style houses bordering a lake three miles wide and seven miles long, and horse-drawn carriages. There were many dirt roads and few sidewalks. One could go fishing, hiking, horseback riding, or skating at the ice rink. This was the country. This was truly living.

I went horseback riding and ice skating when my days weren't full with helping out at my dad's store. After school one of my favorite pastimes was to search for buried treasure. I had a fantastic imagination and always felt there was a treasure awaiting me. My hunch was close.

One day while playing buried treasure, I started digging up an old dirt area located in a garage near our store. Lo and behold, I found $200! I couldn't believe my hunch paid off. The next day I dug again and found more money. And on it went for a week or so. I told my mom about my game and showed her all the money I had found.

At first she didn't believe I had found well over $1,000. As it turned out, we learned later that someone had been stealing from the store and hiding the money. I had been tapping into the thief's mind through telepathy and digging up the loot. Coincidence? No. Psychic? Yes!

We spent only a few more precious years in Lakewood. The few years I spent there gave me a lifetime of memories.

## THE FIRE

Then it happened! My whole world caved in on me.

Mom and Dad wanted me to go with them to visit my two aunts and an uncle in West New York, New Jersey. I didn't want to go to the city; they begged me to go along. "Only if I can take my dog Princess with me," I pouted.

Mom consented, even though she knew my aunts weren't too crazy about animals. So I took Princess and, of course, my favorite pillow with me for the long drive into West New York.

At my aunts', Dad played cards well into the night. Several hours later we were on our way back home to Lakewood. I couldn't wait to get home; after that long drive, I wanted nothing more than to sleep in my bed. As we approached our home, we could see a lock on the door. THEN WE HEARD THE NEWS. The apartment that we were living in just above the store had caught on **FIRE!** It was all gone; nothing was left. We heard later that week from friends that the firefighters were going crazy looking for my dog and me. They thought we were in the apartment. We turned the car around and went back to West New York, never to see Lakewood again. Never, until twenty years later.

That sudden jolt back to reality made me realize that nothing is forever in life. I probably would be traveling the rest of my days, homeless and empty inside, like a Gypsy. Why, dear God, did they take this special place from me? Dad collected the insurance money once again. We lived with Aunt Ceil, Aunt Ida, and Uncle Asher for about two years in West New York.

## MOVING ON!

Living in West New York was very different and lonely for me. I guess that was why I became obsessed with Gerry Turner. This was about the time when Mom and Dad decided to move to L.A. Just another town, just another place. When we reached L.A., I hated it with a passion. The only comfort was my dog Princess.

But even Princess was taken from me one day. When I came home from school that day, my mom told me Princess had run away. I waited two years for Princess to come home. I found out later that our new landlord did not accept pets in the apartment building and my brother-in-law had taken the dog to the pound while I was in school.

For two long, hard years the memories I had of Princess, my beloved dog, kept haunting me. I was beginning to have nightmares of my past, flashes of the fire in Lakewood. *THE NIGHTMARES OF MY PAST KEPT HAUNTING ME.*

## NIGHTMARES OF MY PAST

The one specific nightmare that repeated itself most often was that of 91 Johnson Avenue in Newark, New Jersey. For many years I'd wake up from a dead sleep in a cold sweat. I had been dreaming

I was a child again, running through the corridors and halls of my old apartment building in Newark. I didn't know why this was haunting me. It was as if my past were catching up with me.

I realized there was only one way to stop the dreams that plagued me over and over again; I had to find the answers. It wasn't until JANUARY 4, 1992, that I decided to face whatever the dream was trying to tell me. I asked my husband Blythe to make the trip back east with me.

I was finally going to face the fears of yesteryear, and I was ready for whatever answers awaited me. At this time in my life I could handle whatever was before me.

You see, what bothered me most was the lack of permanency, the lack of roots. I became extremely insecure; there was never anything in my life that was forever. I always wondered what I had done wrong, why everything was always taken away from me. In searching my mind, I realized there was only one time in one place that was permanent. It was a time when we were poor, a time when I had a lot of love, a time when I had it all. That was the only time in my life when changes came about slowly. The place was 91 Johnson Avenue.

I was about to go back in time with my husband to a place that would be very strange to him and even stranger to me. With the new year of 1992 coming up, this seemed to be the perfect time. I stayed focused on New Jersey and New York, with hopes that the new year would bring an answer to my prayers.

**My prayers were answered as the bizarre events began to unfold. This brought me back to memory lane.**

# BACK TO MEMORY LANE, JANUARY 4TH, 1992
## CHAPTER 7

"Twas the beginning of the New Year, a time when everyone's hopes and beliefs would turn toward the tides of new blessings. In all my wildest dreams I would never have believed that the upcoming new year of 1992 would lead me back to memories of my childhood.

The town was all lit up to welcome in 1992. We were sharing our new year in a place that I was all too familiar with, Harrah's Lake Tahoe. It seemed I was moving backwards in time. In my heart I always felt one was supposed to go forward with one's life.

The past year of 1991 had been quite eventful. There was my move from Hawaii to Lake Tahoe, a giant step forward that meant I was ready to go on with my life. I was ready to grow now, to take whatever life had to offer. It was time to face the world. I was looking forward to what the new year would bring.

Over the last ten years I had many unusual dreams, and in those dreams I would always see myself at 91 Johnson Avenue in Newark, New Jersey, where I spent the first nine years of my life. I made up my mind to face my past, although money was very pressing at the time and a trip back East was out of the question.

Suddenly, the phone rang. Much to my amazement there was a gentleman calling me from New York. He informed me his niece had been murdered and asked me to fly immediately to the East Coast. I guess this was a sign; he didn't have to ask twice.

In no time, my husband Blythe and I were on our way to New York. We had at least four days before I would start on the murder case, those four days were mine. As we started our descent into the Newark airport near New York City, I felt very relaxed, more so than usual; this was a feat in itself. I wanted to go back East; this was something I was looking forward to.

I knew I would do the best job that I could for the gentleman. I also needed to go back in time to memory lane. There were pieces missing from the puzzle of my life. There was something in my past that I had to find out; what it was I didn't know. It was as though someone had come along and wiped out half of my memory bank and I had to keep searching to put the pieces back where they belong.

This was the second time in over twenty-five years that I was visiting the East. The first time I visited my relatives in 1989. I was unable to observe my past then; my emotions were overwhelming. I seemed to breeze by my old neighborhoods. This time it was different. I wanted to observe and feel. I needed to visit the slums of Newark; I needed to feel what it was like growing up as a child; I needed to find out what I had left behind.

There lay part of my past that was missing. If only I could find that missing piece, then and only then would I be able to understand who I was.

The evening we arrived in Newark was all too perfect. Everything had gone well from the time we left Reno till the time we arrived at the Newark airport. I was quite proud of myself. We picked up our rental car and drove to our hotel, just thirty minutes away from where my aunt Molly lived.

As we were unpacking our luggage in our hotel room, my husband gasped, then sighed. "Dayle," he shouted, "you picked up the wrong luggage! We have someone else's luggage." **Did You Ever Feel That You Had A Perfect Day?** I really believed that day was as perfect as could be until the luggage caper began. Oh, well, everything can't be perfect. We started laughing; in the last few years we seemed to have critical problems with our luggage. The very next day we went back to the airport to return the poor fellow's luggage and pick up our own.

Next on our itinerary was Aunt Molly's. Aunt Molly was my only living aunt. She was about five feet four inches tall, blond, and as spry as a chicken. She had married very young, and stayed married until the passing of my uncle Benny. With his passing, she became very lonely till she met Sam. Aunt Molly had at least thirty grandchildren and was more active than I was at times.

She had been sheltered all her life. Molly never talked about my father being in the Mafia and refused to accept the idea that my mother was not normal. When I was born, my mother was too ill to take care of me, so Aunt Molly took the responsibility upon herself and cared for me for the first three months of my life. My mother then nursed herself back to health.

As I got older, I began to realize the wealth of information Aunt Molly had about our family. It was incredible what she had stored in her memory over the years.

I suddenly wanted to find out even more about my dad and his past, especially about the repetitive dreams of 91 Johnson Avenue that I was having. I picked up the phone and called Aunt Molly.

"Aunt Molly, get ready for the time of your life," I said. "I'm going to take you to a very special place, a place where we grew up. We're going to our old neighborhood in Newark."

Now, mind you, this is not a place one would go to unarmed. This was serious, dangerous business. Aunt Molly decided to take her boyfriend Sam along for protection. Not a bad idea; there's more safety in numbers.

I was just about to face the one dream that kept repeating itself long after I had left New Jersey. The dream had been endless for twenty years.

In my dream I kept going back to Johnson Avenue and searching the building repeatedly, trying to find my old apartment. I wanted to see where I once lived. In my dream I could never go past the front door of the apartment building. This dream haunted me over and over.

I wanted to see part of my past, something that was so real to me as a child, but now a faded memory to me as an adult. I wanted one last glimpse of my past: something I could hold on to; something I could touch; something that would bring me back to the age that I could remember and feel again. I wanted to be able to hear the sounds of my grandmother, since long gone; listen to what a real mother sounded like. I wanted to smell the aroma of a special home-cooked meal, that very smell which once would tantalize my taste buds. But most of all, I wanted to take a look back at where I once came from.

I wanted to knock on my old apartment door again, go inside, and meet the people who were living there now. I wanted to know who they were and if they were once like me. Most of all I wanted to tell the families of the future that it was going to be all right. I wanted to tell them my story and to give them hope for their future. I wanted to tell them I wished they wouldn't have to suffer as I did. I wanted to tell them that things would turn out just fine, that they would grow up as I did and make it.

I wanted to see, feel, and touch once more. I wanted to make sure that I would not make the same mistakes in my life. The same mistakes that would bring me back again to 91 Johnson Avenue.

Now here I was taking Aunt Molly along with me to Newark. We drove slowly through the old neighborhood, remnants of years past; we were approaching 91 Johnson Avenue. As we came closer to the building, Aunt Molly didn't seem to recognize anything; it was all new to her.

My feelings were greatly enhanced when I reached the apartment building. I started off by sitting on the stoop, or step; I felt comfortable. Then I tried another stoop and I felt more comfortable. Soon the building began to come alive. The tenants were coming out of their cubby holes. As near as I could conceive, the building was now a tenement.

The windows were broken and had no shades, bricks had fallen to the ground, and the main entrance door of the building no longer existed. What was once unique and quaint was now old and tattered.

Aunt Molly and Sam refused to get out of the car. That left my husband Blythe and me. Blythe went off like a hero out of a storybook; he was about to finish that long dream of twenty years that I had been having. He felt that if I didn't try to find out what was behind the doors of horror, we would be bound to spend the rest of our lives on 91 Johnson Avenue. Blythe wanted me to find out what was on the other side of my dream.

We entered the apartment building cautiously, taking one step at a time. Then we inched our way further up another flight of stairs. I glanced at Blythe on my left as he stood in front of the apartment where I was born. As I looked further down the hall, I could see the window that was all too familiar to me—the window I stared out of for the first nine years of my life. I followed Blythe into the dark corridors of 91 Johnson Avenue.

Now I was standing in the hallway, glancing at the stairs to the left of me. My instinct told me to rush up the stairs to visit someone I knew, but I couldn't remember who.

I turned my attention back down the hall where Blythe was standing; he was now facing my apartment. I was shouting in my mind, "Blythe, please knock on the door, please... I want to go in... I want to enter!" But the words wouldn't come out of my mouth.

Blythe said, "We must go now, Dayle. It's too dangerous."

We left the building and walked down the stairs slowly toward the car. Part of me wanted to stay forever. I felt so comfortable. I felt I was home and Mom and Dad would be coming out to get me for dinner soon. The other part of me said it's time to go now; the memory is no more.

Aunt Molly was waiting for me. She didn't seem as curious as I was. She kept shaking her head and saying, "I can't believe what's happened to the neighborhood." I had a very different opinion as I turned slowly and looked away for the last time. We began to drive away slowly.

I realized this was once my home, the only permanent home that I could ever remember. It was the place I had lived the longest with my parents for any one period of time. This was a time I once had a real mother, father, grandmother, and sister. This was once my home; this was once my family. **I now had the answer. This was what I had been searching for all those years—a real family once again**. This was what 91 Johnson Avenue meant to me. There was a sadness within me now, for I truly realized one can never go home again.

Shortly after my visit to memory lane, I worked endless hours on the murder case that I was hired for. The answers were given to the man who hired me, and the case was solved. I was meant to go to New York to solve the murder case, and also to find a part of my past.

**My thoughts were now racing at an incredible speed. I started flashing backin time as Blythe drove away from 91 Johnson Avenue. I centered my thinking toward memories of my family. I tried to remember the good times we once had.**

# ALL IN THE FAMILY
## CHAPTER 8

When my dad passed away, I expected my mother to fall apart. Mom held up rather well. We were close as I was growing up. It wasn't until I was much older when I realized Mom had problems. She was not your normal mother; she was sick. My father contributed to this factor with his endless womanizing. This threw my mom on an emotional roller coaster which led to her countless nervous breakdowns.

I was always the one taking care of her and trying to make her well again. There were times she took out all of her pain and frustration on me. On occasions she beat me regularly with a strap; she would pull my hair and scream at me endlessly. At the end she would always hold me and tell me how sorry she was.

The times I spent with Mom were not all bad. I have a fond memory of her one Christmas Day when I was growing up. We were poor; we couldn't afford to have a Christmas. This never stopped me from believing in Santa Claus. Although no one else in my family did, I never gave up hope. Even now, **Santa Claus still lives in my heart!**

There was this one special Christmas day I recall as if it were yesterday. I remember telling my family I wanted a walkie-talkie doll, but there was no such thing in those days. I hung up my stocking and kept believing. When I awoke on Christmas Day, there were oranges and a bit of change in my stocking; that was all Dad could afford.

I began to cry. I wondered why Santa had passed me by. Suddenly, the doorbell rang; a man wearing a Western Union suit asked for me. He had this huge present wrapped in a gold box with a red ribbon bow attached to it. I opened the box with such joy and anticipation. There she was, a two-foot-high blond doll. She was everything I wanted, except she didn't walk or talk. The card read, **FOR DAYLE, FROM SANTA CLAUS.**

Mom looked at Dad; Dad looked at Mom. They were utterly surprised. You see, neither of my parents nor my sister had sent me this doll. Later that evening Mom was on the phone calling every relative that we knew to try to find out who sent the doll. They never found out, but I knew all along it could only be one person who sent me the doll. It was **Santa Claus!** If you believe as I did, Santa will always come.

Throughout the years we had our good times as well as the bad times. We traveled the highway from New Jersey to L.A. on four different occasions. I missed school most of the time; my education was the road or on the street. Later in life I started to adopt people along the way.

When my parents felt they could no longer take care of me or the money was running out, they would leave me for weeks on end with some relative or friend until the good times rolled around.

One of the more unpleasant times I can remember was when Dad and Mom went out for the evening, leaving me alone as I slept. Mom sang at the Treat Nightclub in Newark, New Jersey. She was extremely talented; she was chosen by a talent scout to be on the Ed

Sullivan Show. This one event might have made her a superstar. Unfortunately, it was not to be.

I woke up early that evening, earlier than expected. This wasn't the first time they had left me alone. I started screaming. I was scared and shaking for about twenty minutes. I screamed for Mom and Dad; no one answered. The door to my bedroom finally opened and there stood Dad and Mom, bruised from head to toe. I started screaming even more as they tried to calm me down. I wanted to know what happened.

Apparently, a man in the nightclub audience kept making suggestive remarks toward my mom. Dad, being quite hot tempered, asked the guy to shut up. The man refused to listen; the next thing anyone knew, Dad was on the ground fighting with him. Mom tried to pull the guy off Dad's back. She reached for a bottle and swung hard to hit the guy over the head and knock him out. It didn't work quite that way. The guy grabbed the bottle, threw it on the floor, and somehow managed to hit my mother in the nose with his fist. Mom found out later that her nose was broken. **That was the end of the ED SULLIVAN guest appearance for Mom.** The show was her only break in life; it could have made her famous.

I never knew where my life was going from one day to the next. The only love that I trusted was the love of my dog Princess. I think this is what helped me keep my sanity. I always hoped she could have been around forever. I knew through Mom's eyes that she would never have any peace as long as my dad was alive, although she always loved him.

When Dad passed on, I thought things would get better for her and she just might be normal again. Unfortunately, she never was;

she always missed Dad terribly. I never seemed to recover from my dad's death, either. Whatever time I had with my dad was never enough. When he was alive, he was so full of life. But he always did such odd things.

Whenever Mom let Dad take me out alone, something would always happen. There was the time he took me to the park. Dad was pushing me on the swing and somehow the swing hit me in the mouth and knocked out my front tooth. I was unconscious when Dad brought me back to Mom. She was outraged. "Why is it every time you take this child out, something happens?" she screamed.

Then, there was the time he took me to Macy's to buy me my first pair of patent leather shoes. The shoes cost $40 in those days. Dad made sure the shoes fit me before we left Macy's. I was so happy to have black patent leather shoes I didn't care if they fit or not. After I had worn the new shoes for an hour or so, my feet were beginning to blister. I complained, and Dad decided to take me back to Macy's. We stood in the exchange line during Christmas for at least thirty minutes. Now, Dad was not the most patient man in town. When we reached the counter, Dad demanded his money back.

The man working behind the Macy's counter refused. He said, "Sorry, no can do. This child has scuff marks at the bottom of her shoes; they have been worn. Sorry, Sir, that's our policy."

Dad asked again, nicely. The reply was the same. Dad was determined not to lose $40, so he picked up the man by his front shirt and held him, literally, two feet in the air above his head. "You'll give me back my money, won't you!" he shouted in anger.

The man was shaking and threw the money at my dad. **I Think The Man Almost Had A Heart Attack!**

Off we went with Dad screaming at me all the way, "The next time we buy you shoes you better make sure they fit and you feel comfortable in them. I'm not made of money."

Then there was the time Dad bought a brand new white 1957 Dodge. The car had push-button automatic drive, air conditioning, and was fully loaded. Early the next morning I asked Dad if we could go for a ride in the car again. He peered out from behind the newspaper he was reading very intently and said, "No, I don't have the car anymore." He went back to reading his paper.

I persisted. "Why not?" I asked.

"It got blown up," he said.

The stories are endless. One of my favorite stories before Dad died was about the day I came home from school and Dad was on his knees spraying the carpet green. "Dad, why are you spraying the carpet green?" I asked. He told me his dog had an accident and the spot wouldn't come out of the carpet. He didn't want my mom to know, so he was spraying the carpet green. She found out anyway.

Another favorite is about the time I walked in and Dad was drilling a hole through the window, which was frosted.

"Dad, why are you drilling a hole through the window?" I asked.

"Because I want to see out," he replied.

Makes sense, I think? Mom didn't think so; she attacked him with a frying pan.

Dad would call Bob and me over to the house to play gin rummy and poker. It seemed whenever I was winning and went to the bathroom, my cards were never the same when I returned. He would switch the hands around and always manage to call out "Gin!" That's when our arguments began. I would yell and scream about

Dad's cheating to the point where Bob would have to pull me out of the room.

The times with Mom were not too pleasurable. She was not always in her right mind. She had breakdown after breakdown; yet, she survived. She just had her eighty-second birthday and is living in a convalescent home in L.A. She is still spry and happy that she has a roof over her head and gets fed regularly.

In her younger days she was quite Psychic, even more so than I. But in those days, the psychiatrists just locked up Psychics and threw away the key. They once gave her shock treatments, telling her there is no such thing as being able to see the future. ("It's impossible to see the future so we will shock you until you tell us that you don't see it anymore.")

I recall the time Mom had breast surgery. She thought she was dying. She sat me down by her side and said, "Dayle, I went through the tunnel. I saw the light. I was with all dead people. I saw Grandma and Grandpa. I was so happy to be with them. I wanted to stay with them. Please, don't ever be afraid of death." She wanted to stay, but Grandma told her she had to come back for me. There was something I would do that she had to live to see. Well, she is still living. I guess she has seen most of what I've done.

But not the main event.

**I began to think back once again, back in time to 1974. Dad had just passed away. I needed a fresh start with Bob. We needed to move away from the city, from all the darkness and despair. It was now time to move to the country.**

# THE YEAR WAS 1974
## CHAPTER 9

I felt within my heart I needed to go back to my roots, back to the country. I needed a place where I felt safe and secure. I needed to find my place in the world again. In my heart I was always searching for a place such as Lakewood.

Suddenly, it happened! We found that special place that reminded me of Lakewood. I would call this new place home for many a year. There she was, high within the mountains—**LAKE TAHOE**. She was hidden away in her own special part of the world. Lake Tahoe is on the border of California and Nevada. In the past Bob and I had vacationed there on numerous occasions. We always had a desire to move and live there, but we never could find a way to make a living.

This time was different. As we were vacationing in Lake Tahoe, Bob decided to submit applications to all the casinos. He knew how painfully I wanted to move to this special place that reminded me of my childhood.

One morning, while we were waiting patiently to hear if Bob would get the job offer from Harrah's Casino in Lake Tahoe, I happened to be going through the Los Angeles Times. An ad in the real estate section of the paper caught my attention. The ad stated: **Two hundred dollars down. Pick up payments of sixty-seven dollars a month. Lot in beautiful lake Tahoe, Nevada. Call for more information.**

Not only did we call, we decided to buy the lot sight unseen. This lot was our nest egg. We were determined to hold on to this piece of property until we found a house that we liked, or we would eventually build on this lot. Since Lake Tahoe is one of the very few places that are still on the barter system, we felt assured that eventually we'd be able to trade our lot if need be.

Now all we needed was for Harrah's to come through and hire Bob, and off we'd go. We waited several months; there was no response from Harrah's. Our hopes were now dashed to the ground. I knew I couldn't stand the thought of living in the city much longer.

As I was driving my car on the L.A. Freeway one day, the smog was beginning to get to me. The traffic was horrendous. As I glanced around while I was driving, I noticed the cement sidewalks were getting longer; the buildings were beginning to magnify. There was too much noise, too many people. What was I doing there? When I arrived at home, I had a long talk with Bob. I was emphatic about how I felt.

I said, "Harrah's or not, Bob, I have to get out of this city. I just can't take it anymore! If we don't move to the country soon and take a chance, then I guess I'll move on my own!"

The next day Bob had a talk with his boss at Diner's Club and told him of my dilemma. Bob's boss responded with an offer. He said, I'll tell you what, Schear. I don't want to lose you as a salesperson, so I'll give you our new Denver office. Go home and talk to your wife. Don't worry, I'll make all the arrangements."

When Bob arrived home, he was exuberant; he couldn't wait to tell me the good news. He said proudly, "Pack your bags, Dayle, we are moving to Denver, Colorado."

The very same day that Bob spoke to me about Denver, Colorado, surprisingly and simultaneously, Harrah's called with a part-time job dealing Twenty-One in Lake Tahoe. Bob was perplexed.

Diner's was about to transfer him to their Colorado office. They were going to move him lock, stock, and barrel with a nice big raise on top of it. Now, here was Harrah's—**No Guarantees,** part-time job, no medical, a salary way below what Bob was making now. However, there were big tips involved, and we would be living where we wanted to. It was a **Big Risk.**

Diner's wanted to fly Bob up to the Denver office within the week to see how he would like it. I remember that day well when I drove Bob to the airport in L.A. We must have circled the airport for at least an hour while he was deciding which plane to board: Continental Airlines to Denver or PSA to Tahoe. What a **Dilemma!** Bob felt obligated to go to Denver. Besides, his boss was waiting on the plane for him.

When I arrived home, I sat by the phone for days, waiting for Bob to call me to tell me where we were moving. Meanwhile, I was packing; but I didn't know where I was going. This was one of the biggest turning points in our lives. I wanted Bob to make this decision on his own without me swaying him one way or another. If something went wrong, I didn't want to be held responsible.

The next day Bob called me from Denver. He told me how beautiful his office was. He told me they had given him a huge welcome-to-Denver party. He made his decision; we were moving to Denver. As I hung up the phone, I was a little bit disappointed. Tahoe was beginning to fade from my memory. I would make do with this new situation if I had to.

It seemed as if I had been packing for days when the phone began to ring again. Bob was on the line. He said, unexpectedly, "Dayle, I quit my job. We're moving to Lake Tahoe. Pick me up at the airport tomorrow at 2 p.m. I'll tell you all about it."

Now I was the one who was perplexed, but happily perplexed.

When I picked him up from the airport the next day, he told me why he chose Tahoe. Bob said Denver-proper had mixed building codes; there were some nice homes mixed in with some beautiful homes. He didn't seem to like the area as well as he liked Lake Tahoe. Besides, he felt he wanted to take that risk.

This was very out of character for Bob. His background did not warrant this type of decision. Bob grew up in New York in a neighborhood called Fort Apache in the Bronx. His family lived in sheer poverty, never knowing where their next meal would come from. The last thing he wanted was to be poor again. Every decision he made in his life was planned and calculated. There were no risks involved, except for this decision, the decision for us to move to Lake Tahoe.

I was very proud of Bob. For the first time in his life he made a decision based on emotions. This was one of the more spontaneous decisions that he ever made. It came purely from his heart and not calculated from his pocket. In my mind this was a very **Brave** decision for him. Besides, Fate is always the answer. If you follow your gut, if you follow your heart, you never will go wrong. Destiny definitely played a hand in this matter.

Within thirty days we were ready to **ROCK AND ROLL**.

As we drove away from L.A., it seemed to be one of the more beautiful days I could remember. We were all packed. The car was full, our dog sat in the back, and we attached a rented U-Haul to our car. The feeling was exhilarating. We were happy for the first time in a long time.

While we drove, we sang along with John Denver as we played his cassette repeatedly. Two of my favorite songs on his album were "Take Me Home, Country Roads" and "Rocky Mountain High." We played his songs all the way to Tahoe. I began to wonder just how many people's lives were changed in the '70's when they heard John Denver's music. I know our lives changed. It was our listening to his lyrics, as well as his music, that warranted our change in life. I was able to see that I was wasting my life all those years living in the city. Everything John Denver spoke about of the mountains and of country life was true.

We were rounding the bend of Echo Summit; this is the very top of the mountain just before you reach Lake Tahoe. We had a clear view of the most beautiful lake in the world. We were homeward bound.

We at last reached our brand new apartment in Lake Tahoe. It was heaven on earth, fireplace and all. No sooner were we settling in than Bob had to start his dealer training school for Harrah's. Within a few weeks I managed to get a job as a telephone operator for the Sahara Hotel. I was in heaven; one of my favorite jobs in the world was being a telephone operator.

Bob's job became permanent within the year. We had medical and dental benefits now, and we were raking in the bucks in those days. Now we were deciding what to do with the property we had bought several years ago. I decided to study for my real estate test to learn the laws of the land. We'd look at houses every weekend. I was looking for someone who would take my lot in trade for a brand new house. I got lucky; I found a builder who wanted our lot on the Nevada side of the lake. I traded him the equity we had built up over the years as a down payment on the new house that he was building. The house cost $37,000. The builder decided to trade. He wanted to build another house, anyway, so he could sell it at a profit. We finally had our very own house, something you dream about all your life. The house was beautiful. It had three bedrooms, two baths, a kitchen and dining room, and sat on one-half acre of property.

Bob continued working as a Blackjack dealer at Harrah's, and now he was learning how to deal a new game called Craps. He enjoyed his work very much. Bob noticed his pay was increasing by leaps and bounds. He was making TOKES, or tips; that's how Blackjack dealers make their living. Bob decided he wanted me to go to school and learn the trade. With two dealers in the family he could look forward to a very secure and wealthy life. However, I had my reservations about this. I was too shy to stand in front of a Blackjack table.

Although Bob kept pushing me and pushing me to get into the business, it took me well over a year before I consented. I rather liked hiding out as a telephone operator; it was fun. It didn't pay much, but I was happy.

It was in the spring when I took my class for six weeks to become a Twenty-One dealer. I must admit it was a great deal of fun. I learned so much about the game. I think most people think it is easy to stand behind a Blackjack table and deal cards, but it is much more complicated than that, as I learned.

The training was not only on how to count to twenty-one, but how to protect your game so the player doesn't steal or cheat from the casino. You learn how to pitch the cards on the table without throwing them off the table. I found out learning to pitch the cards or throw the cards to the player is an art in itself. You learn how to stack chips and how to watch and monitor for counters.

There were many times I became frustrated, but I kept trying. I enjoyed the game immensely. I remember how the teacher taught us to play the game intelligently as well.

**I graduated from dealers school with high honors. I wasn't aware of the lifestyle that was to come!**

# IT'S ALL IN THE CARDS THE ART OF DEALING 21, BLACKJACK
## CHAPTER 10

Living life in the fast lane. Not caring about anything, playing around and having fun; that's what it was all about.

I was a Blackjack dealer, or what some people call a Twenty-One dealer. You know what I mean, the pretty lady that pitches or throws the cards to you while you are still adding them up to count to twenty-one. Well, that was me. Shortly after dealers school, to which Bob sent me, I became a full-fledged dealer.

At that time, it seemed to be a great way to make a fabulous income. Why, **The Bright Lights, All the Action, Drinking, Gambling;** there wasn't even a clock on the wall to tell you what time it was.

There comes a point in everyone's life when you figure there has to be something more than this. I more than reached that point in my life. I'd tease my friends on occasion and say, "It will take a **BOMB** to get me out of this place." This was a running joke with all the Blackjack dealers. We knew once you were in, you were in. It was one big happy family. To become a Blackjack dealer, you have to be part of a very select few. Most dealers had found themselves dealing because of their last trip to Las Vegas, when they lost it all. Or they were penniless from their gambling. They felt they had to make their money back somehow.

Not me. I was selected from the highest of high. I had the killer instinct; I took it personally if I lost the house's money. The casino noticed this was a big plus in the house's favor, so I was chosen to work with the best. I dealt only High Limit games to all the High Rollers. Might I mention, when the casino chooses you, it is an honor. They are swamped with at least one thousand applications per day, and you are one of the few that truly make it.

Becoming one of the select few means you pass the Ken and Barbie doll look-alike contest. That means you reek with some kind of beauty. If you notice, in Lake Tahoe or Las Vegas the casinos have a lot of glamorous young men and women enticing you to their tables to drop your very last dime. In those days I rather enjoyed it.

You were pampered and given extra prime days off if you met the casino's quota of taking enough money in. It was then and only then you had to pass the test of the family, the family of dealers that have been there from day one. They, and only they, had to accept you first; you were the new kid on the block taking away their pampering. Now they would vote you in or they would make your life impossible.

It took me four years to join them. I somehow fell into the trap right along with them. The trap of gambling, drinking, and having affairs! It was then, and only then, I was accepted by the family of dealers. The family would protect, guide, and take care of me.

I know we make our own choices in life; however, my need to be accepted as a person was incredibly high. Having had severe rejection most of my life, this turned me into a follower, not a leader, at that time. My mother had always stressed never to be part of the group. She always wanted me to be different. However, this was the first time in my life I was being accepted by others. I wanted to be a part of this group of dealers. I felt loved and wanted for the first time in a long time on an emotional level.

This group of dealers were more than friends; they were truly my family. I noticed when you tend to fall to the bottom of the pit, you fall all the way. You tend to stoop to other people's levels, but this is what I needed. I had to learn from my own mistakes and experiences.

I remember as a child being very stubborn and having to go to the school of hard knocks to learn any lesson that was to be bestowed upon me. This lesson wasn't any different from the rest.

In the art of becoming a Blackjack dealer, you are not part of a cult of any sort. There are certain jobs in life that may put you in a situation of vulnerability; I felt this was a time in my life when I was very vulnerable. Keep in mind, seventy-five percent of the Black-jack dealers go about their business, go home, and lead normal lives. I am not speaking of those; I am mentioning the other twenty-five percent that I was involved with at that time.

Who in their right mind would want to leave a $500-a-week job, virtually tax free in those days, with all the frills and fun galore? Especially in the 1970's, when inflation was running amok.

I started off my dealing career auditioning for Barney's Club in Lake Tahoe. It was a small club which is now called Bill's. Auditioning is very nerve-wracking. You have to deal to a group of strangers and make the right payoffs. At that point you are called a Break-in Dealer. According to the casinos, you are a Break-in Dealer for about two years. After that point, they feel that you usually can handle a game without much supervision. You see, there's more to the art of dealing the game than just counting to twenty-one.

Dealing Twenty-One is equivalent to a three-Valium-a-day job. There is a lot of pressure; you are always being watched. There is the "Eye in the Sky" who is watching from above. There is the pit boss who is watching you. There are customers who are placing bets and you best be sure they are not padding their bets or pinching money from the bets.

There is always someone watching to make sure you are not cheating or flashing your whole card to your friend or exposing your whole card to anyone at any given time. The rule is never take your eyes off the money, never flash your whole card, and it goes on and on. If the word "paranoia" was invented, it surely was invented when they invented Blackjack.

All this I have described is the tip of the iceberg. To be the best of the best, the casino would like you to win most of the hands that you deal out. Now, if you don't; I mean **If You Don't,** then they send you to what every dealer dreads. It's called Break-in Heaven.

That means, while you are standing at your game, a new dealer is sent in to replace you, the robotic faulty dealer. He or she is the one who is sent in for the kill. In order for this to happen, you would have to be on a losing streak. That means your table is filled to the brim with money, your customers are laughing and having fun, you are depressed and can't win a hand if your life depended on it.

Haven't you ever noticed that whenever you happened to be winning, a new dealer is sent by the side of your old dealer? If this should occur, leave the table immediately, because your dealer, who may have been me, has been sent to Dealer Heaven, never to be seen again.

As you stand in Dealer Heaven, **which is merely a term used for being sent to another part of the casino,** the house tries to put you as far away from people as they can. Most of the time, if you dealt High Limit, which is from $5 to $5,000 per hand, they send you to a game where there may be little or no people. Or you will end up dealing Blackjack to what every dealer dreads, $1 to $200 limit.

No Action! In my case I was sent to a game where there was not a soul but me. There I stood on a game with my arms locked, standard dealer's position, spacing out, overlooking the whole casino, hoping the world would pass me by.

The nice thing about Lake Tahoe in those days was when you did space out, you could look outside through the massive windows and see the beautiful mountains and the snow falling ever so gently. Time almost stood still. In that little space of time that I valued so highly, it was a time I could reflect, a time to think and sort out my life.

As I reflected, I realized that everything was going well for Bob and me. We had it all, everything we wanted. The hard part was we worked different shifts. When you are a Break-in dealer, you don't have a choice. This was the beginning of our problems.

Have you ever noticed when things are going too well, that's the time you'd better worry because **Life Sometimes Changes?** Change it did. As Bob and I were working two different shifts, we did not see each other often; we were like two ships passing in the night.

Bob and I had been married for nine years at this point in time. One day as I opened the door to the house, Bob was waiting for me. He had a somber look on his face. He looked at me like a little lost puppy. "Dayle, I met someone else! I'm leaving you for her," he said.

Whoops! Where have I heard this before? I guess about five years ago. I guess I was wiser now. "Bob, there's the door. Pack your things and never come back!" I shouted.

For some unknown reason, he didn't leave as he finished his thought. "Well, let's talk this over," he said. "Maybe I'm being foolish. I have to look at this logically." And he did. Bob explained he thought he was in love, but he felt that it wasn't worth it to leave me, so he came to his senses.

I was stupid; I let him stay again. Somehow this didn't hurt as much as hearing about Toni Gold; in fact, this didn't bother me at all, for some strange reason. I don't know why, but after Toni and my affair with Gerry, nothing could bother me. Bob and I talked this out. We both got together on the same shift so we could see each other more often and have more of a family life. We realized not being with each other hurt the marriage, and living in the fast lane didn't help matters. The temptation of the casino played a big part in it.

It was then we decided to sell our house and buy a lot on the Nevada side of Lake Tahoe. The taxes were less and you could get more for your money. Bob and I found a one-acre lot with a lake and mountain view for $25,000. Real estate was beginning to boom. We sold our old house within two months for $67,000 without a realtor. Bob had a dream. His vision was to build the house of our dreams. Unbeknownst to me, he wanted to sell our dream house to make a huge profit. This was a major problem. I wanted things to be forever; he wanted to buy and sell. There was never enough money in the world for him.

From day one, Bob was always trying to sell the house out from under us. That's when most of our fights began. The house went up ever so slowly. What was promised for us by the builders, to have the house completed within six months, was now taking well over a year. But the house was worth it. Our house stood on one acre overlooking the lake. It stood four stories high, with 2,600 square feet, three bedrooms, two baths, a jacuzzi tub, three fireplaces, and more.

Money played a huge part in our marriage. Bob was so cheap he wouldn't allow me to buy nice furniture for the place because he always felt that he would sell the house.

There were times when we'd go to the movies and he'd ask me to pay for half the price of the ticket. It seemed I would have to pay for half of everything. I learned to live with this. However, the cheaper he was, the more extravagant I became.

Times were changing. The fights grew deeper and more intense over money. I was beginning to think: If I had to pay for half of everything, why should I be married?

It was at that time I was beginning to fall into the pattern of the "Dealer's Family." I was starting to come home late after shift, hanging around the bar with my friends. I started gambling for fun and profit. I was on a steady decline at this point, although I had several friends that I loved and cherished. Diane Ash was one of them.

Diane was tall, had brown hair, and was very worldly. She had been married several times, and her dad was casino manager of Harrah's, where Bob worked. Diane had three children and a husband named Mike. As we became friends, I started opening up to Diane about my Psychic ability. However, I refused to let anyone in the casino know because of the fear of losing my job. Diane was the only one that I trusted with this information. We became the best of friends. Diane's marriage was on the rocks, so we had a lot in common.

Throughout the years Diane was always there when I needed her. We ate together, played together, and cried together. I was always there for her sad times as well as she was for mine. I couldn't have asked for a better friend. It never seemed to matter to Diane if she had money or not; with three children to feed, her door was always open.

I was beginning to realize that my marriage was **"on the rocks."**

For some reason, I didn't care anymore. All Bob thought about was making money and how he could invest his money to make more money. He didn't pay much attention to me anymore. His whole life was involved in the stock market and wanting to sell our new house for profit.

At work I was beginning to get propositioned by many of my pit bosses, and I must admit there were times I took them up on it. My gambling was getting out of control. I had joyfully gambled away every cent of my precious being. To top it all off, I was teaching myself what it was like to live at the bottom of the trash barrel. Drinking, gambling, and having affairs was the only lifestyle I was accustomed to for at least five years. The funny thing was that Bob was so into Bob he never noticed that our marriage was falling apart.

I realized what I was doing to myself and how I was hurting myself. It was then I decided to join the self-search program. Part of me wanted to stay in the gaming industry; the other part of me wanted out. I was beginning to go through my mid-life crisis. You know the one: "Who am I? What am I doing here? Do I still want to be married?" My search was beginning and I had no control over it. I wasn't sure if I wanted to be married anymore. I was making plenty of money; now I could certainly afford to live on my own, and that intrigued me.

**I wasn't looking to have an affair. But somehow, the pit bosses I worked with were starting to flirt with me. I felt I was ready to find someone new and, just maybe, now was the time once again.**

# BIG RED!
# THE ALL-AMERICAN INDIAN
## CHAPTER 11

I was working day shift as a Twenty-One dealer for Harvey's Casino. This day was a little different from all the rest. On this day I met up with **Big Red, The All-American Indian.**

On this particular day I was dealing High Limit for the casino. I heard through the grapevine there was going to be a big shift-change within the club. There would be several pit bosses from the swing shift that would be coming onto the day shift. This was always a scary time for the dealers because we never knew who our new bosses would be. There was a big discussion in the break-room about our new bosses and who they were.

There was one name that kept blaring up repeatedly; the name was **Gene Ashley**. All the girls warned me about Gene. The word was out: "You don't want to mess with him; Gene is a womanizer. Just stay away."

The next day the shift changed as planned. I was terrified by the name Gene Ashley. I was standing by my High Limit game, waiting patiently for a customer. Suddenly, I was approached by Gene Ashley in person.

He said, "Hi, my name is Gene Ashley. What's your name?"

I spoke ever so softly and politely. "My name is Dayle Schear."

"Nice to be working with you. I've watched you from afar. Would you like to join me for a drink when the shift ends?" He spoke ever so proudly.

"I have to get home early tonight. Maybe some other time, Gene," I replied.

Phew! I got out of that one just in the nick of time. I went straight home that day. My whole objective was to avoid this man at all cost.

The next day as my shift ended, I headed straight for the bar to have a few drinks. I was shooting the breeze with a few of my friends when Gene interrupted our conversation. He bought me a few drinks as he inched his way closer to me and then began to monopolize the whole conversation.

Gene told me he was a Pawnee Indian. I wasn't familiar with what that was. I somehow thought he was telling me he was from India. I asked what a Pawnee Indian was. Gene scratched the table and said "Paw" as he pawed the bar, "nee" as he touched my knee. I began to laugh. I had never met an American Indian before. This was intriguing.

I asked Gene if he was married. He made it very clear that his wife and he were separated. Gene told me they were not getting along; that was why they were on different shifts. Shortly thereafter, his wife approached the bar to speak to Gene, and he introduced me. Her name was Annie. She had worked at Harvey's Casino from Day One. I didn't quite understand their marital situation, but it didn't matter then.

Day after day, week after week, Gene and I talked at the bar after shift. We were getting to know each other. I was fascinated with this man and how bright and intelligent he was. I was more intrigued with learning all about the American Indians. Gene wasn't a halfbreed; he was a full-blooded, one-hundred-percent All-American Indian.

I told Gene I was married and that my husband worked at Harrah's across the street. I also began to tell him of my dilemma concerning my marriage. I stressed on many occasions how un-happy I was in my marriage, that I was thinking of leaving my husband but didn't have enough courage to do so. Gene sympa-thized with me; he somehow could relate to my situation.

There was something different about Gene. He had charisma, a personality that wouldn't quit. He seemed wise beyond his years. Gene had a four-year degree in psychology; he also had an active teaching degree at one point in his life. Yet, for the life of me, I couldn't understand why he would end up being a pit boss at our local casino. I found out later Gene's main downfall was booze; Gene was a heavy drinker.

It was the summer of 1980. Gene asked me to give him a ride to the local bowling alley; he was going to meet some friends there. I was happy to drop him off; it was on my way home, anyway. As I let Gene out of the car at the bowling alley, he reached into the open window of my car and gave me a tender good-bye kiss. I remember blushing and driving off. It was that one little kiss that started it all, a kiss that I could never forget.

Gene was not your handsome he-man. He was dark, short, and walked with a limp. He was quite muscular and athletic in his own way. However, he was very prominent-looking. If you were to dress him up in an Indian headdress, he would definitely look the part of an Indian Chief.

Right after that special kiss I remember so vividly, he began his hot pursuit of me quite actively. All at once our friendship was beginning to dissipate and something much deeper was beginning to set in. I realized he was my boss and one should never mix busi-ness with pleasure. However, I was out of control concerning Gene and this situation; this was going to be my first real affair.

I trusted Gene so much that I began to tell him of my Psychic ability. He told me his father had been an Indian Chief and had some of the same ability that I inherited. His father would practice his talent on the Indian Reservation. He was able to read mail without opening it and that scared Gene terribly. Gene wanted me to pursue my ESP ability. He encouraged me to explore it more and to do everything I could so that I would someday help many. Gene would always say, "If you believe in yourself, let nothing stop you. I want you to be a major success. You have that special gift, Dayle, that ability to help others."

It was then I started to believe in myself. There was something within his voice that made me want to become something other than a Blackjack dealer. I always felt Gene was my best friend. I didn't want anything to change.

On the other hand, I was the biggest challenge in Gene's life. He wanted me sexually and I wasn't going to give in. Gene began to annoy me so much at times; he wanted me to go to bed with him. I almost felt that maybe if I were to give in, I would get him off my back.

Gene was twelve years older than I, a nice age difference but not enough to matter. He began to fall in love with me over a period of several months. We would sit and talk at the bar endlessly. As I recall, he must have caught me off guard. It was at a very vulnerable moment when I finally decided to give in.

That evening after work I remember having my usual battle with Bob. Slamming the door and leaving the house, I drove straight to the casino to look for Gene. Lucky for me, Gene was still at the bar talking to some of his friends. I walked up to Gene and whispered in his ear, **"Okay, Ashley, let's go. You win. Let's buy a bottle of wine and find a motel." What was I getting into?**

Gene followed me out of the casino. We walked to his car and drove around Lake Tahoe till we found a motel that looked empty. With bottle of wine in hand, this was going to be Gene's lucky night. He checked us into the motel; this was very awkward for me. The last time I had cheated on my husband was with Gerry. Now here was Gene. We got undressed rather quickly and I made my way under the nice warm covers. Gene snuggled next to me; he was so warm and cozy.

We were just beginning to make love when, suddenly, I wasn't feeling so well. The wine was beginning to get to me. The room started going round and round. The next thing I remember, I got terribly sick and Gene was cleaning up my mess as I was apologizing. Can you imagine finally getting to go to bed with someone you have wanted and lusted for, for well over three months, and you end up cleaning up her mess? What a dilemma!

I was sure after that night Gene would never want to see me again. I was wrong. What started out in jest became reality. Gene wanted to see me more so than ever. There was no stopping an Indian once he started tracking you.

That whole summer we sneaked away whenever we could get the chance. Whether it was in a car or a motel, it didn't matter as long as we were together. In between making mad, passionate love, we would talk for hours about the love we had for each other. Gene seemed to be more of a husband to me than my own husband Bob.

Speaking of Bob, for some reason in the beginning he thought I was out gambling, not having an affair. Gene's wife thought he was on an alcoholic binge. I was falling madly in love with this man. Making love to Gene was a unique experience, an experience I could never put into words. Gene was so gentle and kind, he even made my job at work bearable. It was fun going to work; he was always there by my side.

Our relationship grew by leaps and bounds. He began opening up to me ever more. Gene began to go deeper into his family life. Apparently, there had been an incident at work many years ago between Gene's son Billy and another boy. There was an argument and Billy shot the other boy. I remember Billy was in prison for this crime, but the one who suffered the most was Gene. He claimed this is why he drank so much.

Well, three months turned into three years faster than one could blink an eye. I recall I'd meet Gene during the day when my husband was working. However, I would always make sure I was home in time to make dinner for Bob. In the beginning I thought this was exciting. I was losing weight, starting to feel like a woman again, a woman who was wanted and loved by two different men.

Gene was beginning to get sloppy over this situation. We both were leaving tell-tale signs all over the place. Lake Tahoe is a small town; there isn't anything that doesn't get by when you really want to find out something. Pretty soon everyone at the casino was talking about our affair. Gene's wife was definitely beginning to suspect. From what I understood, Gene had had other affairs before me, but his wife always knew that he would come home to her. This time was different; Gene was not coming home anymore except on occasion. Annie was getting wise and she felt threatened for the first time. It was okay, for some reason, for Gene to play around, as long as no one knew about it and as long as it didn't embarrass her. But this was different. The whole town knew about us, except Bob. I don't know why Bob didn't suspect. I think he was trying to make more money; he was in his own little world.

Gene and I had a code. He would call my friend Diane whenever he wanted to see me. Diane, being the romantic that she was, wanted me to be happy with whomever I was with. We would then meet at Diane's house and listen to music and make love well into the night until Gene went to work.

I was beginning to develop a conscience over this situation. I wanted to leave my husband and be with Gene forever. I couldn't stomach making love to two different men anymore. I needed Gene more than I needed my life. Gene wasn't prepared to leave his wife until his son Billy was released from prison.

Gene would pull some major stunts so he could have me all to himself. It was at this point Bob was beginning to wise up. I couldn't wait any longer; I had to speak to Bob about our marriage. I wanted out. I finally confronted Bob one day.

I shouted, "Bob, I want a divorce! You can have the house. Just leave me alone!"

Bob began to beg and cry. "Please don't leave me. I'll do anything. I'll change; I promise I will."

I was beginning to feel sorry for him once again. I decided to cool it for a while with Gene. I needed to think to sort things out. I then met with Gene and we had a long talk. I spoke to him about how Bob was feeling and that I couldn't leave him yet. Bob got to me again; I don't know what it was, but I felt obligated. I also told Gene I wasn't going to see him anymore. Gene was smart enough to know I would be back.

Bob finally figured it out; he asked me whom I was seeing. I couldn't deny it any longer. I finally told Bob I was seeing Gene Ashley. He went into shock. "How could you love an alcoholic like him! I can't believe you're embarrassing me with a person like that."

All of a sudden Bob didn't feel threatened anymore. He was out to win me back. He would do everything in his power to keep me from leaving him. I was very receptive to this. However, the want and desire to be with Gene was greater than the want of Bob. A light was beginning to shine and Bob finally realized that he was going to lose me.

Hardly a day went by that I didn't think of Gene. I finally gave in. I had to see him. Here I had a man, Bob, who was in love with me; we had been married for fifteen years, but somehow I lost respect for him. Then there was Gene who wanted me and filled my endless void. He was wonderful sexually, and he would encourage me to use my Psychic potential. The only problem we faced: Gene was married, and so was I.

I knew in my heart I loved them both very deeply, but I also knew someday I would have to make a choice. It was very hard to live two different lives and pretend to the world that everything was fine. I was always honest with Gene; I would tell him how I felt. He never once swayed me. He always told me it was my decision.

Early in the morning the very next day, I heard the doorbell ring. Bob answered the door and there stood Gene, asking to speak with me. Bob called me: "Hey, Dayle! Your Lover Boy is here. I'm leaving! So the two of you can be alone." I couldn't believe this was happening. There was Gene, standing inside my house, challenging my husband. **Boy, was he drunk!** Gene had this stupid look on his face, half his shirt was hanging out of his trousers, and his legs wobbled so badly I thought he would fall down. Bob slammed the door and off he went. I was left alone with Gene. I've heard of A **Knight In Shining Armor,** but this was ridiculous.

I decided it was far too dangerous for us to stay in the house; Bob might come back with a shotgun. So Gene made his escape in his truck and I followed him in my car. Off we went to a nice secluded place where we could discuss this matter. I didn't know how I was going to get out of this mess. Gene had disrupted my life. I barely had a husband, and now this crazy Indian was trying to make me his

**Squaw.**

But I loved him. I asked Gene if he was willing to leave his wife. He never answered. Gene was concerned that Bob was on his way to tell Annie what happened. He knew this was one mess he might not get out of. I knew he couldn't leave Annie just yet. He didn't want to hurt her, but what he didn't realize was he was hurting her more by being dishonest, and she was no dummy.

**I must say, for three years our love affair was wild and crazy. I could write over three hundred pages about all the crazy things Gene and I did during my mid-life crisis.**

I decided that I had to be honest. At this point I was in no position to move out financially. But I couldn't stay there in the same house with Bob any longer. Gene had a great excuse; he drank to oblivion. I didn't have any excuse, except, I was **STUPID!**

It was at this point I decided I couldn't live like this any longer. When I arrived home I had a long talk with Bob and apologized for what Gene did. I explained to Bob it would be better if I left the house for a while, but I never mentioned divorce. I just didn't want to hurt him anymore. Bob wanted me to stay. He wanted us to work things out. He thought if we could go to counseling and if I would give up Gene, everything would be all right.

This was the problem; I was not willing to give up Gene. I needed time to think. As I was packing my suitcase, Bob asked me where I was going. I told him I was going to move in with my girlfriend Diane for a while. I wanted him to give me time to sort things out. Somehow I couldn't look Bob straight in his eyes. My head was down as he grabbed me and said, "I love you. Please don't leave!"

**I decided to stay. We came to an understanding for a while. All Was Well Until The Day The BOMB Went Off!**

# BOMBED OUT!
## CHAPTER 12

Just imagine what it would like if you awoke one day and suddenly your whole life was just about to change. All the comforts you once had, all the security that you once felt would no longer be there for you. This major catastrophe happened to me in just a fleeting moment in time. This event was a major turning point in my life. On this day my whole life changed right before my very eyes.

Not only did my whole world change, but the new journey that was chosen for me also came unexpectedly. The event that was to occur also affected well over forty-five-hundred other people. Their lives were altered in time as well. This was a learning experience and a spiritual experience, one that would virtually throw me off my present course onto a new beginning. It would give me a new outlook on life, one that would last for more than a lifetime.

Unbeknownst to me, this journey was now beginning. I was thrown from the pits of hell, taken out of my body to be shown my life right before my very eyes. This realization of my new life-to-come was astounding to me. I was shown by this one event how I was hurting myself as well as all the people around me. I was given a second chance. I now had a choice: whether I would allow myself to fall deeper into the pit of Hell, or whether I would follow the light of knowledge into the new path that had been given to me.

It happened one hot summer day. I call it the beginning of my new life. It was a time of reflection, a time to heal, and a time to take a long hard look at what I had become. For without this event that gave me a second chance, I don't know how much more damage I would have done to myself and others.

I feel we are all given second chances at one time or another in our lives. We sometimes do not recognize them when they come. I call them miracles. But it is not often you are given the opportunity to realize what life may hold for you. I have learned when one door closes, another will open. But you must believe me when I tell you that this was one of the very few chances I had to change my life.

## SECOND CHANCE

It was August 27th, the year 1980. The day started out like any other day; I awoke as usual. I was getting ready for work at Harvey's Casino. My shift was from noon till eight in the evening. This particular day was just beautiful. I started out by drinking a cup of coffee, lighting a cigarette, and staring out my window for about an hour or so. The view from my dining room was very picturesque. I stared out the window upon the lake as I was pondering over my life. I then took time out to play with my dogs. I made my way into the living room, listening to some music while I got ready for work. I had already decided if I could get out from work early I would head down to the lake and lie on the beach.

I was finally ready. I grabbed a quick cup of coffee, kissed the dogs goodbye, and off I went in my car. As I was making my way down the hill toward the casinos, I turned on the radio. I heard our local deejay announce: "Attention. If anyone is heading toward the Stateline Nevada area toward the casinos, turn around immediately and go back. Please turn around and go back! There is a bomb in Harvey's Casino."

I kept driving as I heard the warning again. "There is a bomb in Harvey's. It can go off at any moment. Please, people, turn around!

Keep away from the Stateline area."

At this point I turned the car around and headed back up the hill toward home.

This must be a joke, I thought. I can't believe this. A bomb? They have to be joking; maybe the station's taking ratings. I kept driving as I heard it again. I finally reached my home. As I was parking the car, Bob ran out to greet me.

"Did you hear about the bomb?" he asked.

"Yes," I replied. "I can't believe it. Is it true? Is it really true?" I was shocked.

We both ran into the house and turned on the radio simultaneously. We sat listening intently to the radio. We listened and listened as our whole life began to flash before our eyes.

What was being transmitted across the radio wires was most unique. Apparently, this was not your everyday bomb that was placed in Harvey's Casino. We always had bomb threats in the past, but nothing to speak of. The bomb that was placed in the casino was the size of a HOTEL ROOM. The news that we were hearing for three long days was devastating to everyone within the town.

The FBI was called, as well as the CIA and the bomb squad. There were specialists from all over the world being flown into our tiny little town of Lake Tahoe. For some reason, there wasn't anyone knowledgeable about how to defuse the bomb. Lake Tahoe was now the center of attention; we were now being televised throughout the nation.

Days went by, although it seemed like weeks. Harvey's Casino for the first time in history shut down. Each day became more and more of a nightmare. At one point the bomb squad was going to evacuate the whole town. No one seemed to know what to do; it was very chaotic. Who could make a bomb like this? We did know that there was a timer on the bomb set to go off within a specific time frame, but no one was quite sure when.

What would happen to the town? We could all be unemployed. And then there was the safety of the town that was at stake. It was a very scary time. There was constant news from the radio stations coming across the wires minute by minute. The Feds had to come to a decision, one they didn't want to make. It was then the bomb squad decided there was no other solution but to evacuate a portion of the town and blow up the bomb.

This was devastating, just thinking about the place where you have worked every day for a period of five years going up in smoke in a matter of minutes. We were given a specific time that they would detonate the bomb. The bomb squad was in the process of clearing several city blocks. They seemed to know in which direction she would blow, and where the safe areas would be.

There were several dangerous situations that might occur, but they seemed to have them well under control, so they told us. My husband Bob was a pit boss at Harrah's across the street from Harvey's Casino. There was a string of other hotels and casinos that were in the path of the bomb. All could go in a matter of minutes. Although Harvey's was not in operation, Harrah's was, and so were the other casinos within the area.

On the day they chose to detonate the bomb, only a few select dealers were asked to go in to work and deal cards. I, of course, was one of the **LUCKY ONES!** My job was to work at Harvey's Inn, several blocks away from the main hotel and casino. It was business as usual. The streets were lined with on-lookers and many curiosity seekers. Most of the town was out and about. Bob's job was to secure some of the main pits for Harrah's and to tape up the windows. It flashed on him that they weren't paying him enough money to risk his life; somehow, he managed to go home and watch the event on television.

As for me, on this historic event I drove to work for one of the last moments in my dealing career for Harvey's Casino. As I drove, I noticed the streets were lined with wall-to-wall people selling shirts that said, **"I survived the bomb at Harvey's in Lake Tahoe."**

I was told by my pit bosses that we were safe at Harvey's Inn; the blast would never reach us. For some reason, I believed them. It was just a few minutes before countdown. The bomb would be detonated; Harvey's Casino would be no more.

My boss, Wil Seadman, approached me and whispered in my ear, "Dayle, when the bomb goes off, you might feel a rumble. What I want you to do is cover your tray of money with this plastic cover and duck under the table if need be." He spoke calmly.

My reaction to that was **"Oh, I see, you really mean I should kiss my pretty little white ass goodbye."**

Wil laughed and said, "Don't worry. We picked you to deal to our customers because we knew you could handle it."

It only took an instant for it to dawn on me: What the hell was I doing here, dealing cards to women in their bathrobes? I was only making $45 a shift and risking my life. There was no telling how far the bomb blast could reach. I was dealing cards just as if it were any other day. I couldn't believe people were gambling under these circumstances.

The customers I was dealing to had been evacuated and sent down from Harvey's main hotel and casino. I was dealing to people in their nightgowns. I wanted to leave, escape; but it was too late. **There she blew!** The only casino in the history of the world to be blown up and, of course, it had to be the one that I worked for.

As my whole life flashed right before my eyes, I just couldn't believe this was happening. There was nothing left of **Harvey's Hotel and Casino,** just a pile of ashes. All the other casinos were intact and there weren't any injuries. The bomb squad had done a fine job of blowing up Harvey's.

My shift now ended in more ways than one. As the bomb blew, so did my job. The reaction of the people watching it go off was like that of an audience at a three-ring circus. Everyone was in awe; maybe the shock of it all hadn't set in yet. I recall feeling devastated and lost. It was at that moment I took off my dealing apron for the last time, folded it so neatly, and took one last look around me.

I made my way outside of Harvey's Inn and looked up the block toward the remembrance of what used to be Harvey's Hotel and Casino. I shook my head in disbelief, turned around slowly, and headed back into Harvey's Inn and Casino. I decided to sit down at the bar and have a drink. What else was left to do but sit and drink and talk about what had happened. Several dealers joined me at the bar. Time went by so quickly. Many dealers began to gather at the bar. Gossip was beginning to spread widely.

Several drinks later I came up with what I thought was a brilliant idea for the moment. "Let's go to the unemployment office and file for unemployment," I said.

My friends seemed to like the idea. With drinks in hand we all walked to the unemployment office, figuring we might get the upper hand if we were the first in line.

As we were approaching the unemployment office, several reporters seemed to be following us. I, of course, was feeling no pain when the reporters started asking me questions.

"What's your name?"

I responded with "Dayle Schear."

They asked me what I felt really happened in regards to the Harvey's bomb.

I responded with **"It Was An Inside Job."** Whoops! Wrong move. The liquor was talking. No sooner did those five little words leave my mouth than I realized I was in a heap of trouble.

"Trouble" was my middle name. I knew that would be the last time I would ever deal again at Harvey's. Why did I say that? After that statement to the press, I knew my time was up. This was my turning point. In a matter of days all would change, including my life.

I somehow made my way home. My head was spinning not only from the booze, but also in my heart I knew I should have never spoken to the press. I broke a cardinal rule, the dealer's oath never to tell what really goes on inside the casinos. Most of all, never speak to outsiders about your job and how you feel about it. The damage was done.

Throughout my dealing years I would always joke with my dealer friends. They would tell me that once you were in as a dealer, the chance of getting out without returning was slim and none. Because the money was good, a large percentage of dealers always came back to deal the game.

I, of course, was defiant. I believed I was at the peak of my career; I was considered to be one of the best, one of the top five dealers on the hill. I knew I was reaching burnout. I was looking for ways to get out of the casino and I was positive that I could find a way out. However, my dealer friends would always say, **"It Will Take A Bomb To Get Us Out Of This Place."** The funny thing was we'd all laugh about it and go back to our games. Since we were always dressed in black and white, we called it "The March of the Penguins."

When I arrived home, I explained everything to my husband Bob. He felt that I shouldn't worry; we would get by at that time. Bob and I stayed glued to the television and radio for at least a week. We watched intently as they were trying to find out who placed the bomb in Harvey's. In the weeks to come, somehow they would manage to open up one pit at Harvey's to make the casino operational. And slowly, out of forty-five-hundred employees the casino was beginning to call, some people went back to work but not enough to matter. Bob was thankful that we both worked at different casinos. At least he had his pit boss job at Harrah's. As for me, I didn't have a clue as to what I was going to do. Part of me was relieved that I could stay home for a while; the other part of me was devastated.

A few more weeks went by and we were beginning to hear horror stories about the employees who worked for Harvey's. Forty-five-hundred people were out of work. They were losing their homes, wandering the streets, homeless, without jobs; people were leaving the town to look for work elsewhere. This took a toll on the community; businesses were going bankrupt. Till this day the town has never fully recovered.

It was early in the morning when Bob went to work. Shortly after, there was a honk outside of my front door. There sat Gene Ashley in his car. I walked over to him; I hadn't seen Gene in well over a week and I was happy to see him. He asked me to get in the car and we drove to a secluded spot.

"What happened?" he asked. "I looked for your name on the list at Harvey's. You were supposed to be called back to work, then I found out you were fired. What happened?" He was very concerned.

I told Gene about what I had said to the press. I told him I didn't mean to talk to the press; it was the liquor speaking. Gene understood. He felt he could find a way to get me back to work. I knew that it wouldn't work, but if he wanted to try, that was up to him.

We ended up making love in the car for hours. It seemed as if he didn't want to let me go. He kept telling me how much he loved me. He wanted to know what I was going to do for a job. I didn't know. I told him I needed time to think.

Days were passing. I spent most of my time thinking about what I was going to do with my life. I was able to see Gene as much as I wanted, since I wasn't working. We became extremely close. Later, it dawned on me I somehow had to go back to work.

Now that I was unemployed, my obsession with Gene was overwhelming. Bob was still at my side, but my heart belonged to Gene. We began talking about being together. But I knew I had to find myself for the first time in my life. I didn't know what I was supposed to be doing with my life.

Meanwhile, over the months there was much talk about the bomb. Everyone wanted to know who did it and why. The tourist trade was picking up by leaps and bounds every day. People were coming to Lake Tahoe from all over the world to see the remnants of Harvey's Casino.

Within a month I found a job dealing Twenty-One in Carson City for the Ormsby House. The only problem I faced was it was a graveyard shift; graveyard was something I wasn't used to. I found I was sleeping once every three days. This definitely was not for me. I would go to work half asleep; I knew I wasn't long for this job.

It was one of those months: I was in the wrong place again at the wrong time. I was just finishing up my shift and heading toward home when several of my friends called me. Guess who was in town. Gerry Turner. It seemed he took his own jet up to the Lake and the word was he was searching the casinos for some Blackjack dealer that he knew at one time. He apparently didn't have any luck, so he left. I must have had the luck of the Irish. Shortly after that, I was laid off from my job at the Ormsby House. And, by the way, I thanked them.

It was several years later when they found out who planted the bomb in Harvey's. The man was John Virges, someone I was familiar with. In fact, I dealt cards to him on many occasions. John was into Harvey's for well over a million dollars, which he failed to pay back. He was then kicked out of his room and he felt insulted after spending well over a million dollars over the years at this one hotel. He had a vendetta against Harvey's.

John Virges had acquired demolition skills in World War II and was clever enough to have escaped at one time from a Nazi prison camp. He devised this bomb with timer and had it sent into Harvey's hidden in an immense IBM box. The innocent-looking box with the bomb in it was sent to the storage area in the basement till someone just happened upon it. John was arrested and is still doing time in a state prison. A sad person; he was a compulsive gambler.

**As for me, I had to make a decision. Life was getting extremely hard until Diane Ash opened her door and let me come into her life so I could grow.**

# PEOPLE I'VE MET ALONG THE WAY
## CHAPTER 13

My head was spinning. I didn't know in which direction to turn. Everything hit me at once. The year was 1980; my life was in shambles. I was living on unemployment benefits and didn't quite know what I was going to do with my life.

My marriage of fifteen years to Bob was on the rocks. The $82 a week I was living on was barely enough to meet my needs. I needed my space; I needed to get away for a while. I had a long talk with Bob that evening. I explained to him the pressures of my everyday life were getting out of control. I wanted to move in with my best friend Diane for a while to get my head together.

Bob understood where I was coming from. This was the first time he consented to letting me have my space. He was sure I'd come home in a few days, after I was cast out in the cold with little money to survive on. He felt I'd finally see the light in our relationship and I'd never want to stray again. Maybe he was right, but I had to find out for myself.

When the bomb blew at Harvey's, I felt I had to keep on going. I felt safe and secure moving in with Diane; we were the best of friends. As I left my house, I held on for dear life to my faithful hair dryer. I was carrying a mixture of clothes in one hand and my favorite pillow in the other hand. There I stood, right outside of Diane's window, as she welcomed me. Although she had three children to feed, her door was always open.

Diane was tall, had brown hair, and was very attractive. She had been married several times and was now going through a divorce. Diane was special. We would manage to get into the most unusual situations. Far be it from me, this was one of the most interesting parts of my life.

I felt I was there to help Diane through her divorce. I feel that people are sometimes thrown together in this big world for some special purpose. Diane was the sister I never had. We had more fun together as friends. I needed her to help me grow. Diane taught me all about the real world and what my role would be in it.

Diane and I wanted to find something different to do around town. We grabbed a newspaper, the "Tahoe Tribune," and looked through the day's events. There it was, the Great Wagon Train Party held once a year in Lake Tahoe. We decided to go. Diane suggested we get all spruced up in our fancy western wear and mosey on down to the party. This would be a great chance to meet all the right people in the town; some of the most influential people in town would be there.

This event reverts back to the old Pony Express days in Lake Tahoe. The townspeople dress up in costumes and take the original Pony Express ride all over again. They actually deliver mail as in the olden days of yesteryear.

I recall it was a hot summer day early in July. The pine trees were beautiful; the sun was shining; the lake was as clear as glass. When we arrived, I noticed everyone from the sheriff's department happened to be there. We sat down at one of the picnic tables and gazed around in fascination. Across the crowded picnic table sat a very handsome man wearing a sheriff's uniform. I wanted to meet him. Of course, Diane just happened to know every eligible bachelor in town.

Diane introduced me to the officer. His name was Lieutenant Stan Pope from the Douglas County Sheriffs Department. Stan was about 35, tall, dark, and handsome, with blue eyes. It's hard to describe someone who is simply gorgeous.

When Diane introduced me, she decided to add to my mystique and told him I was Psychic. Stan politely introduced himself, then mumbled, "If you're so Psychic, why don't you read me and give me a little taste of your ability."

As the saying goes, "I nailed him to the cross."

I held on to Stan's Chapstick while I gave him a reading. That was all he was carrying on him that day. When I blurted out a crime which no one knew about, I amazed him. Stan asked me if I could meet him at the sheriff's station in the morning.

"Yes," I said. Well, I turned to Diane and mumbled under my breath, "Another fine mess you got me into." Here I was trying to stay low-keyed about my Psychic ability, and Diane threw me into the lion's den. Within a few hours I would be mincemeat for the lions.

We mingled some more and Diane introduced me to a local deejay, Mark Lennartz. Diane made her pitch again and was telling Mark how talented I was as a Psychic. Mark showed an interest in me and asked if I were ever on the radio before. I told him "yes."

I explained to Mark that I was tuning in to his radio station one evening and I heard a Psychic on the air. His name was Ken Bittinger, and he was taking live calls from his radio listeners. I listened intently. I decided I had to meet this guy, so I set up an appointment with him. I wanted to trade readings with him. Ken recognized my talent and asked me to join him on his radio program. We talked for hours on end. Ken felt I was just as good as he was, even though I had no experience. The funny thing about this was that we were both born on the same day, same month, and same year, and had similar personalities.

Much to my surprise, Ken scheduled me to be on the radio with him and the response was overwhelming. I appeared for several weeks with him. Ken later decided to move on to the islands of Hawaii. He foretold that within two years I would have my own radio talk show. I, in turn, predicted he would be a success in the islands.

Mark listened intently to my story. He liked the idea of my performing on the radio along with him. Mark asked me to call him within a few days; he wanted to check with the owner to see if it would be all right. "Thank you, Mark; it was a pleasure meeting you," I said.

Well, it was time for Diane and me to mosey on. Whoa, what an eventful day! In the course of this one day I went from an ex-Blackjack dealer to a professional Psychic. As Diane and I made our way back to the car, I discussed with her the embarrassment I could face. I had never declared myself as a Psychic, since I only dabbled in it once in a while. There might be some casino workers who would laugh at me. I could see the headlines now:

**"EX-BLACKJACK DEALER BECOMES PSYCHIC."**

Diane tried to calm me down. "Don't worry, Honey, you're good at what you do; you're talented. If they laugh at you, you can laugh all the way to the bank."

That evening Diane helped me get prepared to meet the sheriff. I was nervous. The next day Stan was excited to see me. The first thing he did was lock me up in a jail cell along with some clothing that belonged to a suspect. This case was known as the "John Robert Powers Case." I was told that they found the body but they wanted to know how to find the killer.

I went into a detailed description about the killer and his approximate location. Several months later the killer was found. It was then that Stan assigned me to a detective named Steve Kibbi. Steve and I worked on several murder cases after that. What was most important, we became the best of friends.

To describe Detective Kibbe: He is the most honest, incredible detective you would ever want to meet. I noticed he didn't have a big ego like most cops I have encountered. Steve was willing to work with Psychics. He would do anything within the law to solve a crime. Steve reminded me of **"COLUMBO"**; they even looked alike. There wasn't much that ever escaped him. Our friendship is still on-going.

One case we worked on together was called "John's Tahoe Nugget Robbery." Steve happened to be visiting me in my home in regards to a different case, when all of a sudden I blurted out, "John's Tahoe Nugget is going to be robbed within the next thirty days. Please, Steve, be aware of this." It was July 6, 1982. I stated many things at the time and most of it panned out. I seemed to be picking up on robberies. I also picked up on a robbery at Harrah's in Lake Tahoe, for which I was given credit.

This was the beginning of my Psychic detective work, mostly connected with Detective Steve Kibbe. Steve was amazingly Psychic. I think that was why he solved ninety percent of the crimes that he worked on. If ever there was a dedicated detective, Steve Kibbe was the one. You see, being a detective was more than a job for him; it was a way of life. He wanted to be the best at whatever he did in life. He gave up many things for his job; he gave up his family at times and just plain living. (My highest wishes for the future, Steve. If there is a medal for your classification, **YOU SURELY DESERVE IT.**)

# Letter from Douglas County Sheriff's Office,
# Detective Steve Kibbe

September 30, 1983

ON MAY 27, 1982, WHILE WE WERE INVESTIGATING, TWO UNSOLVED ROBBERIES AT HARRAH'S, LAKE TAHOE, THE SUSPECT IN THE ROBBERIES WAS UNKNOWN, AT THAT TIME.

PICTURES THAT WERE TAKEN BY THE CASINO CAMERAS, SHOWING THE ACTUAL ROBBERY IN PROGRESS, WERE SHOWN TO DAYLE SCHEAR, IN HOPES OF LEARNING MORE INFORMATION ABOUT THE SUSPECT.

UPON REVIEWING THE PHOTOGRAPHS, WHICH AT BEST WERE VERY POOR, THROUGH DAYLE SCHEAR'S INFORMATION, DAYLE STATED THAT:

1) **THE SUSPECT WAS A LOCAL**

2) **KNEW THE CASINO OPERATION**

3) **DRUG RELATED/ GAMBLING PROBLEMS**

4) **THAT HE WOULD SHOOT, IF GIVEN THE CHANCE.**

5) **MIGHT BE MORE THAN ONE PERSON INVOLVED.**

6) **THE SAME SUSPECT WOULD COME BACK TO HARRAH'S AGAIN AND ROB AGAIN.**

7) **THE SUSPECT WOULD BE CAUGHT AND ARRESTED WITHIN A SHORT TIME.**

ON JULY 4, 1982 THE THIRD ROBBERY TOOK PLACE AT THE SAME CASINO. WITHIN A MATTER OF TWO HOURS, MICHAEL LOPEZ WAS ARRESTED AND CHARGED WITH THE ARMED ROBBERIES WHICH, AFTER A JURY TRIAL, WAS CONVICTED OF THE LISTED ROBBERIES. THE 96,000 DOLLARS THAT WAS TAKEN BY LOPEZ IN THE THREE ROBBERIES, HAS BEEN LOCATED IN VARIOUS DEALINGS.

DET. STEVE KIBBE

DOUGLAS COUNTY SHERIFFS DEPARTMENT

# From Douglas County Sheriff's Office, Stan Pope

**July 6, 1982:**

Detective Steve Kibbe met with Lake Tahoe Psychic Dayle Schear, to discuss an active case that Steve Kibbe and Dayle Schear were working on.

This date, I Dayle Schear informed Detective Kibbe that John's Tahoe Nugget would be robbed within a 30 day period of time, by a local individual. I informed him at the time to please watch the Tahoe Nugget.

**July 15, 1982:**

John's Tahoe Nugget was robbed, on July 17,1982. The following information was released to Stan Pope, of Douglas County Sheriff's Office, by me through psychic revelation, by the use of pictures, signatures & clothing. This information was recorded on tape, July 17, 1982:

**Personality Profile of suspect:**

1) I stated that the suspect had a name change, (suspect used other names) and that he had a criminal record.
2) I also stated that there were two or more people involved in the robbery.
3) The suspect was on his way to Las Vegas, Nevada
4) There had been a change of cars

**Motive for Crime:**

1) The suspect had a grudge against the casinos and wanted revenge.
2) Suspect was a gambler, involved in drugs and owed people money.

I stated that the suspect would be caught within 30 days; and that Stan Pope should "UP" the bail, or the suspect would be let go.

The suspect was caught on July 19, 1982.
This information is documented by Stan Pope, Douglas County Sheriff's Office.

STAN POPE

I was overwhelmed by the new people Diane introduced me to. I was well on my way to a new career. Night was falling and shortly there was a ring on her doorbell. There was my long-lost Indian; he had tracked me to Diane's house. I told Gene of all the happenings at the Wagon Train; I must have rambled on for hours on end.

Gene was encouraging me to pursue my destiny as he carried me to the bedroom and began undressing me slowly. Our love-making was getting better and better. I began to notice he was not going home at all to Annie. It seemed while I was living with Diane he wanted to be with me more and more. Gene loved my living with Diane. He felt she would protect me and he could see me as often as he wanted now. He had the best of both worlds.

I was addicted to him. He was the best lover I ever had back then. He certainly knew how to please a woman. And please he did. I think our record for making love in one day was seven times, and each time was better than the next.

Diane began to warn me to be careful of getting pregnant. I looked at her and laughed. Bob had convinced me that there was something wrong with me, that I couldn't bear children. Even though the doctors deemed him sterile, he had an operation to increase his sperm count, which went to almost normal at one time. He claimed I was now the faulty one. I truly believed I would never become pregnant. Here I was, making love to Gene for two years and nothing ever happened. I reassured Diane she had nothing to worry about, but she kept giving me strange looks. "The way the two of you go at it, you never seem to come up for air. I would be surprised if you didn't get pregnant," she said. I laughed!

The lean times were setting in. Diane suggested that I give it a shot at the radio station. She wanted me to call Mark Lennartz. I did. For once, I was in the right place at the right time. He wanted me to be on his radio show. Mark was going to allow three hours of air time, all devoted to "ESP & ME."

This was it, make no mistake about it. I was given a date and time for my first appearance on radio in Lake Tahoe. It was July 18, 1981, Saturday morning from 9 a.m. till 12 noon. I was nervous, but it was do or die; I had to take the chance. I was going to read Mark's Tarot cards on the air.

**In the deck of Tarot cards, there is one card that I love the most. That card is The Fool. When The Fool card comes up in the spread, it means you will be placed in a foolish position: whether you choose to remain a fool or venture inward onto a different path. You could travel all the roads, highways, and byways onto the greatest heights; but the choice, my friend, is up to you whether you choose to remain a fool or not.**

**For some reason, that card and only that card kept popping up out of a deck of 78 Tarot cards and kept landing on our table. I had to heed the warning. Only time would tell, but I had to take that chance.**

**RADIO, HERE I COME!**

# THE GOOD OLD RADIO DAYS
## CHAPTER 14

### JULY 18, 1981

"Live on the radio with Psychic Dayle Schear." Mark Lennartz announced me that morning. Mark was the first deejay I had ever worked with. He was a skeptic who was going through some hard emotional times in his life.

### "ENTER PSYCHIC"

One thing I noticed: I would always turn up when someone was in trouble. I had a knack for that. The universe always placed me where I belonged. Mark was six-foot ten inches tall; I was five-foot two inches and 98 pounds dripping wet. What a crazy pair we were. The interview began. Mark asked the usual questions about ESP and Psychic ability. Then he asked me to read for him.

From that moment Mark the skeptic became a believer. I hit home on too many occasions. I started to go for his jugular vein. "Enough!" he shouted. Mark opened up the radio phone lines. The calls began pouring in. The listeners called me "Amazing! Unbelievable! Fantastic!"

The radio show was an overnight success. People were talking all over town about the new Psychic, how "right on she was." They definitely wanted more. What surprised me most was that the townspeople never associated me with the casinos. For some reason, they thought I was someone entirely different. I recall I even blew away John Parker, the owner of KOWL Radio Station.

I waited three weeks for the radio station to call me back, hoping that they would hire me on a permanent basis. I paced the whole time, waiting for the call. I had noticed while I was on the radio that I was helping a lot of people. I received an enormous number of calls for readings. This kept me alive financially for a while, anyway.

The phone finally rang. John Parker, the owner, called me personally. He offered me a job at the radio station every Saturday morning. John was unique and eccentric. He was 37 years old, a self-made millionaire, and cheaper than Jack Benny. John made a living out of creating radio stars. He would build your ego until there was no tomorrow, but he would pay the least amount of money he could to his radio people.

John thought I was a fantastic performer. He didn't care if I was a Psychic worth a damn. All John cared about were his ratings. He would compliment me on my radio presence and tell me I had a fantastic radio voice. John would say, "Dayle, I'd pay you any amount of money for you to be a female deejay rather than a Psychic performer." John felt by building me up as a radio personality, fame would come my way. He also knew that if I were to give out my phone number on the radio, people would call and book appointments with me; therefore, he wouldn't have to pay me a salary.

John was more than right. The radio show was a **Great Success**. I was booked solid with readings for well over a year. It never dawned on me that I just might become famous doing this radio show. The purpose of my doing the radio show was to help people. I must admit when this all started, it was sink or swim. I never knew where this radio show was going to lead. As I got further and deeper into my desire to help people, they responded overwhelmingly.

I never imagined in my wildest dreams that there were so many people crying for help out there. As Mark and I created more of a market, the number of people that would call the radio station crying out for help was beyond our comprehension. The phone lines would be lit up for well over an hour before I arrived at the studio. People were just waiting on the phone lines, hoping I would choose them.

A realization came upon me one day. The old adage that Psychics are not supposed to make money for helping people was crazy. I found out my Psychic ability worked better if I ate three meals a day and paid my rent.

For a Psychic, the radio was a great means of communication. Individuals placed calls to the radio station; I then picked up on their voices and told them what I saw. Within my ability, there lies a special gift. Many people have commented over the years that any-one can listen to a question from a caller and give them an answer. This is true. However, the way I worked was different from the rest. I would only allow the callers to give me their first names and where they were from. No questions. I then would tell them what I saw in their past, present, and future.

I was unique. There were very few Psychics in the world that could read a person by phone just by saying **"HELLO."** I was very serious about my work and helping people; the money was secondary. After a while I truly believed that this was my calling all along.

This is the way I felt about working on the radio and how I wanted to help people even more:

**To help, to give of yourself when people are down and there**

**is no hope. They cry, "Help me!"**

The radio calls come pouring in by the hundreds. With a lot of help from the man upstairs, I open their eyes to a brighter day. For just a moment in time I reach out and touch them. I can see where they can not. I give them a future.

**To help just one person and put that person on the right path is a greater deed, more than one can perceive. That is my destiny.**

To utilize the radio air waves to make people aware of their own human potential is my quest. To make them realize that they should also help mankind by opening up their own Psychic ability. **That, Too, Is My Destiny.**

To give them a future when they are at their wits' end. It's just a little hope that goes a long way. I will get them over the hump for a brighter tomorrow. I am one of many who have been chosen for this gift. To utilize my ability to further mankind, to make their paths a little more comfortable along life's road. **That, Too, Is My Destiny.**

When the people came to my home for a personal reading, they were at their wits' end. They cried, "Please tell me my future." So I gave them one. Little did I know that their reality was my reality, and the future I so perceived was their future.

People expect help and comfort when they come to see me. As a Psychic I am expected to give them all the answers and make all the decisions for them. That way, perchance if I am wrong, they can blame the Psychic rather than themselves.

There are people from all walks of life that go to Psychics. Most people want direction in their everyday lives. Some are at a crossroad of a major decision and within their own hearts have known the answer to their problems all along. They want the Psychic to confirm what is already in their minds so they can feel at ease. Since ESP is readily being accepted all over the world, people are more open to Psychics.

When people come to me for a reading, I do not tell them the answer. I tell them what I see. I give them more than one path, the best option for them to follow at that time. And most importantly, I give them the outcome of their situation along with direction.

The whole point of a Psychic is to allow individuals to make their own choices in their lives, to pick and choose of their own free will. A Psychic should not judge the clients in any way.

There are times when someone is so lost that I am guided to give that person a future and help make a decision. When my clients are not capable of making decisions, I search my mind to find out where their talents lie to help them along their paths, to be able to give them positive feedback and insight into the future. I teach them to help themselves.

When I let myself be guided to help them on their new paths, somehow through the help of God their futures are shown to me. I am able to pass the information on to them. There have been many occasions when I felt I was just making something up; but, lo and behold, much to my surprise the person's future turns out exactly the way I saw it. I guess it was the individual's destiny all along.

I have chosen several ways to help mankind with my gift. The radio has been one way. As I hear their voices, I have been able to help people with extreme accuracy. I felt my calling. I was destined to deal with the masses on a one-to-one basis to affect their lives.

This was chosen for me on a spiritual realm; also through live shows, seminars, television, or in any other medium. I am enlightening and educating the public. Whatever medium of communication it takes, I will be there as long as someone out there needs my help.

Radio and television allow me to help the troubled at the time of their need. People look forward to some friendly voice coming over the air waves, someone that they feel will help them through a rough time in their lives. THIS IS MY WORK. THIS IS MY LIFE-LONG QUEST.

I found out radio was where I belonged. This was how my first radio show with Mark helped me along my path. Slowly but surely, through helping the masses of people I began to learn how to help myself.

Compared to what I used to be, a Blackjack dealer, working with Mark and the staff at the radio station was a whole new world opening up for me. Mark didn't quite know what to make of the whole situation.

I started off every Saturday morning reading his cards on the radio; and sure enough, the events that I predicted were coming true. There was a point where Mark would consult with me on a regular basis if he was confused about something in his life.

Our routine on the radio was simple. I would start with an opening song that pertained to the Psychic realm, such as "Read My Mind" by Gordon Lightfoot. Mark and I would chat about upcoming events that pertained to ESP. It was more of an educational process than anything else. I was beginning to educate the listeners on facts and fallacies regarding ESP. People were actually learning.

Going into our second hour, we would open up the phone lines and I'd speak to the callers live on the air. We allowed each caller one question for time purposes. However, my answers went far beyond answering the question. The show was becoming so hot it was unbelievable. I mean, in a small town like Lake Tahoe, it was turning into the biggest soap opera ever. People actually looked forward to every Saturday morning with Mark and Dayle.

We started to expand our show into different areas. I utilized Psychometry, which is the art of holding onto objects belonging to an individual to see into the past, present, and future of that person's life. The callers would drop by with jewelry that they owned and give them to Mark, who then handed them to me during the show. I knew nothing about the callers.

We would contact the callers at home and I would proceed to tell everything I saw for those individuals through holding of their objects. The accuracy was most amazing. Following Mark's time slot was a deejay named Ken Hunter. Sometimes I would end up on his show as well. Ken and I also became close friends.

**I was finally where I was supposed to be, on the radio. The radio was good for me and within three months my ESP was increasing by leaps and bounds.**

# FRIENDS
# THAT MADE A DIFFERENCE
## CHAPTER 15

In each and every one of our lives there is always someone in the background to help you when you need help the most. In my case throughout my life certain people have always been there when I needed them the most. Whenever I was at a major crossroads of a decision, there were friends who played a key role in my life.

## TONI YORK

When Toni York arrived at my doorstep, she was a pretty little blonde standing about five feet four inches tall. Her beauty was overwhelming. Toni was sent to me by a gentleman named Tom. Tom was having an affair with Toni and he wanted me to check her out to make sure he was doing the right thing. Tom wanted to leave his wife Kathy and marry Toni, but there was a doubt in his mind.

I asked Toni to be seated. I learned from Toni she had been going to Psychics all her life. I began my reading; I saw a clear picture of Toni in my mind. No matter how hard I tried, I couldn't see Tom and her together. I saw a man from the past standing by her side. I described this man in detail to Toni. She admitted that she had always been in love with this person I described. His name was Cole Smith. Deep down inside, this was the man she would always love. She couldn't get him out of her mind.

Toni was strikingly beautiful. There wasn't a man that she couldn't have, except for Cole Smith. She began to break down and cry. Toni admitted that she did love Tom, but deep down there would always be Cole within her heart. I tried to teach Toni to deal with the situation about Cole and to confront him so she could release him and go on with her life. I kept seeing a vision of Cole and her together in the future. I mentioned to Toni, "I know you will find this very hard to believe, but somewhere in time you will marry Cole Smith." The reading was over; Toni began to leave.

Then a series of bizarre events began to happen. It was snowing outside as Toni thanked me, made her way to her car, and drove off. Within a matter of minutes I heard the doorbell ring. There she was again. It seemed her car got stuck in the snow. Since it was getting late, she decided to accept my offer to stay the night.

We talked for hours. We noticed the similarities within our lives, the many things we had in common. Toni needed direction. She was 21 and I was 32. I wanted to guide her further so she wouldn't make the same mistakes that I had made. I taught her to the best of my ability to confront the situation with Tom and how to deal with Cole Smith.

Toni ended up living with Bob and me for several years on and off. The funny thing was that every time she tried to leave my house, she was always bounced back, either through a freak snowstorm or a car accident. We then decided she was meant to live with us until she got her head straight.

It turned out Toni was to help me and guide my life to some extent. We both decided this was a Karmic lesson. We needed each other in our lives at that point in time as well as for years to come.

Toni learned that her love affair with Tom was not meant to be. Within six months it faded. She also learned to confront Cole and go to **"The School Of Hard Knocks,"** graduating with a lot of hurt and pain. She found out that the man she loved, Cole Smith, was living with another woman. The woman was just being used as a play toy for Cole. The pain of loving someone who really didn't give a damn! Toni learned a lot, living with me. For years she was looking for Cole in every man she met.

## HOWEVER, IN 1989 TONI MARRIED COLE SMITH, JUST AS I PREDICTED.

### DIANE ASH

I have spoken about Diane on many occasions, but there is something within me that cries out to say more. If ever there was a friend in this world, one I could go to even now, Diane was surely one of them.

Diane was a friend, mother, and sister all wrapped into one. Most of the fun we had together can't be written in any book, unfortunately. The good times we shared, the times we cried, the times we laughed. Diane had all those qualities of a wonderful human being. She was special. Diane believed in love in its highest form. What a Romantic she was.

I learned my first lesson about Karma through Diane. Diane and I would have these discussions about Karma. She was a strong believer in "what goes around comes around"; I was not. She once said, "Someday I'll be able to prove to you what Karma is." I didn't expcct it to be so soon.

That afternoon I needed to leave Diane's house for a while to feed my dogs. I told her I would be back in a half hour or so. On my way home I stopped at a liquor store to pick up a bottle of wine. As I was pulling out of the parking stall, I backed straight into another car. I left a tiny dent on the other car. Since no one was around, I took off like a bat out of hell. I then ran up to feed my dogs and was soon on my way back down the hill with the bottle of wine packed neatly away in my car. When I reached Diane's, I told her about the car I dented and laughed about my getaway. "See, I told you there's no such thing as Karma," I said.

Several drinks later Diane was beginning to believe me. It was time for me to go home. Diane walked out to the driveway with me; we were far from drunk. I started up my car and backed out of her driveway. I heard a crash. I had backed into Diane's car, totaling out my tail lights. Diane's car was heavier than mine; not a scratch on her car. I turned around, quite ashamed. Diane said, "Well, do you believe in Karma now?" I did.

Diane also reminded me of the time I was so mad at Gene that we ventured over to his house one day and decided to toilet paper his car.

One of the saddest days of my life was many years ago shortly after the bomb went off at Harvey's. I noticed that Diane's health was fading. There wasn't a doctor around who could figure out what she had. She seemed to be growing weaker and weaker by the day. Some doctors thought she had palsy; others thought she had low blood sugar; and the rest plain didn't know. Finally, after doctor after doctor, they came to the conclusion it was all in her head.

She ended up in the hospital one day. That day I received a phone call from the hospital; the doctor told me Diane tried to kill herself. I couldn't believe what I was hearing. I rushed down to the hospital and stormed into Diane's room. I demanded an answer. "Is it true, Diane, what the doctors have said about you?"

Diane couldn't remember. She looked up at me and pleaded, "Dayle, you're Psychic. Please concentrate. Tell me what you think is wrong with me. Please, get me some help!"

I sat quietly and concentrated while I held her hand. I then looked her straight in the eye. "Diane, I believe you have multiple sclerosis," I said.

"Does that mean I'm going to die?" she asked.

"NO! I won't let you die," I said emphatically. "Let's get out of this place. I'll find a doctor to help you."

Within a few weeks I found an MS doctor in Reno; he was able to confirm my findings. All the other doctors thought Diane had a brain tumor.

**As of March 1992, Diane is living in Santa Barbara. Her MS is well under control. Diane and I are still the best of friends.**

### PHIL AND ESTHER SIMPSON

Phil and Esther Simpson own one of the finest jewelry stores in all of Lake Tahoe. It was a fine morning early one July when I first met Phil and Esther. I was still working for Harvey's at that time in my life. I wanted to buy some jewelry. In those days I was a Blackjack dealer; our hands were our prize possession and jewelry enhanced my look. I was looking around the store and noticed a nice gentleman with curly blond hair sitting at a jewelry showcase counter. I asked if he could help me. He was Phil Simpson, the owner of Simpson's the Diamond House.

We were soon talking about everything under the sun. I took a liking to a ring of black onyx and diamonds and bought it immediately. Phil asked what I did for a living. I told him I was a Blackjack dealer for Harvey's, but in my spare time I did Psychic readings. Phil was quite a bit perceptive himself. He asked me if we could trade some of his jewelry for a reading. While I was making my purchase, I did a mini-reading on Phil. He was very impressed.

For many years to come, Phil became a regular client. I would do a lot of readings for him regarding the store and other ventures.

We became the best of friends. The funny thing about Phil was that if you took a picture of him and me together, we looked like brother and sister.

As for his wife Esther, she was as fine a lady as could be, a lady with lots of class. Esther was the one who held the store together. A good portion of Phil's life was spent being an alcoholic and the load was always on Esther. She had to run the store and take care of things. Phil eventually joined Alcoholics Anonymous and was successfully recovered. Phil and I became very close; he was very spiritual and very deep into ESP.

It was now the year of the gold and silver crash, somewhere around 1979 or 1980; you know, the one where gold was soaring and the stock market was crashing. Phil came to me and said, "Dayle, how about predicting the gold market."

I looked at Phil and said, "That's one thing I never touch with a ten-foot pole."

Phil looked at me and said, "I know you can do it. Why don't you try."

I explained it was against my God-given gift to predict the market. "All will be taken away from me if I do this."

Phil wouldn't take "no" for an answer. "How about you try just this one time. I'll only put a little in the market and no one will get hurt," he said.

"Okay," I said, "as long as you don't put much in the market."

Gold was at $900 an ounce; against my better judgment I predicted it would keep going up. As you know, within a couple of months gold went crashing down. The look on Phil's face was of one who had lost his best friend. I asked him what was wrong.

"I put an enormous amount of money in the gold market," he replied.

"Phil, you promised me you wouldn't do this!" I shouted. "I told you I have no experience in the stock market."

"I know," he said sheepishly.

I then advised him to short the gold so he could make money on the way down. Phil never did. This caused Phil to be in a financial crunch bigger than even I could imagine. I didn't know how to save him.

I really thought that he was going to take a drink again and go off the wagon after ten years. When it rains, it pours. Suddenly, out of left field, Phil found out that his best friend had died. This added another trauma on Phil. I think this was one of the more trying times that I had ever seen Phil go through.

I was really worried. Here was a man who was kind and good, always helping everyone else in town from the bottom of his heart. Suddenly, he was down to the bottom of the pit. I don't think Esther knew what was happening then, but Phil seemed to be falling apart and no one, including me, could help him.

**Phil figured he needed to get away. The pain he was feeling over his friend's death and the money he lost was getting to him. He told me he was going away for a while and that he would call and tell me where he was. I begged him not to drink; just call me instead. Phil escaped. He never told Esther or me where he was going.**

# MORE ABOUT BOB, GENE, PHIL, TONI, AND DIANE
## CHAPTER 16

In all my years of counseling people, I have never heard of several people at once going through a mid-life crisis. It wasn't only me, but also Bob, Phil, Gene, and Toni. We were all going through it together. I was trying to get away from Gene, as well as Bob. I wanted to find myself. Toni was trying to get away from Tom and Cole. Gene just wanted a normal life; he wanted Annie and me together so he would never have to make a decision.

I was still living with Diane. My radio show was well on its way, thanks to her. She encouraged me to believe enough in myself and to give it a try on the radio. Thanks to Diane my whole life changed.

I was no longer the Blackjack dealer from Harvey's Casino. I now was the "Lake Tahoe Psychic." Offers were coming in from all over Nevada and from as far away as the Bay area. It seemed everyone wanted to meet me. I was asked to appear at every local function in town. Everyone wanted to say that they knew me or had a reading from me. But the most interesting job offer I had was from the Lake Tahoe Community College. The college wanted me to teach a mini-course on the Tarot in the late summer.

I was honored. Here I had only a high school diploma and the community college was asking me to teach. I accepted. With the help of my friend Diane we pulled it off. I was filled with excitement when I walked into the classroom. My classes were overbooked; it was standing room only.

There were professors and teachers and the dean of the college welcoming me personally. What an honor! Fame was now bestowed upon me in every honorable way that could be conceived.

Before I left Diane's house, we sat down and had a long talk. I told her I needed a break; I needed to get away for a while. Helping all those people forced me to look at myself in a different light. I decided to go back home and pack my things and take a quick three-day weekend in Santa Barbara. But first, I needed to speak to Gene.

That evening at Diane's, I spoke with Gene about our relationship. I told him I loved him very much and probably would want to spend the rest of my life with him. I understood his excuse that he couldn't leave his wife because his son Billy was still in prison. I accepted that, but I told Gene I needed him more now than I ever needed him. My fame was getting out of hand. I didn't know what to do anymore. I felt loved and wanted when I was in his arms; I knew he would always protect me.

At the same time, I needed to get away from him for a while. I needed to think things through. Gene never understood; he just wanted me to be patient and wait this thing out. I told him we had been together for two years now and both our marriages were breaking up. What was the point of being patient? Gene said, again, "When this is all over, I want us to be together. Just give me time. You have got to give me time, Babe."

My problem was I was running out of time. I put my foot down and said, "Gene, I love you, but I have to leave you for a while. Please don't try to find me, and I can't tell you where I'm going." I kissed him goodbye, waved to Diane, and headed for home.

As I was driving, I began questioning myself and my marriage. Was loving Gene the right thing to do? Or should I go back to Bob and make it work? I was giving everyone else help through the radio;

yet, I couldn't even help myself.

I didn't want to give up sixteen years of marriage, but at the same time I wanted to be with Gene. The question arose in my mind: If I don't learn to help myself first, how can I help other people? These were very trying times. What started out as a fluke with the radio was seemingly so real. I was actually giving of myself and changing people's lives in a positive way. I knew I wanted to help Gene stop drinking and to be honest with himself. I argued with myself on many occasions about this. I wanted to give him up, knowing my chosen path was helping others. I couldn't; I loved him.

I was tired of fighting off his wife, tired of sitting and waiting for the phone to ring, and tired of wondering when he would come to Diane's house to see me again. Gene knew he was losing me to the Psychic Realm. As much as he encouraged me to go on with my career, a part of him wanted me to be with him.

The more fame that came my way, the harder Gene tried to keep me with him. This wasn't easy for him. He wanted someone to stay by his side and hold his hand; he was a man who couldn't handle responsibility and had to be shown the way. I was the stronger of the two in regards to my career. As for me, my growing desire to learn about ESP was overwhelming. I was torn between my career and Gene. It finally came to me. I thought long and hard about my relationship with Bob as well.

In all the years I was married to Bob, the one thing that stood out the most was that he was **CHEAP**, so cheap he drove me nuts. I mean, one can deal once in a while with a husband who is thrifty. But every day of your life? It gets old fast. When Bob and I would go to the movies, he'd ask me to pay for half of the ticket price. If we bought furniture for the house, he'd ask me to pay for the chairs and he'd buy the table.

During our marriage the most outlandish thing that happened was during the time of our coldest winter in Lake Tahoe. I was bathing in the tub when I noticed that it was quite cold in the house. I got out of the tub to turn up the heat so I wouldn't freeze and Bob started yelling like there was no tomorrow. He claimed our heating bills were so high and I just was adding to it.

Now, it wasn't like we weren't making money. I was still employed at Harvey's just before the bomb when this incident occurred. We were knocking down $4,000 per month between the two of us. There was still plenty to go around. I informed Bob that I'd get sick if the temperature fell below 40 degrees. He went ranting and raving all over the house about the heating bill and demanded that I pay for at least half of it. That was the straw that broke this camel's back.

I needed to go somewhere warm and far away from him. I told Bob I was going to Santa Barbara to get away from him. I was packing my bags to get away from this madman when there was a knock on the door. It was Toni.

Bob was getting ready to go to work and opened the door to let her in. "Hi, Toni," he said on his way out, mumbling all the way.

"What's with him?" Toni asked. I told her about the bathtub caper. She just laughed. "Why are you packing? Where are you going this time?"

"To Santa Barbara," I replied.

"Oh, goody! Can I come too? We could have fun," she said.

I looked at her for a moment out of the corner of my eye. "Yes, why not? The more, the merrier."

At that moment the phone rang. It was long-lost Phil on the line. "Phil! Are you okay?" I shouted. He didn't know. He asked me what I was doing. I told him that Bob lowered the heat, I was fed up with

Gene, and Toni and I were heading to Santa Barbara for the weekend.

Phil had a suggestion. "I have a better idea. I'm in Sacramento with some of my Oakland Raider friends. Why don't you girls come down here for a few days and we can all talk this out?"

I repeated what Phil had said to me on the phone to Toni. She said, "Let's do it! What do we have to lose anyway?"

I picked up the phone again and said, "Okay, where do we meet you?"

Phil said, "Meet me at Bobby McGee's in Sacramento. I'll see you kids there in a few hours."

As I hung up, I said, "I can't believe I'm doing this."

Toni had no doubts in her mind. "Come on, be a sport," she said. "Do something crazy for once in your life."

She then reminded me we didn't want to get Phil in trouble since Esther hadn't heard from him in a while, and here he was inviting us to party with him in Sacramento. We decided we wouldn't tell anyone where we were going. The only thing anyone knew was that we were going to Santa Barbara. We were going to keep it that way. I still couldn't believe I was doing this. It was so out of character for me. I was beginning to miss Gene; I didn't know what he was going to think. All I knew was I had to get away from everyone I knew. Phil needed our help and I didn't want him to take a drink.

Toni and I were on our way to meet Phil in Sacramento. I just couldn't believe this was happening. This was the most bizarre thing I had ever done: lying, cheating, and traveling with my friend. We arrived at Bobbie McGee's restaurant around five o'clock in the afternoon. We had no problem finding Phil; he was waiting for us. We sat with him the whole evening and he introduced us to many of the Oakland Raiders and friends that he knew.

It seemed we partied the whole evening. Toni and I told Phil about our problems at home, and now it was Phil's turn. Finances had hit him hard, and he wasn't accustomed to that at all. He had been born with a silver spoon in his mouth and didn't know what it was like to spend less than $200 a night for dinner.

It was getting late. Phil decided we should check into a nearby hotel. He got Toni and me a room and reserved one for himself as well. A lot of good that did; we ended up talking all night long about our problems and how we were going to resolve them. Finally, about five in the morning, we all went to our rooms and somehow managed to fall asleep.

Just before I drifted off, I asked Toni, "What do you think we should do tomorrow?"

Toni answered, "It is tomorrow, Dayle. Let's go to sleep and think about it later."

I didn't get much sleep. I thought about Bob and Gene the whole night through. Why was I running away, anyway? I thought I should resolve this matter; but the more I thought, the more insecure I became.

When we awoke that morning, I remember Phil calling our room, asking if we wanted brunch. We did.

**Phil was a man of few words, but when he spoke it was mighty important. As we ate brunch together, Phil said, "Did you girls notice that there's no sun outside? I have a great idea. Let's go to the Islands."**

# THE HAWAIIAN ISLANDS
## CHAPTER 17

**"Let's go to Hawaii!** It's warm and beautiful in the Islands. We can think our problems through," Phil said.

Toni and I looked at each other in disbelief. "Are you serious?" I asked, stunned.

"I'll show you how serious I am!" Phil shouted. "I've booked the flight. Now, let's hurry and get packed. We're leaving for Hawaii within the hour!"

Toni and I didn't have much to pack; we just had an overnight carrying case. Until Phil called, we only had intended to go to Santa Barbara for the weekend. Money was a factor; we each had only $100 to our name. Now, at a moment's notice, we were running breathlessly to catch our plane at the San Francisco Airport. **Bound for Honolulu, Hawaii.**

As we boarded our flight for Hawaii, First Class, my fear of flying began to kick in. Whenever I fly I tend to get extremely nervous. I also knew if I got excited about the trip I could possibly set off some electrical or mechanical equipment on the plane. I knew all the Psychic energy that I had built up over the years was extremely strong.

When a Psychic gets upset, all kinds of things start to happen to electrical and mechanical equipment. I didn't want to take any chances, so I decided to calm my nerves with a few drinks before I boarded the plane. I began to drink excessively. Somewhere between the awakened state and the passing-out state I was aware of the plane taking off.

I barely remember being semiconscious as we flew over the Pacific Ocean. Toni and Phil abruptly awakened me, and Toni reached into my purse to retrieve my Tarot cards for me. The one thing I learned was to always carry my cards with me almost everywhere I went, just in case someone would perhaps be in need of a reading. Toni propped me up, placed the Tarot cards in my hand, and asked me to do a reading for a flight attendant. I complied.

Before long, the plane was on its final approach into the Honolulu Airport. I couldn't believe we were actually in Hawaii!

## "WHOA, WHAT A CRAZY TRIP!"

The thing I love most about arriving in Hawaii is the beauty of her islands. Whenever you get off the plane, there is this aroma, this fragrance, that the wind blows quietly toward you. It's the aroma of the island flowers reaching out and touching you all at once.

After being mesmerized by the aroma, we proceeded to retrieve our luggage and Phil decided we should hail a taxi. The taxis in Hawaii are unique; some are limousines and some are Cadillacs. We managed to catch a limo to Waikiki and the Sheraton Hotel. There was a doorman to greet us at the hotel; I'd never seen such a splendid place like this before. The Sheraton was so exclusive and so plush.

After we checked in, a bellhop took whatever little luggage we had down a long corridor that led to the main part of the hotel. Phil made sure our rooms were next door to each other. Our room was unbelievable: huge and pink. We had two queen-sized beds and a basketful of fruit. Everything we wanted was at our disposal. It was now getting late in the evening; we had such a tiring and wonderful day, we decided to retire early. Toni and I said goodnight to Phil and said we would see him in the morning.

The next morning we awoke rather early and ordered some coffee and donuts from room service. I remember the charge for that simple breakfast was just outrageous, about $25 for a pitcher of coffee and a few donuts. Toni and I looked at each other and said, "This is crazy!"

We couldn't stomach spending that kind of money on our budget. We called Phil to tell him how expensive breakfast was. Phil simply said, "Don't worry; this is my treat."

We managed to convince Phil that we should move to a more moderately priced hotel. I just couldn't bear the prices where we were. We decided to move on to the Hawaiian Regent Hotel just two blocks away.

Phil was a wonderful person, although he was born with a silver spoon in his mouth. He never knew what it was like to go hungry. Toni and I did! This trip was so enlightening to all of us. We were teaching Phil what it was like to live as a normal person. Phil was teaching us what it was like to live the life of luxury.

As we were leaving the Sheraton Hotel, we noticed the Hawaiian Regent Hotel was within an eye's view from where we were. Phil wanted to catch a cab for the two-block run, but we convinced him that the exercise would do him some good. Besides, we could walk in the beautiful Hawaiian sunshine. It took some fancy talking to convince Phil, but off we went on our next adventure.

On several other occasions I had frequented the Hawaiian Regent Hotel in Hawaii with my husband Bob. We found it to be pleasant and comfortable. The service was excellent and the rates were very reasonable.

Now Phil, Toni, and I were checking in all over again. We were ready to hit the pool; we wanted to soak up some of the beautiful

Hawaiian sunshine. Instantly, Toni and I realized we didn't have any bathing suits or clothes to wear. We had only packed a few things for Santa Barbara.

When Phil called and asked if we were ready to go to the pool, we explained to him that we hardly had any clothes in our luggage; we were plumb out of bathing suits. Phil told us to meet him downstairs in the dress shop. When we did, he said Toni and I could each pick out a bathing suit and one outfit. Now we would be prepared for our wonderful outing at the pool.

As we were trying on our new outfits, Phil happened to catch the news on a nearby radio: "The Gold Market has plunged." All at once, there was this strange sound coming out of Phil's mouth. We asked Phil what was wrong. He found out he had lost the hefty sum of $10,000 in the market. But he shrugged it off. "Who cares," he said. "We're on vacation anyway." We all ran swiftly toward the pool.

I think we had been basking out in the sun till we turned into red lobsters. At this point I don't think we cared one bit about solving our problems. The peace and serenity of the beautiful blue Pacific were all we needed now.

Toni and I took turns trying out the delightful Hawaiian drinks; you know the ones: Blue Hawaii, Chi-chi, Mai Tai, Hawaii Itch with the back scratcher. Every drink we tried was just marvelous. We stayed at poolside from sun up till sun down for three days, wondering why our lives were so screwed up.

In the evenings we got all dolled up for a night out on the town in Waikiki. Phil took us to fabulous restaurants like The Library, Spats, John Dominis. Oh, I don't want to leave out Michels.

One day we all went to a coffee shop where we couldn't get any service. Phil got angry and said, "I'm going to buy this place and fire that waitress." We agreed it was a good idea.

One morning, instead of sitting and eating by the pool, we decided to take Phil to McDonald's for breakfast, just to break the monotony of a pampered life a little. From Phil's reaction I swear you'd think we were taking him to some low-class dive. He just didn't want to go to McDonald's. He finally gave in and agreed to go with us and try some breakfast there.

About a week into our trip we were beginning to get a little bored of lying in the sun, getting tanned, peeling, and re-tanning. Then bizarre events started to happen to us.

The first occurred on a day that Toni and I were shopping. We stopped at a clothing store and decided to make a purchase. As the salesperson handed me my change, she started to tell me my future for some unknown reason. I looked at Toni and Toni at me. I couldn't believe this was happening. Out of the clear blue, this salesperson started telling me that I was going to be famous and that I would be living in the Islands. I looked at her in amazement, then asked, "Are you Psychic, Lady?"

She replied, "No, just in tune with the universe." Toni and I decided maybe this woman was just a little bit off.

We decided to resume our shopping and headed toward the International Marketplace. We were told that the International Marketplace was one of the most famous shopping areas in the United States. There isn't anything you can't get there. We enjoyed just looking around more than anything else.

All of a sudden, Toni shouted, "Hey, Dayle, look up there!" Right where we were standing, just above our heads, was a sign: "Psychic Reader." This was beginning to get redundant. As you guessed, we went in for a reading.

Toni decided I should go first. I gave the Psychic my $15 and listened carefully as she spoke: "I see you have traveled to the Islands, Little One, to find yourself." I remained silent. The Psychic continued: "This trip to the Islands will change your life. When you go back to the Mainland you will be a different person. I see you will become quite famous."

I just couldn't buy into what she was saying. After the reading I told Toni, "Don't waste your money. This woman has a screw loose. Me famous all over the world; can you imagine that? I'm going to move to Hawaii; can you imagine that? Come on, let's go." As we started to leave abruptly, I noticed an attractive woman awaiting her turn with the Psychic Reader. She introduced herself as Beverly Maden and asked if the Psychic was any good. "Not for me, Lady!" I replied.

She asked me if I knew of a good Psychic reader. I told her I was Psychic and I'd help her out at no charge. We went to a local bar and I read her Tarot cards. Beverly was pleased about what I saw in her future. Ironically, she was a hooker and in the midst of turning her life around. Since we both were trying to turn our lives around, we became friends, hoping we would meet again.

"It's a good thing you always carry your Tarot cards with you wherever you go. You tend to make a lot of friends this way," she remarked. I wondered what else was in store for Toni and me. This trip was beginning to become most unusual, even better than our wildest imaginations.

"I think it's time we go back to the hotel. Let's find out what Phil is up to," I said. "We can all decide where we're going for dinner tonight." We couldn't wait to tell Phil all about the Psychic we met. I just couldn't believe I was getting a reading from a salesperson without my asking her; all I wanted was to buy something in the store.

By the end of the first week in Hawaii, we had astounding tans and an established routine. We would awake by 12 noon, then lie by the pool and have several drinks; except Phil, who had his club soda and lime. We would then get dressed and ready for a night on the town. We ate and drank at the most elite places in town. Life was one big party for the rich and famous. However, all parties must end, especially when you begin to crave a plain old hamburger.

One morning I awoke rather early. Toni wasn't up yet, and Phil and I wanted to talk about our problems alone, so we decided to take a walk. As we were walking down the streets of Waikiki, we saw a sign that read: **"PSYCHIC RICHARD IRELAND."** Phil and I looked at each other in amazement. "Why is it that everywhere I turn I either get my fortune read or I run into a Psychic reader? I just can't believe this, Phil." He shook his head in disbelief.

We followed the sign that directed us to Psychic Ireland. Right above the hotel entrance a sign stated that Dr. Richard Ireland would be appearing tonight. Phil and I were really excited; we couldn't wait till we got back to our hotel to tell Toni all about this Psychic that was appearing at the other hotel.

I turned to Phil and asked, "What does all this mean? Everywhere we go there seems to be a sign pointing in the direction toward our destiny."

Phil replied, "It's time we started paying attention to all the signs along the way."

This is known as "Forks in the Road." I've noticed when one is troubled there are answers out there that lead us to our destiny, if we only choose to pay attention to them.

Wild with anticipation, we finally made it back to our hotel. We told Toni about Dr. Ireland and asked her if she'd like to join us. Our excitement was now her excitement. For the first time in a long time I had the feeling that this Psychic was for real. I knew within my heart he could answer my questions.

Evening was approaching at a very quick pace. Toni and I got all dolled up for this major event in our lives. Phil hailed a cab and directed the driver to take us all to the hotel where Dr. Richard Ireland was appearing. The anticipation was growing; our nerves were on edge. We sat in quiet contemplation of this event, now growing ever so near. When we reached the hotel, we were excited.

As we entered the showroom, we searched the audience for three available seats; lo and behold, there they were, three tiny seats right up front. We hurried to capture the seats, knowing all along that we were meant to sit there. The lights were beginning to dim; show time was approaching.

The hotel was proud to introduce Dr. Richard Ireland, Psychic. Within moments an assistant led Dr. Ireland onto the stage. We never took our eyes off him. What a showman he was.

He put a blindfold over his eyes and asked the audience to open their wallets and take out any bill they had on them, such as a $1 bill or even a $20 bill. He then asked the audience to concentrate on the serial number of whatever bill they were holding. Although he was blindfolded, he would read the serial number of the bill.

Dr. Ireland called this Billet Reading, something I was not at all familiar with. I couldn't believe what I saw with my very own eyes. Dr. Ireland read the serial number of the $20 bill that Phil was holding. This was unbelievable! This must be a trick; why, no human being could do this. I was trying to figure it out.

For his next feat Dr. Ireland asked the studio audience to write down any question they wanted answered. We were all provided with pencil and paper to do so. This was the part I was waiting for very patiently. My question was, "Who will I end up with, Bob or Gene?" Toni asked if she would end up with Cole. Phil asked about his business.

We waited with anticipation. Toni and I wanted our questions answered first, so we started concentrating on Dr. Ireland. We knew we could reach out with our minds through ESP. We were right. He was beginning to feel our presence. He was also rather annoyed.

He finally asked us, "Why are you doing this to me? I can feel your thought waves. You are beginning to disturb my thinking pattern."

I answered him. "Dr Ireland, we just want you to answer our questions."

He shouted, "Okay!" and, still blindfolded, reached his hand into his fishbowl of questions. Lo and behold again, he came up with the question I asked. He then began to read my question aloud, blindfolded: "Who will I end up with, Bob or Gene?"

Dr. Ireland paused, then said to me, "Bob is okay, but Gene is a great lay."

I died a thousand deaths as I fell to my knees onto the floor, laughing all the way down. How did he know this? How did he know that Gene was a great lay? I just couldn't stop laughing. But he never did answer my question.

As for Toni, he told her that after much trouble she would end up with Cole. And he responded to Phil, "You, my dear friend, need to book an appointment."

Now, mind you, this was all being done while Dr. Ireland was blindfolded. What a show! I never in my life, not even till this day, have ever seen anything like him. I still wonder how he did what he did. Although it didn't matter, I did know he used a bit of telepathy and ESP. The showman part of him was exceptional. That is what he used to bait people for his readings.

We couldn't stop talking about Dr. Ireland during the cab ride back to our hotel. The next morning Phil booked an appointment with Dr. Ireland. Toni and I wanted to see him so badly, but we couldn't afford his prices. We waited for hours for Phil to come back and when he did we questioned him. We wanted to find out what Dr. Ireland had told him, but Phil said it was too private to share with us.

We were now approaching our second week in Honolulu, with more suprises to come. Time was passing much too quickly; we knew that we would have to be going home soon back to the Mainland. Toni and I still wanted answers to our lives.

After the Psychic show Phil and I wanted to find more fun and entertainment. We started checking the newspaper to find out what else was happening around town. I noticed an ad; it read: **Trapper's For Fun And Enjoyment. Come Join The Party.** This intrigued me. I turned to Phil and said, "Let's check out this place, Trapper's, tonight." Phil was game. Toni opted to spend a nice quiet evening in the apartment.

I started to get ready. Suddenly, I began to feel hypnotized; I started to stare out at the ocean from our lanai. Phil shouted my name; I didn't hear him. Phil approached me and shouted again, "Why haven't you changed your clothes yet? What's wrong?"

I was startled out of my trance. "I don't know, Phil. I keep hearing this name in my head over and over again. The name sounds like Alazo, Alonzo. I don't know what it means. But it sure keeps annoying me."

Phil located a phonebook and looked in the yellow pages for a restaurant named Alazo or for a person with the same name. Nothing came up. "Don't worry, Dayle, we'll figure it out," he assured me. "Now go on and get ready. Do you still want to go to Trapper's?" I said I did.

Off we went on our next adventure. I was beginning to like the inside of a cab. When the cab driver let us off at Trapper's, we walked into one of the more unique and "happening places" in Honolulu. It had a bar and a dance band and the floor was alive with people dancing. The whole place was buzzing with gaiety. There seemed to be a lot of Mainlanders inhabiting the place, including several visiting entertainers.

Phil began mingling with some people that he met and I was left alone. All of a sudden, a tall black man approached me and introduced himself. "Hi, my name is Alonzo."

I was stunned. I couldn't speak. Finally, I managed to mumble, "What's your name? What was your name again, please?"

"Alonzo."

I freaked out. I said, "I know this sounds strange, but I've been looking for you all night."

Alonzo looked at me with an amused frown. "What exactly do you mean you were looking for me all night? I thought that would be my line."

I explained. I told Alonzo I was somewhat Psychic and for some reason I kept shouting his name aloud all day.

"I understand, Dayle," he said. "It seems you must be in need of some help. Have you been troubled?"

"Yes," I answered.

Alonzo told me this wasn't the first time that this had happened. There had been several other occasions. I listened intently as he spoke. "I seem to have a knack for being at the right place at the right time," he said. "Maybe I was meant to be here to help you tonight." He explained he was a professional hypnotist and he was somewhat Psychic as well.

It was then I shouted for Phil to come to me. Phil sensed something wasn't right. "Phil, remember the name Alazo? The name I was shouting out earlier?" I asked. "Well, I want you to meet Alonzo Demello."

Phil just looked at me in disbelief. Not only was this person that I was speaking to called Alonzo, he was the one I was looking for all this time without knowing it.

Alonzo was now sizing us up. The chatter was dying down at Trapper's; it was nearly four o'clock in the morning and they were getting ready to close. I didn't want to leave. Alonzo asked me to put my hand in his; he would tell me what he saw in my future.

He told me of my troubled romance with Gene. He told me of my upcoming fame. Then he made a profound statement. He said I would be returning to the Islands for many years to come; I would return to help the people of the Islands with my gift. That was my destiny. I would perform and entertain. He also said I was having trouble making a decision about a man that I loved; and if I were to go back to this man who drinks heavily, he would pull me down with him. My true destiny was the Islands. Alonzo then told me to go back to the Mainland and straighten out this situation. If I were to go back to my husband, it could work.

I was shocked again. I had told Alonzo nothing! Yet, he knew everything!

Alonzo said he had one warning for me: If I chose to be with Gene, my gift would be taken away from me. If, on the other hand, I chose to become a Psychic by profession and help people, my path would be lined with fame and glory.

Phil couldn't believe what he was hearing. He didn't want to interrupt Alonzo, but he wanted to know what his future would hold. Alonzo stated Phil and I would be friends forever, that he was my teacher and spiritual guide for many lifetimes to come.

I thanked Alonzo for opening my eyes and answering all my

questions without my asking. I hoped that we'd meet again. Alonzo turned and walked away, saying, "Don't worry, Little One, our paths will cross again." And so it turned out just like he said; ten years later we did meet again.

Phil and I left Trapper's. This time we decided to walk to the hotel. We were overwhelmed by what we had just heard and witnessed. We tried to analyze the situation.

I asked, "Why does this keep happening to me?" I was beginning to believe that I was on some kind of spiritual trip, one that was not of my choosing. Where was this leading? What was going to happen next? I began to get scared all of a sudden. I began to think that I had no control over my life at this point. Everywhere I went Psychics were popping up and reading my future. Why?

Phil explained how he saw the situation. "Can't you see, Dayle, what's happening to you? We all came to the Islands for answers; that's what you wanted. Now the universe is taking over and you're getting the answers that you've wanted. Can't you see this? Everywhere you go, people are telling you the same thing. Wake up, Girl. Pay attention to the signs in the road; they're leading you toward your true destiny."

I said, "Phil, do you realize what you've just told me? You want me to believe that this is all happening for a reason. I don't know if I can buy into this."

"Looks like you don't have much of a choice," Phil said. For the first time I was beginning to believe!

The very next evening I decided to stay by myself in the hotel to just sort out the past few days. I needed to get in touch with my true feelings about life now.

While I was contemplating everything under the sun, Toni and Phil went to Bobby McGee's for dinner. After dinner they decided to take advantage of Bobby McGee's huge dance floor. The place was mobbed. While Toni was dancing with Phil, she noticed a gentleman who had been eyeing her all evening. When she excused herself from Phil and proceeded to the ladies' room, the man followed her. He stopped Toni for a moment. "Excuse me," he said, "I've been watching you from afar. My name is Eric. Could I have this next dance?"

Toni looked up at the gentleman; she found him to be quite handsome. She replied, "Just give me a few minutes and I'll be glad to dance with you." She then returned to Phil and told him about the new man she met.

Phil said, "Go right ahead. He seems to be a nice looking fellow."

Toni danced with Eric for the rest of the evening and gave him her phone number when he asked for it. When she and Phil made their way back to the hotel, she couldn't wait to tell me about Eric. She hoped that he would call her.

The next day we noticed a leaking pipe in our room. The hotel suggested that we change rooms, so we did. We didn't realize that our changing rooms would cause such a fuss. The problem was when we changed rooms, for some reason the hotel did not inform the switchboard operators. Naturally, they thought that we had checked out. On any other occasion, this wouldn't have mattered. But today of all days, it did matter.

Phil, Toni, and I were soaking up rays at poolside. I was beginning to sort things out in my little mind; everything was beginning to make sense to me. Now, keep in mind that Toni and I had a new room and a different room number. Bob was trying to locate me; he was told by the operator that I had checked out. Eric was trying to get in touch with Toni; he was also told that she had checked out.

Somehow the mess got straightened out and Toni and Eric made connections. Eric, who turned out to be quite wealthy in real estate, had summoned his whole staff to find Toni; if they didn't, it would be their jobs.

Toni wanted me to meet Eric, so we arranged for lunch. Eric seemed very nice and I believed that he wouldn't give up on his hot pursuit of Toni. (I was right. Eric followed Toni till the ends of the earth, literally.) Toni found him very attractive. They promised to stay in touch.

Our stay was coming to its end and it was time to head back to the Mainland. Phil had resolved a lot of his business problems. Toni had met her new love. As for me, all the readings that I received pointed me in the direction of helping people. I had a lot of work to do if I wanted to return to the Islands. This was all too bewildering for me. I wanted to believe so badly. But then again, did I really? I wasn't sure if I had found what I was looking for.

Our last night in Honolulu was just as crazy as it all began. We went to a restaurant to say goodbye to the Islands with hopes that we'd all return. The evening was so special, no one really wanted to go home. It seemed we all wanted to experience more of the spiritual adventures that had been occurring on a daily basis.

I mentioned to Phil that there was one thing I felt badly about; that when we arrived in the Islands, we never got "lei'd" with beautiful flowers. I no sooner got the words out of my mouth when an Hawaiian lady came around our table and asked us if we wanted to buy some leis. What was most unusual, she had only three leis left.

As we talked over dinner, we knew we had learned some important lessons. We learned to believe in ourselves. We also learned to take life one day at a time. Most of all, we learned to trust our intuition.

Our farewell to the Islands was now played out. It was time to get back to reality, pack our bags, and head for home the next morning. I did notice that my luggage was just a little bit more hefty now. We all tried to get a good night's sleep, but there was a sadness among us. "It can't be over. Why can't this experience last forever? Farewell to the beautiful Islands of mystery and intrigue."

The morning arrived. After grabbing a quick breakfast, we hailed a cab in front of the Hawaiian Regent Hotel. As we entered the cab, we took a long, hard look back at what was.

On the way to the airport every light was red. Then there was our cab driver who spoke very little English. Toni and Phil were sitting in the back of the cab and I was in the front, directing the driver to the airport.

All of a sudden, I smelled smoke. I turned around and looked at Phil and Toni. "Do you smell smoke, or is it my imagination?"

Phil responded, "I don't smell anything."

But Toni replied, "I smell smoke, Dayle."

"Well, look around," I directed.

They did. Phil opened the ashtray on his right. It was on fire! I mean on **FIRE**.

I tried to tell the cab driver to pull over because the ashtray was on FIRE. He ignored me and kept driving faster and faster. I think he thought if he got us to the airport at record speed all would be well. I then began screaming at him, "You pull this cab over right now! WE ARE ON FIRE! Do you hear me!"

The driver just glanced at me and began speeding even more, to 90 miles an hour. Not only were we on FIRE, he was trying to kill us as well!

I turned to Phil and Toni in the back seat. Phil was trying frantically to put out the **FIRE**. He looked at me and yelled, "What do you want me to do? Pee in the ashtray?"

Toni then shouted, "This is an omen! We're not supposed to leave the Islands. I'm not getting on the plane if we make it to the airport, especially if it's delayed!"

We did make it to the United Airlines terminal a few minutes later. The driver stopped the cab abruptly, brakes screeching as he pulled up to the curb. He leaped out from the cab, opened up the trunk, and threw our luggage out onto the street.

He then proceeded to make his way to the back seat of the cab, where he picked up the ashtray that was on fire, single handedly. How brave he was! Then he threw the ashtray on the ground, stomping on it the whole time. If looks could kill, we would have been dead as he stared us down. He pointed his finger in each and every one of our faces and warned us in a heavy accent, "Don't you ever come back here again. You people are CRAZY!" We couldn't help but laugh.

We boarded the plane for San Francisco on the way back to Lake Tahoe. Thank God there were no delays; Toni would have left. There was so much room on the plane we all spread out and were able to get comfortable.

As Phil was falling asleep, he mumbled, "Hey, do you guys want to go to Mexico?"

Toni and I, both at the same time, replied, "NO!"

When our plane landed in San Francisco, we caught a cab to where we had left our cars, but Phil decided he wasn't ready to go home yet. He wished us well and said he would be in touch. He then caught the next plane to Arizona. Till this day I don't know why Phil went to Arizona.

Toni and I were more than ready to go home now. What was supposed to be a three-day vacation in Santa Barbara had turned into a two-week adventure in Hawaii. We had time to think in our car; the drive to Tahoe from San Francisco was about four hours.

**We wanted to absorb, to take it all in, what really happened to us. I decided to make an effort to work things out with my husband. I would try to forget Gene; I knew our relationship was on its way out. I couldn't wait to see Diane and tell her about all the amazing things that had happened in Hawaii.**

# BACK TO REALITY
## CHAPTER 18

I was home at last in beautiful Lake Tahoe. I felt extremely refreshed, even somewhat enlightened. The series of events that took place were just mind boggling. Bob was quite happy to have me back home. I told him that I would try in the marriage with him as much as possible.

In my heart I still felt that I was missing something, but I didn't quite know what it was. You see, through it all Bob did love me and care for me with all his heart and all his soul. We had been married for over fifteen years, and that meant something to him. He understood what I was going through.

This was a very painful time for him. Each and every time I left him he knew a part of me would never come back. Why was he that fool that everyone made him out to be? I even questioned him on many occasions. I knew that part of me still loved him, and that I couldn't bear to be without him. I honestly believed that in my heart I could make it work.

I kept punishing myself over and over again for allowing Gene to come into my life. I always thought that Gene was the answer to my problems. I thought Gene was my Knight in Shining Armor.

The biggest shame and embarrassment that I felt was knowing that everyone in town knew about our love affair. I felt at times there was no turning back. I had put so much hurt upon Bob, why would he even want me? What started off in my mind as a way to get even with Bob had now turned into a full-blown love affair with Gene.

I was out of control. Part of my life depended on Gene; this was something I wasn't prepared for. I chose to stay away from Gene deliberately when I got back in town. I began to analyze everything, I thought about Gene a lot; I thought about my career; and I wondered if Gene would ever leave his wife. I also wondered if our love affair would ever be more than just an affair. Thinking, thinking, thinking; my brain felt as though it was going to explode.

Well, it was time to go back to work for the radio station. Everyone was excited to see me. The popularity of our show had increased by leaps and bounds. So had my readings. I was beginning to help people from all walks of life; that was very encouraging. I began to realize that I was contributing very heavily to mankind through my radio work. I took my work very seriously, although there were many individuals who made fun of me at times.

The majority of the townspeople were beginning to understand ESP. It was largely due to the educational process and how I was educating them. It was about four weeks since I had returned from the Islands; I had made no contact with Gene whatsoever.

However, it was on this warm beautiful summer day in August of 1981 that I decided to take a drive along the country roads. All of a sudden I heard someone honking at me. I looked in the rearview mirror of my car and realized it was Gene. "Oh, God, not now. I don't want to see him now," I said to myself. I began to drive faster and faster, but somehow he managed to catch up with me. I pulled the car over as he shouted, "Hi, Babe! Where've you been? I have to talk to you. Have a drink with me."

I didn't want to, but I was compelled to do so. I followed Gene to Kingsbury Lanes, a bowling alley that was our usual meeting place for years, and pulled the car into the parking lot. He grabbed me as I was getting out of my car and put his arms around me. As we walked slowly toward the bar, Gene said, "I've missed you, Babe. Why haven't you called me?"

I told Gene about my adventures in Hawaii with Phil and Toni. I also told him it would be better if we didn't see each other for a while. I wanted to make my marriage with Bob work.

Gene had a sad look on his face. "Good luck with Bob!" he remarked. Then he added, "But I know you love me. You'll be back."

Gene was right. I did love him, all too much. I just couldn't help myself. One drink led to another. The next thing I knew, we were off to find a motel in the area. Gene and I made love for seven hours non-stop. I barely came up for air. How could I stop loving this man when it always felt so right? Gene fulfilled an emotional need within me.

I looked up at my watch in horror; it was now seven o'clock. "Gene, we have to get out of here; it's getting late," I said.

Gene would have none of that. He begged, "No, Baby, stay the night. I want to wake up to you in the morning. Please stay with me."

"No, Gene, we can't. Let's get dressed and go home," I urged. But I gave in; we made love one more time.

He was ready to go now. "Let me take you out to dinner before you go home," he said.

We had a wonderful steak dinner in a secluded restaurant just out of town. After dinner Gene and I went back to Kingsbury Lanes for just one more drink. I glanced at my watch and realized it was almost midnight. I mentioned again that I had to go. And again, when Gene said, "Please just stay a little while longer," I stayed. I decided to throw a few quarters into the juke box to play our favorite song. However, the song that started playing on the juke box was not the one I had selected. Instead, it was "Heartbreak Hotel" by the Eagles. I paid attention to the lyrics: "There's going to be a heartbreak tonight; someone's going to get hurt." The lyrics raced through my mind. That same song played over and over again, well over ten times in a row. I brought this to Gene's attention.

"It's just your imagination," he said.

"No, it's not!" I shouted. "I heard that song at least ten times tonight." To my knowledge I never played that record at all in the course of the evening. I believed it was a warning.

I left the bar rather abruptly and made my way to the ladies' room. When I came back, I sat down beside Gene, turned toward him, and out of the corner of my eye I saw someone approaching. I screamed, **"OH, SHIT!"**

Gene looked at me in surprise. "What's the matter with you, now? Why are you cursing?"

I could barely contain myself. **"Your Wife Just Walked In!**

Now it was Gene's turn. **"OH, SHIT! SHIT! SHIT!"** he said.

I became extremely nervous. I hadn't been drinking the whole evening that we were together, but I decided now was a good time to have a double. "Remain calm. No matter what happens, remain calm." I managed to look calm, but my hands were shaking badly.

Gene's wife was now standing between Gene and me. "So this is your lover, the one you've been seeing all this time," Annie said. She was speaking to Gene, but looking at me. "I thought I'd never have the pleasure of meeting her."

Gene looked at her and said innocently, "No, Annie, you're wrong. I was just having a beer and Dayle was sitting next to me. We were only talking."

Annie started chasing me around the bowling alley. Gene then began to chase the both of us. I don't know how he finally did it, but he somehow calmed Annie down. He actually made her believe I was just someone at the bar he was talking to.

As Annie left us for the ladies' room, I looked at Gene with disgust. "I'll be seeing you around, Gene. It's over."

"Don't bet on it," he replied.

It was three in the morning when I arrived home. Bob was waiting up for me. He fired question after question at me. "Where have you been all this time? The last I heard from you, you were at the radio station. What do you mean coming home at three in the morning? I thought we resolved your problem."

I asked Bob to sit down and I told him what had happened. "I'm sorry. If you want me to leave, I will," I said.

Bob laughed at the situation, almost like I was amusing him. "No, I don't want you to leave; I love you. I guess it's over with you and Gene. Rest assured it's over, Dayle. I think his wife will kill you. It sounds like she's a lot less patient than I've been." Bob sounded somewhat relieved.

The next day my conscience was bothering me. After Bob left for work I realized I couldn't go on like this much longer. I called Annie to tell her I was giving Gene up and asked her to meet me at Kingsbury Lanes.

When I arrived at Kingsbury Lanes, Annie was sitting at the bar, waiting for me. I sat down next to her. At first I didn't know what to say. Annie started the conversation; she wanted to know everything about Gene and me. I began by telling her how we met and how he had told me that he was separated from her.

Annie stopped me. She said to her knowledge they were never separated. I told her everything from the beginning to the end. This was very painful for me as well as for her. Annie had heard of my Psychic ability from the radio. She then took off her wedding ring, handed it to me and said, "If you really believe in this stuff, why don't you tell me if I'll stay married to Gene?"

I reached for her marriage ring and held it tightly in my hand. I gazed at her, then I bent my head slowly toward the floor and shook my head knowingly. She knew the answer as well as I did. I told her I was sorry. Annie asked me if I was going to make my own marriage work. I told her I hoped I would.

I said goodbye as I turned and walked away. I looked back at Annie sitting by herself, drinking at the bar. I flashed on Gene even though he wasn't there. My eyes fixed on Annie once again. Poor, pathetic Annie, married to a **Heavy Drinker.** That could be me sitting there ten years from now waiting for him. A flash of reality set in.

I never wanted to be in that situation ever again. I got in my car and drove to Diane's house. I wanted to tell her everything that happened to me. I started off telling her about Phil and Toni and ended with Gene and Annie.

Diane stared at me. "Whoa, this has been one hell of a month for you. Let's just hope you're not pregnant!" she said.

"Pregnant?" I began to get emotional. "Where did that come from? I've been with Bob for fifteen years and with Gene for three. Why all of a sudden would I become pregnant?" I was shouting by now.

Diane replied, "I don't know. It just came out of my mouth. Don't worry about it. I just thought that this would be the icing on the cake."

"Some icing!" I said. "Wipe those thoughts from your mind,

Girl." Little did I know that Diane's bizarre comments were predictions that were about to come true.

After the incident with Annie I didn't see Gene at all. I was beginning to get used to the idea that our affair was over. I began working regularly for the radio station, every Saturday from 9 a.m. till 12 noon. I was quite content. The requests for readings were coming in rather steadily. There was order now in my life; it was beginning to feel good and not so crazy.

Then my life changed. I somehow caught the flu, which is rare for me; I was sick as a dog. On the fourth day of not feeling well, I went over to Diane's house for a visit. She asked me if I had heard from Gene, and I told her I hadn't. She asked me how I felt about it. "Not that bad," I replied.

Diane commented that I seemed to be putting on a little extra weight. As she spoke, her daughter Lisa passed by me and said, "Dayle, I bet you're pregnant."

I screamed, "Get out of here, Lisa! I'm just getting over the flu. I am not pregnant!"

Because Lisa had blurted out that I was pregnant, Diane insisted I should purchase a Daisy II test; you know, one of those tests that check for pregnancy. I complied to humor her. We even had a bet going. We tested my urine the very next morning. Within an hour we would know one way or another. This was the longest hour in my life. I wasn't ready for the result: **PREGNANT.**

"I can't believe this, Diane. There must be something wrong. I know I'm not pregnant." I was into the denial stage.

"Well, according to this test, you are," Diane said.

I began to go into shock. I was in my early thirties and pregnant for the first time in my life. What was I going to do? I knew that Bob was sterile. There was only a ten percent chance that the baby could be his. I was dumbfounded, overwhelmed. This couldn't be happening to me. I didn't know what to do.

Diane then asked me if I wanted to keep the child. "Of course," I said, although I had mixed feelings at the time. First, I had to get used to the idea that I was pregnant. This was too overwhelming; everything was hitting me at once.

I thought back to all those years in my early twenties when I wanted to have a child so badly. But now I was older and wiser, and I had said goodbye to Gene. Diane suggested I go to the doctor to confirm the pregnancy. The doctor verified what we already knew. His telling me I was pregnant never lessened the shock one bit.

I was confused. "Diane, what am I going to do?"

"Let's think this through," she said. "First, I think you'd better tell Gene, then let's see what he says."

"Diane, I can't do that," I said. "I promised Annie I'd never go near Gene again."

"Sorry, Dayle, I want to remind you that this is half Gene's baby. He has a right to know."

I pleaded with her. "Diane, I need you to tell him. I just can't."

She was determined. "Okay, I will! We're talking about a child here. Now things are getting a little complicated. What are you going to tell Bob anyway?"

"I don't know, Diane; I just can't think right now."

Diane was used to pregnancies; she had three children, and every time I turned around, someone in her family was pregnant. I, however, had to think through my situation.

Gene finally called me at Diane's house within a week of my knowing I was pregnant. Diane answered the phone and said,

"Gene, I think you'd better come over to my house. I have something to tell you. It's quite urgent." Not only was Gene getting over the shock of my meeting with Annie and of our discussing him inside out and upside down, but now Diane was also going to tell him he was going to be a father.

Diane told me later that when Gene arrived at her house, she asked him to sit down. He just wanted to know how I was. He told her he wanted me back at all costs and that he loved me. Diane decided this was a good time to tell him. Her voice was firm. **"Gene! Dayle Is About Six Weeks Pregnant With Your Child."**

Now it was Gene's turn to go into shock. **"WHAT!** Are you telling me I'm going to be a father? I'm too old to be a father. I have three kids of my own. What are we going to do? Diane, help me, please." He put down his head and held it in his hands.

"That's up to you," she said.

"Where is she anyway?" he asked. "I've got to see her; I'm going crazy without her."

"She's at home."

"Does Bob know?" Gene asked.

Diane answered, "I don't know."

Well, Bob did know because I told him the whole story. I told him that after I gave up Gene I found out I was pregnant. Bob asked, "Is there a possibility that this child could be my child?" I said "no." Bob and I talked. He wanted me to stay; he wanted to take care of me, no matter what.

Shortly after, Diane called to tell me that she had spoken to Gene and that he wanted to see me. "Gene is sitting in my living room now. I think you had better come over."

When I arrived at Diane's house, Gene was waiting. He held me in his arms and told me how much he loved me. He asked me how I was feeling. I told him I wasn't feeling so well; I was beginning to have some spot bleeding.

Gene said, "I think we should talk about this." I agreed, but he did all the talking. "Dayle, this situation we're in. We're both married; we'll be hurting a lot of people. I'm too old to be fathering a child. This doesn't mean I don't love you. It just means I'm fourteen years older than you. This isn't right."

Diane jumped into the monologue. "Well, Gene," she said, "you should have thought about that while you were having your fun and games. What do you want her to do, anyway? Give up the child?" Diane was stern.

Gene bent his head in shame. "I don't know, Diane; I love her. I have to think for a while." He stood up and walked out the door.

Diane turned to me. "I'm sorry, Dayle, but that man has to take responsibility for something sometime in his life. I'm sorry I was so harsh," she said. "Always remember, Dayle, you can replace a man, but you can never replace a child." Words to the wise. These words rang true.

Months passed; I saw Gene on several occasions. He never made a decision one way or the other. I was getting to the point where I just didn't want to see him anymore. I wanted to be left alone.

Meanwhile, I was bleeding almost every day. It was questioable at this point if I would be able to hold the baby. I was approaching my fourth month with much cramping and pain. Bob was there to see me through. Diane told me Gene was calling her house on a regular basis to find out how I was. I didn't want to talk to him. I was in pain, but I still worked for the radio. I kept on with my readings and kept myself busy. I was now approaching my fifth month.

Unexpectedly, my water broke at home. I began to bleed profusely. There was no one who could take me to the hospital, so I called my doctor and asked him to meet me at Barton Memorial. Gushing blood, I drove myself to the hospital. I just made it; I was beginning to hemorrhage. The doctor was there waiting for me and for some of his staff to come aboard to assist.

I was in terrible pain. I knew I was losing the baby. It seemed like hours before the doctor took me into the operating room. My only words to him were, "Please don't let me bleed to death."

Within moments the bleeding stopped. The baby had died. In my heart I always knew that although I had tried so hard to keep the baby, this child was not meant to be.

I lay within the four walls of the hospital. I had nearly three days to think upon the matter. I kept wondering why my doctor wouldn't give me a blood transfusion. I had lost so much blood. When he came into my room to ask me how I felt, I said, "Okay, Doc, but why won't you give me a transfusion? Why do I have to lie here and suffer?"

The doctor became very stern at this point. "You'll stay here in this hospital no matter how long it takes. You'll manufacture your own blood. Dayle, there seems to be some bad blood going around. I don't want you to get infected." He added, "Someday you'll thank me for this."

He was right. It was the beginning of the **AIDS VIRUS.** God only knows what might have happened if I had had that blood tranfusion. **THANK YOU, DOC.**

I was ready to go home. Gene never knew that I lost the baby. He was on vacation with his wife Annie at that time. Diane and Bob were the only ones who really cared for me. When I got out of the hospital, they were there to nurse me back to health.

I had all the time in the world to think things over now. I thought of Gene quite a bit. I realized he wasn't man enough to want to be with me now. He was never by my side. If anything in life would endanger his well-being, off he went.

Diane was able to reach Gene by phone several weeks later. She told him about the loss of the child. I'm sure he was relieved. He still told Diane how much he loved me and wanted to see me. In my heart I had lost total respect for Gene, but I still had a slight ray of hope. I don't know why. Diane's words kept going around and around in my head, over and over again: "You can replace a man, Dayle, but you can never replace a child." **The pain of it all.**

As I was getting better and better, recovery-wise, I began to throw myself into my work. Full steam ahead! I wanted to learn more and more about my field. I wanted to help people more so now than ever before. The radio work and helping people were my only means of escape. It was the only way that I could try to forget about Gene.

Times were changing at KOWL radio. The station wanted me to go to Hawaii and make an appearance on their affiliate radio station, KIKI. This was beginning to sound interesting. John Parker, the owner, offered me his condo in Honolulu and offered to pay my airfare if I would appear on KIKI. He knew I would be an overnight success in the Islands. I guess what the Psychics had told me in Hawaii was now about to come true. I decided to take up John Parker's offer and go to Hawaii, especially to get away from Gene and to be able to think clearly. I asked Toni York to assist me in the Islands, all expenses paid.

My business was escalating by leaps and bounds. I never needed or wanted for anything. In fact, I was making more money than both Bob and Gene put together. Money was not what I wanted, however. I wanted love and happiness in my life. I was beginning to think it was impossible to have both.

I then began my spiritual search. A few weeks before Toni and I were to leave for the Islands, I began to seek out every Psychic that I could get my hands on. I found one Psychic, Pam Kenni, in Carson City, Nevada. Pam was a Spiritual Psychic, quite different from myself. The work that I did with helping people on a Psychic level was more isolated. I worked with their everyday problems, giving them choices to better their future. Pam dealt with helping people find their own spirituality.

All I did was give Pam my first name and where I was from and left her with a few questions I wanted answered. Within a week or so, she called and told me that my tape was ready. After I picked it up in Carson City, I sat down in a quiet room of my house and listened to what she had to say. Keep in mind that this girl knew very little about me. She just told me to ask a few questions, then she would have her spiritual guides or friends answer.

My first question was about my future: "Will I be with Gene in the future?" My second was about my present: "What is my purpose in going to the Islands of Hawaii?" My third was about my past: "Why was I bombed out of Harvey's?" I turned on my tape recorder and began listening intently. It was mind boggling.

I was scared. This was a new experience for me, my first with a Spiritualist. I didn't even know if I believed in spirits talking through human beings. Was she just going to make up things? Webster's Dictionary defines "spiritualist" as one who believes "that the dead survive as spirits which can communicate with the living with the help of a third party; a **MEDIUM."** In 1981 Spiritualism was flourishing.

Most of the public is as uneducated as I was in regards to Spiritual Psychics. There are many different kinds of Psychics, such as an Astrologer, Spiritualist, Psychometrist, and Numerologist. The field is endless. I found out throughout the years that there are different times in one's life when one needs different types of Psychics. They can help guide one along the way when reaching a crossroad of a major decision.

If you want to consult with different types of Psychics, you should ask around and try to find a Psychic that is credible. When one is referred to you, you should ask what method that Psychic is using. If this coincides with what your needs are, you are ready to try your Psychic.

This is how I found Pam Kenni. I was in need of a deep spiritual awareness at the time. This reading was given in part to me by Pam's spiritual guides. What I am about to tell you was the beginning of my spiritual awareness.

The tape began with my name and the date. Pam then went into a trance-like state; her voice began to change and other voices began to materialize on the tape. Pam then asked the question to her spirit guides:

**TELL US OF THE SPIRITUAL QUEST IN REGARDS TO ONE DAYLE SCHEAR... IN REGARDS TO HARVEY'S AT LAKE TAHOE... IN REGARDS TO GENE ASHLEY... IN REGARDS TO THE ISLANDS OF HAWAII.**

**Answer that was given:** WE SEE DAYLE TO BE A VERY ADVANCED SPIRIT. SHE WILL BE A TEACHER ON THE

EARTHLY PLANE. THAT IS HER DESTINY. THE SITUA-
TION AT HARVEY'S WAS SET UP SOLELY FOR THE PUR-
POSE OF HER GROWTH. SHE WILL BE GIVEN A PERIOD OF
TIME TO CHANGE, A PERIOD OF TWO AND ONE-HALF
YEARS FOR HER GROWTH. IF IN THAT PERIOD OF TIME
SHE CHOOSES SOLELY ON HER OWN TO FOLLOW A
DIFFERENT PATH, THEN THE SPIRITS WILL NOT DEEM
HER WORTHY OF SPIRITUAL GROWTH.

WE RECOGNIZE GENE ASHLEY AS A LOST SOUL THAT
DAYLE HAS COME INTO CONTACT WITH TO HELP. HOW-
EVER, ALL WILL BE TAKEN AWAY FROM HER IF SHE
CHOOSES THE PATH OF ONE GENE ASHLEY. THE SPIRITS
HAVE SET UP CERTAIN SITUATIONS FOR DAYLE IN THE
NEXT FEW MONTHS. WE WANT TO SEE IF OF HER OWN
FREE WILL SHE WILL MAKE THE RIGHT CHOICE. SHE
WILL FIND THAT HER LOVE FOR GENE IS GROWING LESS
AND LESS AS TIME GOES BY. IF IN THE GIVEN TIME
FRAME SHE REFUSES TO LET GO, WE THE SPIRITS WILL
MAKE IT ALMOST IMPOSSIBLE FOR HER TO REMAIN
WITH GENE. THIS IS NOT HER DESTINY.

SHE WILL EVENTUALLY MAKE A MOVE TO THE IS-
LANDS OF HAWAII WHERE THERE ARE MANY WHO NEED
HER HELP AND GUIDANCE. THE PEOPLE OF THE ISLANDS
WILL LOVE HER VERY MUCH. THIS IS WHERE HER OWN
SPIRITUAL GROWTH WILL BEGIN.

IN MANY WAYS IT HAS STARTED ALREADY. IF SHE
CHOOSES TO FOLLOW WHAT THE SPIRITS SAY THERE
WILL BE MUCH LOVE AND RECOGNITION. HER OWN
TRUE PATH WILL COME AS SHE GROWS WITHIN THE

ISLANDS OF HAWAII.

HER TRUE DESTINY IS TO HELP AND SERVE OTHERS THROUGHOUT THE COURSE OF HER EARTHLY LIFE. SHE WILL THEN HAVE A CHOICE TO STAY WITH HER HUSBAND; OR IF SHE CHOOSES, ANOTHER MATE WILL BE GIVEN. THE PERSON THAT WILL BE PICKED FOR HER WILL BE HER SPIRITUAL TEACHER FOR MANY LIFETIMES TO COME. THIS PERSON WILL BE SENT FROM US TO HER TO HELP GUIDE HER LIFE. WITHIN THAT THERE WILL BE LOVE. THAT IS ALL.

**The tape blew my mind away. It felt so right; it felt so true. I knew that Pam was gifted. I also knew that I couldn't go on living the way I was. It was time to face the truth of the matter. It was time to go back to the Islands.**

**"Toni, are you ready to go!" I shouted.**

# BACK TO THE ISLANDS
## CHAPTER 19

Toni and I were finally packed and ready to go. We said good-bye to Bob as he dropped us off at the San Francisco Airport; he was planning to join us in a few weeks. This time Toni and I were flying coach on United Airlines to Honolulu. We would be reaching the alluring islands of Hawaii just in time for the holiday season. The month was early November; the year 1982. The weather was picture perfect, beautiful as always.

John Parker, owner of the radio station, had a car waiting for us. I remember we had the use of his car for the whole duration of our stay. We couldn't wait till we reached our apartment at Discovery Bay.

This building that we would call our home for about four weeks was a high rise set right in the heart of Waikiki, which was considered the more exclusive center of town. It was a secured building and we were situated high up on the thirty-fourth floor. The lanai of our apartment overlooked the blue waters of the Pacific Ocean and we had access to a pool, sauna, and Jacuzzi. What more could we ask for?

Toni and I got prepared for my radio show on KIKI. This would be my debut, my first performance on radio in Hawaii. I was nervous; this was all new to me. I had hoped with anticipation that the people of the Islands would accept me.

As we unpacked our clothes, Toni reminded me that I would do just fine. She said, "Remember, Dayle, people are the same all over the world. They have the same wants and needs as you and I do. Why don't you and I go to Trapper's. We can have a refreshing Hawaiian drink, sit back, have a few pupus, and relax."

I thought it was a great idea. Toni and I had many fond memories of Trapper's. It had been several months since we were in the Islands. This was very exciting for us.

Off we went in the car that John had supplied for us. Driving around the island in our own car was refreshing for both of us.

When we got to Trapper's, Toni and I saw two empty seats at the bar that we claimed for ourselves. We were unaware that in those days in Hawaii it wasn't considered proper for women to sit at the bar. You see, in the state of Nevada no one thinks twice if a woman sits at a bar. This is how our trouble began that evening.

Toni and I were having a wonderful time munching and talking away when a fellow came by and asked our permission to sit next to us. He introduced himself as Regis Connally. "And what are you two beautiful women doing here, sitting at the bar?" he asked.

Great line! We liked him immediately, even though he was giving us a line. As we made general conversation, I asked Regis what he did for a living. "I'm in the process of starting my own airline," he replied.

As Regis spoke, I focused along with him; I began to visually see his dream as well. Instantaneously, his dream came alive right before my very eyes. I told Regis that I did see him starting his airline and that his dream could become a reality. He asked me how I knew this.

"Because I'm a Psychic," I said.

Regis was intrigued. "You really do see this happening?"

"Yes, it could," I replied. "But you need some money backers. I have a strong feeling in time this may come to pass."

The minutes turned into hours as Toni and I got deeper and deeper into our conversation with Regis. We found him to be utterly fascinating and amusing. He told us he was a professional actor at one time; I was impressed.

Regis was a good-looking man in his forties, with black hair, beard, and mustache. His personality was more of the ethnic persuasion. He seemed to have an East Coast sense of humor, something I was very familiar with since I had spent several years in the New York and New Jersey areas.

Toni and I really took a fancy to Regis. This was very important to us. There was something unique about him, something I couldn't put my finger on. I really liked him. Have you ever met someone and instantly developed a fondness toward that person, but not know why? This is the way Toni and I felt about Regis.

Well, it was time to go back to our condo. Regis asked where we were staying. When we said Discovery Bay, he said, "That's funny, I'm staying across the street at the Hotel Lanai." He asked for a ride home since we were heading in the same direction.

We asked Regis if he'd like to come up to our apartment and have a drink. We wanted to learn all about him and his new airline called "Wings of Paradise."

Regis was happy to have met us. We spent the whole evening talking about my career. We even managed to sneak in a little conversation about his new airline. During the course of the evening, I managed to tell him everything about Gene. We spoke at length about why I was running away from Gene. Before the night was through, Toni, Regis, and I were the best of friends. We somehow knew that we were going to know each other for a long time.

Before Regis left, we asked him for his phone number and he asked if we could have dinner tomorrow evening. Toni and I said, "Yes. In fact, why don't you let us make you dinner?" Regis was delighted; it had been a long time since he had a good home-cooked meal.

Toni and I had to get to bed early. I was mentally preparing for the radio show in the morning. I don't think I slept a wink that evening. The next morning I was alert and ready for whatever I'd have to face.

I made my way to KIKI radio station, which was located in the downtown area of Honolulu. I was able to find my way to the elevator that took me to the fifteenth floor of the high rise. When I got off the elevator, I saw the sign: KIKI Radio. A receptionist greeted me in the lobby.

I was extremely nervous. I sat and waited patiently for the deejay to come and get me. I looked up for a moment and there was a young man waiting to greet me. He said, "Hi, you must be Dayle Schear. I'm Ron Wiley. I've been waiting for you. Come on in."

Ron showed me to a seat in the control room. He explained that he had been promoting me throughout the week in Honolulu and the response was overwhelming. Ron wanted me to sit back and relax. He gave me a headset. The phone lines were beginning to light up.

"Well, Kid, it's time for you to do your thing," he said. The next words I heard were directly from Ron Wiley: **"You're Live On The Air With PSYCHIC DAYLE SCHEAR."**

There were 15 lines into the radio station and they were all lit up. I just couldn't believe it. Everyone who was on the line was asking to speak with me. At first I had a hard time understanding the local callers. They spoke a dialect of their own called pidgin English. I wasn't familiar with this new language yet. Before long, however, I fell into the pattern right along with them. Pidgin English sounds something like this: "You the Psychic Lady. Oh, Lady, you spooky." Translation: "You're Psychic. Oh, you scare me."

During the course of the two hours I was on the air, Ron Wiley would translate periodically. The show was another overnight success. People wanted more and more.

I was different from most Psychics. There were times that the radio audience would ask me a question, but instead of giving an answer, I'd ask them something off the wall, like why their tooth was missing. I was able to tell them things no one ever knew. The accuracy was most amazing, even to me. There were times I blew myself away.

When I arrived home after the show, Toni was waiting for me patiently. She said, "That was one hell of a show you put on, Lady. Don't you feel proud of yourself?" I certainly did.

I asked Toni how many people she had booked for readings. She replied, "I booked you for the duration of your stay, with a waiting list to boot." I just couldn't believe this.

Ron asked me back on a weekly basis. I had a slot of my own once a week on Friday. Every Friday morning for two hours, Honolulu was mine. I gave out my telephone number for private consultations. After the show I'd always check my messages. There were too many to handle. I had more requests for readings than I knew what to do with in the short duration I planned to be in town.

I was different, all right. I guess they never had heard of a Psychic like me in the Islands. My schedule was incredible; from 9 in the morning till about 2 in the afternoon, all I did was see clients.

In the evening Toni and I had a little time for ourselves.

We somehow managed to meet Regis for dinner almost every evening. Toni and I also made sure we had time to lie by the pool or go to the beach. With my schedule it was quite hard at times. People were calling me from all over Oahu and the neighbor islands. I barely had time to think of Bob or Gene.

Suddenly, a strange series of events was about to happen to me. Since I was considered the new kid on the block, a large number of Psychics in the Islands wanted to check me out. One by one they called me. They wanted to see if I'd trade readings with them. I was always eager to meet new Psychics, so I always said, "Yes, of course."

Within a two-week period, there were Psychics coming out of the walls of my apartment. I'm not exaggerating. I must have been doing at least two extra readings per day. Each Psychic was different; each was unique. I was becoming extremely discouraged. Among the whole lot of Psychics I couldn't seem to find one that was accurate. I started to pawn the Psychics off on Toni. Maybe I was hard to read; maybe I was blocking them. Toni would now become my personal guinea pig. Seven Psychics later, Toni became just as frustrated as I was. She finally said, "I don't want to do this anymore. There hasn't been one Psychic who has been accurate yet, Dayle."

We were down to the last Psychic; she was Lauralie, a black reader from Los Angeles. I decided to give this one a try. I sat down at my dining room table; Lauralie pulled out a deck of regular playing cards. She asked me to shuffle the deck of cards and make a wish. She then laid the cards out in a spread and proceeded to read for me.

The reading went as follows: I SEE THAT THERE IS A MAN WHO IS WAITING FOR YOU. THIS MAN IS A LIBRA. (Very good, I said to myself. She's zoomed right in on Gene.) THIS MAN WALKS WITH A LIMP. IT SEEMS HE HAS LEFT HIS WIFE. HE IS NOW LIVING WITH A DARK-HAIRED WOMAN MUCH TALLER THAN HIMSELF. LOOKS LIKE HE IS GOING TO GET A DIVORCE. I CAN'T SEE YOU WITH THIS MAN AS MUCH AS YOU WANT TO BE.

THERE IS ANOTHER MAN WHO SITS AND WAITS. HE IS AN AQUARIUS. HE WANTS TO BE WITH YOU VERY MUCH, BUT YOU CAN'T MAKE UP YOUR MIND WHO YOU WANT TO BE WITH.

SOON THERE WILL BE A CAPRICORN MAN WHO ENTERS YOUR LIFE. THIS IS THE MAN YOU WILL END UP WITH. I SEE MUCH FAME FOR YOU.

Lauralie read me for at least two hours. When it was over I thanked her. Shortly after she left, I looked at Toni, she at me, and we tossed Lauralie's tape out of the window. We watched it free fall thirty-four stories and smash into a million pieces.

"Come on, Toni, we need to take a nice walk on the beach," I said.

As we strolled along the edge of the water, Toni said, "Penny for your thoughts."

I was angry, infuriated. "I just can't believe what Lauralie told me; Gene's leaving his wife and he's with another woman. Can you believe this? Are all these Psychics lunatics just like most of the skeptics claim them to be?"

Toni replied, "No, Dayle, I just think there are so few of them that are genuine and real, such as yourself. Why don't we forget about all this and call Regis tonight?"

I did as Toni asked. We called Regis and asked if we could finally cook him the long-promised meal that we were planning all along. That evening Regis came over for a wonderful prime rib dinner. After dinner we had a few glasses of wine. I remained silent throughout all of this.

Toni noticed that I wasn't participating in the conversation. She and Regis both asked me what was wrong. When I didn't respond, Toni said to Regis, "I know what's bothering her. You see, we had this Psychic come up earlier to tell Dayle her future. The only problem was she told Dayle that Gene was with someone else. Dayle became very depressed over the matter."

Regis then stepped in and said to me, "Is there anything I can do for you to help matters along?"

By now I had had a few too many glasses of wine. "Yes, Regis, you can help me out," I said in a very sarcastic tone.

"Great! What do you want me to do for you?"

I said, "I know, why don't you call Gene for me. He's at work. I'll give you his phone number. You can tell him that you found his number in my wallet and you wanted to know who he was. You might add that you've been seeing me exclusively whenever I've come to the Islands. Oh, remember to mention that you met me on my last trip when I was here with Phil and Toni."

Regis said, "Are you sure you want me to do this?"

Yes, I was sure. I said, "You might also mention that you are in love with me and what does he want to do about it."

Regis made the phone call. Toni and I sat in the living room while Regis talked to Gene in the bedroom, so we couldn't hear the conversation. We waited patiently. Toni asked, "Why are you doing this?"

I said, "Because I'm tired of this whole mess. It's showdown time."

I remembered that Regis was once an actor; I knew he'd do a great acting job for me. Within ten minutes Regis came out of the bedroom and slowly made his way to us. We were waiting with anticipation. "Well, what did he say?" I wanted to hear all the details.

Regis said, "Well, you're mine; all mine, Dayle." He said Gene seemed to be in shock throughout most of the conversation. Regis asked him, "What do you want to do about this?" And Gene replied in anger, **"You Can Have Her!"**

Toni started laughing; she thought it was funny. I began to think that this was one hell of a mess that I managed to get myself into.

Regis was very serious. He said to me, "I think you've lost him."

Toni stopped laughing. "Dayle," she said, with an urgency in her voice, "I think you'd better call Gene and tell him this was a joke."

I waited for two hours, trying to think this situation through. I finally went into the bedroom and placed a call to Gene. He answered the phone: "Gene Ashley, Harvey's Pit 5. How can I help you?"

I said, "Hi, Gene, it's me. I'm calling you from Hawaii."

Gene replied, "That's funny. About two hours ago your friend called me from Hawaii also. Except he wouldn't give me his name. Maybe you want to tell me who he is?"

I could tell he was angry. I explained that I had been drinking and this was a very poor joke I had played on him.

Gene didn't believe me. He wanted to know who the man was that I was involved with. I told him several times that it was nobody.

Gene said, "I'm at work. I'll call you later and we'll discuss this person who is **NOBODY.**"

I gave him my number and sat back to wait for his call. Several hours went by. Regis apologized and said he hoped that I could work things out. Toni was shocked at Gene's response. When Gene finally called, he was drunk.

"I want you to tell me who this guy is that you're seeing," he demanded. I kept telling him it was nobody. He then said, "Don't you know by now, Babe, that I love you very much? I want you here with me now. If you're telling me the truth, then I want you to make plane reservations. Call me within the next few days so we can be together. Just let me know which flight you'll be flying in on and I'll be there to meet you."

Gene went on. "I love you; I don't want to lose you. I have a wonderful surprise for you when you get here. I can't wait. We'll make love all night long. Please find a way. If you do this for me, I'll forget about the other guy. I'll be waiting for your call. **Remember, I Have A Big Surprise For You! I Love You, Babe."**

I told Gene this would be very difficult for me now. I had hundreds of people who were waiting to see me. Gene wouldn't listen. He said, "If you really love me, you'll be there for me. I'm sure you can take a few days off if you really wanted to."

I gave in. "I'll try to arrange my schedule so that I can be with you in Reno. I'll call you in a few days with my flight schedule," I said. What else could I do? I was in love with the man. I would have walked to the ends of the Earth and back for his love.

I walked back into the living room where Toni and Regis were sitting. I said to Regis, "You did one hell of an acting job. Gene really believed you." I told Toni I wanted to fly to Reno for the weekend to be with Gene and asked her if she could rearrange my work schedule. Toni said she would manage somehow. She turned to Regis and said, "The girl is hopeless!" Regis agreed.

Regis had to be going. "This was one exciting evening we had. I'll see you girls tomorrow. Thanks for the amusing entertainment and the wonderful dinner." He laughed knowingly.

After Regis left, Toni wanted to know exactly what Gene had said. I told her everything, then I excused myself. "I'm going to call the airlines and make reservations for Reno next week. I'll call Gene back in a day or two and tell him what flight I'll be on."

That was exactly what I did; I called United Airlines and booked a flight for Reno. I felt relieved. I tried in my wildest imagination to visualize what kind of surprise Gene would have for me. In all the time that I had known Gene Ashley, he never once surprised me with anything. I searched my mind for the answer. "What could it be?" I knew in my heart he would never leave Annie, especially since his son Billy was still in prison. Oh, well, I guess it would have to wait till I saw him in person.

Several days later, I called Gene at Harvey's. It must have been my lucky night; Gene answered the phone. "Hi, Gene, it's me. I'm sorry I bothered you at work."

"No problem, Babe," Gene replied. "I've been waiting for your call. Did you book the airline reservations?"

"Yes, I'll be coming in next Friday on United Airlines, Flight 185 into Reno Airport about 2:30 in the afternoon."

"I'll be waiting for you. I miss you so much, Babe. I really want you. I need you badly. I can't wait till Friday." Gene purred into the phone, sensuously. "Don't worry about anything. I'll book us into the best hotel. We'll spend the whole weekend in bed making love.

I'll make sure we never leave the room. We'll have breakfast in bed, lunch in bed, then there's me and you in bed." He sounded romantic.

God, this sounded too good to be true. I felt his every word.

"When I'm through loving every part of you, then I'll tell you of my long awaited surprise," he said.

As I listened to Gene's words, I couldn't help but fall in love again. There was something about this Libra man. Within my heart and soul I somehow knew he must have been Bogart in his last life. Our life was just like Bogie and Bacall's.

Nothing mattered anymore; I knew I would be on that plane. I also knew I would swim to get to him if I had to. There wasn't a mountain I wouldn't climb. I truly loved him.

I hadn't forgotten what the Psychics had said, but I knew that they were wrong. I knew that Gene and I belonged together. This man had something that no other man had. He was the only man that really loved me. He knew how to make love to me. He knew how to make me believe in myself. He knew how to make me feel special. When we made love, the minutes, hours, and days were no more; time stood still.

Damn him! He was doing it again! I wanted to stop loving him, but he was pulling me right back in again. I sometimes wondered if I had ever learned anything in life. Here I was, about to fall into the same trap again. Damn those Libras of the world. I was powerless against them; I never could get away from them.

I was going to do it. I was going to board a plane and travel three thousand miles for a weekend of endless pleasure. My decision was made. Now I would work as hard as I could throughout the week helping people.

Toni and I worked our hearts out seeing client after client. The week was drawing to a close; just four more days and I would be in his arms. The phone in our apartment began to ring. It was Bob. He said, "Dayle, I'll be in Honolulu tomorrow. Will you pick me up?"

I had forgotten I was supposed to meet Bob in Honolulu. I was in shock. I remember telling Bob that we were having a bad connection on the phone; I would call him back within the hour. Then I screamed for Toni. **"Help! What Am I Going To Do?** Bob wants me to pick him up at the airport tomorrow. I'm supposed to fly out and meet Gene on Friday."

Toni started to get nervous. She blurted out, "Another fine mess you've managed to get us into, Schear! We need to sit down and think this dilemma through." She thought for a while, then said, "Let me see if I have this situation correct. Bob wants to fly into Honolulu tomorrow and he wants you to pick him up at the airport. Gene will be waiting for you at the Reno Airport on Friday. Why don't you try to delay Bob by one week? That should solve your problem."

I was relieved. "That sounds good to me. I can tell Bob that my business is overflowing and that you and I have things under control. Besides, it would be better for him if he could fly in next weekend. Then I could spend a lot more time with him."

Toni said, "Now that we've finally resolved the situation, I think, let's sit for a few minutes and have a glass of wine."

While I was searching in the kitchen cupboards for some glasses, Toni turned on the radio searching for some mellow music so we could kick back and relax. She tuned into our favorite radio station, KIKI, and what we heard was mind boggling. Ron Wiley was issuing a bulletin:

"ATTENTION. THERE IS A STORM NOW APPROACHING THE HAWAIIAN ISLANDS AT A VERY PRECIPITOUS

PACE. THIS FAST MOVING STORM IS A VERY GOOD INDI-
CATION THAT A HURRICANE IS RAPIDLY APPROACHING
THE ISLANDS. WE ESTIMATE THAT HURRICANE IWA
SHOULD BE NEARING THE ISLANDS SOME TIME AROUND
FRIDAY. PLEASE SECURE ALL OUTDOOR FURNITURE
AND LISTEN FOR FURTHER NEWS BULLETINS."

I was frantic. "Toni, did you hear what I heard on the radio?
There's going to be a hurricane. I can't believe this. I just can't
believe this! What do we do now?"

Toni began to run around the apartment like a chicken without a
head. I asked her what she was doing. "I'm putting away all the lounge
furniture. We'd better get some masking tape for the windows."

I was watching Toni panic when I was the one who should have
been panicking. This was getting to be amusing. Hurricanes didn't
fluster me because I grew up in New Jersey and as a child I had
weathered several hurricanes. This was Toni's first real big one.

The hurricane was going to wallop us between Thanksgiving
Day and Friday. The timing couldn't have been worse. I wondered
if Gene would believe this. The cards were definitely stacked
against me. I had to think quickly. What was I going to do? How was
I going to get out of this mess?

I placed a call to Bob in Lake Tahoe. When Bob answered the
phone, I'm sure he detected the panic in my voice, a panic he misin-
terpreted. "Bob! There's a hurricane heading right for the Islands.
What should we do?"

Bob said, "Don't panic! I'll be in the Islands way before the
hurricane hits. Just pick me up at the airport tomorrow at 12:30,
United Airlines."

My thoughts began to wander as Bob spoke. I thought of Gene

and how much I would disappoint him. I began to fantasize while visualizing our love-making. My thoughts were weighing heavily upon the wonderful time we would have together. This beautiful picture suddenly began to fade and reality was just about to set in. "Dayle. Are you listening to me?"

I awoke abruptly from my daydreaming. "Yes, Bob, I am. I'll pick you up tomorrow at the airport. See you then." I hung up. I sat in silence for just a few moments to gather my thoughts. I had to find Gene; but I was reluctant to tell him I couldn't meet him in Reno because of the hurricane.

I tried endlessly to reach him by phone. He was nowhere to be found. I later began to get a fix on him. He had two days off, apparently, and no one seemed to know where he was. I panicked for just a moment, then I realized I would probably reach him before the storm hit.

Just as I was about to leave the phone, it rang. This time it was my long-lost buddy, Phil Simpson, on the line. "Phil, how the hell are you? Where are you?"

"It's a long story, Dayle," Phil replied. "I found out that you and Toni were in the Islands so I decided that I wanted to be there with my buddies. I'm in Lake Tahoe now, but Esther and I will be flying into Honolulu tomorrow."

"ESTHER!" I was stunned. "When did you go back with Esther?"

"I told you it's a long story. I'll tell you when I get there," Phil said.

Now, not only was Bob coming in, so were Phil and Esther. Gene was still floating around the universe somewhere. This was turning out to be one eventful afternoon.

I finally was off the phone. I located Toni and said, "You're not going to believe this, Toni."

Toni was glued to the television set watching all the updated information about Hurricane Iwa. She said, "Dayle, I'll believe anything right now."

All of a sudden for a brief moment in time, I forgot about what was happening with the people in my life. I sat down with Toni to watch the latest updates. The local television channels were reporting on the weather situation every few minutes.

**UPDATE: HURRICANE WATCH. HURRICANE IWA IS NOW HEADING FOR HONOLULU. WINDS PREDICTED TO BE AT LEAST 70 TO 90 MILES AN HOUR. THE STORM IS CENTERED OVER THE PACIFIC, EXPECTED TO HIT THE OUTER ISLANDS BY FRIDAY. THEN ON TO HONOLULU. TAKE ALL PRECAUTIONS. THIS IS NOT A STORM WATCH. THIS IS AN ACTUAL HURRICANE. PLANES THAT WILL BE FLYING INTO THE HONOLULU AIRPORT MAY BE RE-ROUTED DEPENDING ON WIND WARNINGS. STAY TUNED FOR REGULAR UPDATES. PLEASE MAKE SURE YOU HAVE PLENTY OF CANDLES, BATTERIES, RADIO, AMPLE FOOD SUPPLY ON HAND. IF YOU ARE NEAR ANY GLASS WINDOWS MAKE SURE YOU CAN GET TO A SAFE SECURE PLACE.**

I was engrossed with what was coming across the TV screen. The phone began to ring. I left Toni watching the television to answer the phone. "Hello," I shouted.

Regis was on the other end. "Did you girls hear the news?"

"Yes, I can't believe this is happening," I shouted. "On top of everything, Bob is flying in tomorrow to be with me. I haven't been able to get hold of Gene yet. Can you come over for a while? This is getting scary."

"Just give me a few minutes and I'll be right over," Regis replied.

I went back into the living room to see what else was going to happen. I reminded Toni about what the Psychics in the past had predicted for me. I told her of the spiritual reading Pam Kenni gave me. "Toni, remember what the spirits warned me about? This is beginning to make sense to me now. They told me if I were to continue my relationship with Gene, all would be taken away from me unless I complied. It's happening just as Pam said."

Toni turned to me and said, "Get a hold of yourself. Do you really believe that this storm coming in has anything to do with you and Gene?"

I said, "Toni, how many coincidences have to occur before I begin to see the light? Maybe you're right and it is a coincidence, but there's always a hidden message in such happenings."

Within moments the doorbell rang. It was Regis. I let him into the apartment and he naturally gravitated to Toni and the TV. While they sat and watched the news bulletins, I excused myself and went to the bedroom to try to locate Gene by phone one more time.

It was as if he had disappeared off the face of the Earth. Everywhere I called trying to locate him, no one seemed to know his whereabouts. I hoped that Gene had been watching the news bulletins all across the nation regarding the hurricane approaching the Hawaiian Islands.

I made my way back into the living room where Toni and Regis were engrossed in the news. They didn't take their eyes off the TV for any length of time. I pointed out to them that within two days

Thanksgiving would be here and I thought it would be a good idea if we went to the market to buy some food before the storm hit. This statement seemed to grab their attention. They both agreed, so off we went shopping for our Thanksgiving Day turkey.

I remember telling Toni and Regis that hurricane or not we were going to celebrate Thanksgiving. Regis asked, "What happens if the power goes out?"

I said, "Don't worry, I have it covered. I'll make sure our turkey is done on or before Thanksgiving and way before the power goes out. Remember, Regis, I'm a Psychic. I promise you, hurricane or not, we'll be eating turkey."

When we arrived at the market, the lines were overwhelmingly long. I guess everyone on the island was stocking up with groceries. I told Regis we were going to have lots of company for Thanksgiving. "Phil and Esther, Bob and I, you and Toni. So we'd better buy enough to hold us over till the hurricane passes."

I don't know how we made it upstairs with the amount of groceries that we had. When we finally opened the door to the apartment, we were completely exhausted. For several hours we sat and watched the latest updates on the storm.

The next day was Wednesday. I went to the airport to pick up Bob and waited for him at United's baggage claim area, my usual spot. Bob spotted me immediately and leaped into the car. We had a casual conversation on the way back to the apartment.

When we arrived, Toni answered the door and Bob gave her a kiss. Then he noticed there was a man in our apartment. Regis happened to be doing his laundry in our place.

"Why is that man doing laundry in your apartment?" Bob asked. "Who is he, Dayle?"

I remembered that I never did mention Regis to Bob and how we met him. I introduced Regis and began to tell Bob that Regis was in the midst of starting his own airlines called "Wings of Paradise." That's all Bob needed to know; he was impressed. Regis and Bob began a long and involved conversation.

While the two men were talking, I pulled Toni over to the side and asked if Gene had called. When she said "no," I told her I was very concerned. Toni told me not to worry; we would handle the situation. The phone rang at that very moment; it was Phil. He had finally made it in and wanted to tell me that he was safe and sound. Phil said he would meet us tomorrow sometime for Thanksgiving dinner.

Well, everyone was accounted for and we could now brace for the upcoming storm. We kept watching the television. In the next few hours things began to get quite unsettled.

BULLETIN: UPDATE ON THE HURRICANE. THE STORM IS NOW APPROACHING AT A MORE RAPID PACE. HURRICANE IWA IS EXPECTED TO HIT THE ISLANDS SOMETIME TOMORROW, THANKSGIVING DAY. BE PREPARED. SHUT OFF ALL GAS LINES AND BRACE YOURSELF FOR POWER OUTAGES. MORE NEWS TO COME FOLLOWING THE 6:OO PM NEWS.

I decided it would be best if Regis spent the night with us; it seemed to be too dangerous to leave at this time. Everyone agreed! Bob really liked Regis; he had a friend and someone to talk to. Last I heard, Regis was offering Bob stock options in his company, "Wings of Paradise." Bob was willing to help Regis any way he could.

Thursday, Thanksgiving Day, the winds were blowing quite

heavily. I arose early in the morning to bake my turkey. I knew I didn't have much time before the power would go out. We were already beginning to experience rolling blackouts on the island. It was around 3 p.m. when Phil and Esther finally made their way to our apartment. Toni and I were so happy to see Phil; we hadn't seen him in months. We introduced Phil and Esther to Regis and told Phil about his new airline.

The next thing we knew, the power went out, the oven went off, and the elevators shut down. The winds were kicking up to at least 50 miles per hour. It really didn't matter because my turkey was fully cooked and ready. Then the phone lines came down. Oh, well, so much for Gene. If he hadn't figured out by now that I wasn't coming, I didn't know what to tell him.

Toni and Regis wanted to get a bottle of wine for our turkey dinner from the liquor store downstairs. I said, "Are you **CRAZY?** The elevator is out and we're on the thirty-fourth floor."

Toni said, "Don't worry. Regis and I need the exercise. We'll be back shortly."

We waited two hours for Toni and Regis to come back. We were all very concerned. We were living on candlelight and battery-operated radios at this point, and they were missing. We were just about to have our Thanksgiving feast when my front door suddenly flew open. There stood the long overdue Toni and Regis. What had happened to them?

Toni explained, breathlessly, "Are you aware that Discovery Bay has two completely different towers?"

I said, "Yes."

"Well, Regis and I took the wrong tower to our apartment. First, we walked **34** flights down the stairs to the liquor store. Then we walked **34** flights up the stairs back to the apartment. We discovered there was no such apartment number. We looked at each other and felt we were in the **Twilight Zone.**

"We then realized we were in the wrong tower. I thought Regis was going to kill me. We regained our breath, and we proceeded to walk down another **34** flights of stairs till we located the correct tower. By this time Regis was **HALF DEAD.** I was carrying him, literally. We then walked up another **34** flights of stairs till we found our apartment. And here we are."

Regis had collapsed on our sofa. I thought he was going to have a heart attack. He just lay on the sofa in a semi-conscious state, gasping for air, while we applied cold compresses to his forehead. I would have called 911, but all our phones were out. We knew he'd recover, so we decided to have our Thanksgiving dinner. I was determined to have that Thanksgiving dinner, even though the wind was now racing at 70 miles per hour and we were experiencing rolling blackouts.

The only thing that was accomplished that afternoon was our finally having our turkey dinner. The evening worsened with high winds and torrential rains battering the apartment. All we had were several candles and one radio. There was only one channel open on the radio at that time. As bedtime neared, everyone found a safe place to sleep. I nestled on the floor and left a window open so it wouldn't blow out. I noticed everyone was asleep by now. I was cozy and stayed awake, listening to the only station broadcasting on the island.

I heard some wild stories that night over the radio. Planes were being detoured to the neighbor islands; a lot of planes couldn't make it into Honolulu; some air carriers were being told to turn around when they reached the halfway point over the Pacific. All in all, it was quite exciting. I was glad I stayed for the excitement alone.

The following day, everything was back to normal, except for a lot of debris, uprooted trees, and a few shattered roofs. The black-outs continued for a week, but the winds had died down and Honolulu was safe once again. We found out later that the island of Kauai had been hit the hardest.

Within a week our visitors all decided to head back home to Lake Tahoe. Toni and I stayed on to finish up my work at the radio station. Although we had been hit by a hurricane, the number of people who were coming to see me for private readings was incredible.

Toni and I stayed on for at least two more weeks. Regis decided to go home and try to market his airline somewhere else. Bob had to go back to work. And Phil and Esther were happily back together. As for me, I was unable to make contact with Gene. All in all, hurricane or not, the radio show was extremely successful and I was invited back. The radio station wanted me to appear again in the next few months. They wanted me to split my time between Lake Tahoe and Honolulu.

**After being on the island for well over a month, I knew it was time to go back home. Besides, Toni and I were getting jumpy. I wanted to go home to find out just what happened to Gene Ashley. I said my goodbyes to the people of the Islands. Toni and I were headed for Lake Tahoe, Nevada.**

# YO! GENE, WHERE ARE YOU?
## CHAPTER 20

Toni and I were back in the real world once again. Bob was concentrating on his new business venture. He wanted to get a gaming license so he could put slot machines in some of the small local places around town. Toni decided she wanted to go to beauty school and I plunged into my work for the radio station and kept myself busy.

One day I paid a visit to Diane. She was packing and getting ready to move to an apartment a few miles away from where she was living now. The rent at the new place was much cheaper. I decided to help her pack and that weekend we were getting ready to move.

While we were packing, Diane asked me, "Have you heard from Gene?"

"No," I said. "Diane, I've been searching this town. I don't know what happened to him. He's not at work; I don't think he's with Annie. I don't know what to make of it."

Diane remarked, "Maybe Annie killed him."

"That's not funny!" I said.

That weekend as I was helping Diane move into her new apartment, I spotted Gene's car right around the block. I shouted, "Diane, come here! You're not going to believe this. I just saw Gene's car parked right around the block. What should I do?" I was panicking.

Diane said, "Go find out where he is. Don't worry about me; you find him. Hurry up now."

I went racing in my car around the block and pulled up right behind his car. I walked into the building and looked at the name tags of each apartment. There he was; the tag said "Gene Ashley."

Oh, my god, he moved out from his wife Annie. I was in shock. I didn't know what to do next. So this was his surprise for me; he really moved out. We could be together now. I was ready; I would leave Bob and move in with Gene. My excitement was overwhelming; I could barely contain myself.

I knocked on the door slowly. Gene answered. He was surprised to see me but he invited me in. I ran into his arms and he held me ever so tightly; he hugged and kissed me like there was no tomorrow. Gene asked me, "So when did you get back from the Islands?" I mentioned about a week or so ago. He asked how I found him and I explained about Diane being his next-door neighbor.

As he was holding me and staring right into my eyes, he said, "There's something I have to tell you. I just want you to listen to me and not get excited."

Gene went on. "After Regis phoned me and told me he was your lover, I was extremely depressed. As much as you were trying to convince me that he never existed, I found it very hard to believe. Then when you didn't show up at the airport, I knew that you were really seeing someone else."

I interrupted. "Gene, there was a hurricane! Didn't you hear it on the news?"

"Yes, I did," he replied, "but I also knew if you really loved me you would have been here for me, hurricane or not."

I started to interrupt him again, but he said, "Let me finish; this is hard enough. I had already moved out from Annie. That was going to be my surprise to you. But I sat and waited at the airport and you never showed up. I guess what I'm really trying to say is I met someone else, Dayle. I'm seeing someone else."

Was I dreaming? Was this really happening to me? I waited almost three years for this man. I thought he loved me. I started flashing back to what Lauralie told me in Honolulu. She was right. She told me Gene was with someone else; she told me I would lose him. Why did I throw her tape out of the window? Why didn't I believe her? My head was spinning. I sat silently for a while and began to think about this situation.

My first thought was that this was all my fault because I had pulled that silly little stunt on Gene with Regis. I began to believe that I deserved everything he was dishing out. But I started to wise up a bit. I realized this was just an excuse. Gene was using me as an excuse to get away from Annie. He was dumping me, as well as his wife. He found a new play toy, someone who would stick to him like glue. That was the real reason. Gene knew that I traveled a lot and he was scared of flying. He also knew he could never be with me, so he decided to shack up with someone who was more passive.

I wondered if he ever loved me or if this was one big joke. I looked up at Gene. For the first time in my life, I was scared. Who was this woman that he was seeing? Did I know her?

Gene interrupted my thoughts. "Dayle, did you hear what I said? Did you hear a word of what I told you?"

"Yes, Gene. I heard everything that you've told me," I said. Gene wanted to tell me whom he was seeing. I refused to let him. I shouted, "Please don't! Because if I know, I'll kill her!"

I demanded to know if he loved her. He said, "No."

"I don't understand. Is there hope for you and me, or do you want to be with her?" I asked.

"I don't know at this point, Dayle," he replied. "All I know is you hurt me badly with your Regis stunt. I need time to think." Gene could see I was hurting now. He said, "Come here. I didn't mean to hurt you." He kissed me. We then began to make mad, passionate love for hours on end.

I was determined to win him back at this point. I felt his new girlfriend posed no threat to me whatsoever. As long as I didn't know who she was, it didn't matter. I knew I could win out if I tried. Gene gave me his new number and told me to call before I came over in the near future. There would be many occasions when his girlfriend would be coming over; he didn't want the two of us to meet. I agreed.

I left Gene's apartment somewhat dazed and headed back to Diane's. When I went running into her apartment, she asked, "Well, did you see him?"

"Yes, Diane," I said. "The only problem is Gene is seeing someone else!"

**"WHAT! THE SON-OF-A-BITCH!"** Diane was angry. I told her the whole story from beginning to end. She said, "Dayle, this is war and you can win at the end if you listen to me. We fought too hard to get this man. He left his wife; the rest is easy. Besides, I think he's just trying to punish you for all the hurt you put on him. I think you should continue to see him and be as nice and sweet as you can be. At the end he'll be begging you to come back. Meanwhile, I'll do some digging around and find out who this girl is."

Several weeks passed and I followed Diane's advice. It was working. Gene was falling more and more in love with me as time went by. As soon as his girlfriend left, I'd sneak into his apartment and make amorous love. When I knew she'd be returning, I'd sneak out of the apartment as fast as I came in. I would leave him love notes all over the pillow and underneath his pillow so she'd know that I had been there. **"All's Fair In Love And War."** And this was war; at least my war.

Within a week Diane called me to come to her apartment. As I walked in, she said, "I have some news for you. I found out who Gene is dating. You know her very well; in fact, all of Harvey's knows her."

**"WHO, DIANE, WHO?"** I was beginning to sound like an owl.

"Her name is Betty Inn-White, also known as **Blow-Job Betty.**" Diane and I laughed hysterically. She was no match for Diane and me.

Day after day, night after night, I would see Gene. I was winning him over. Until I got **CRAZY.**

It was New Year's Eve, the start of a brand new year for me. I spent most of that day with Gene Ashley. Gene told me he was working that evening but right after work he'd come and get me and we'd spend all of New Year's Day together.

By now he knew that I knew of Betty. He warned me that Betty would be using his apartment that evening; however, he would be working. He was honest. I was slowly winning Gene over; he told me he loved me more and more as time went by and he'd soon be getting rid of Betty so we could be together.

That **CRAZY** New Year's Eve Diane and I and a friend named Sandie, were really boozing it up. The more I drank the angrier I got that Betty was in Gene's apartment. Diane didn't help matters any; she was really fueling the fire and feeding my anger. One thing led to another and we all piled into Diane's car; we were on a Witch Hunt. Betty Inn-White, beware!

We reached Gene's apartment in record time, the three of us all drunk out of our minds. We parked the car right in front of the apartment and turned on the headlights so they would beam right into Betty's face. All three of us then began to pound on the door. We shouted, **"Betty, we know you're in there. Did you know that Gene has been sleeping with you and he's been sleeping with Dayle as well? You Bitch! You better come out of there or we'll break the door down."** And it went on and on. I think we woke up the whole apartment building.

There was no response from Betty. We decided to go home. We laughed the whole time as we were driving home. A few hours later, Gene called Diane's apartment; he wanted to speak to me.

"Dayle, I can't believe you did that to Betty. Why did you do that? I told you I was going to spend New Year's Day with you. Now you went and spoiled the whole thing. I don't ever want to see you again."

Diane asked what Gene had said. **"Oh, I think we really did it this time!"** I said.

Gene didn't call me for three weeks. Finally, he called me at Diane's and said he wanted to speak to me. I went to his apartment and listened while he bawled me out. He said he didn't know why, but he still loved me; he couldn't get me out of his mind. We made love once again.

Then, I somehow came to my senses and realized that I was no toy. If Gene wanted to see Betty, that was fine with me. Besides, she'd make a better wife for him. She would be at his side while I would be traveling around the world as usual. Lauralie was right, and so was Pam Kenni. I knew the spirits would never allow me to be with Gene. It was my final realization. I had to accept this, no matter how much I loved him.

I decided to leave Betty and Gene alone and go on with my life. This was very painful. I learned a great lesson. That was the last time I ever got drunk.

**Several months later Gene's son approached me and asked why I had pulled that stunt on New Year's Eve. I said, "I was drunk. Sorry." His son told me I was one half inch away from marrying his father before I did what I did. That made me feel wonderful. I thanked him for his insight and went on with my life.**

# PETER HURKOS,
# WORLD FAMOUS PSYCHIC
## CHAPTER 21

After I left Gene I was depressed for weeks on end. I still had the radio show and my popularity was growing by leaps and bounds. Bob was by my side, patiently waiting to be approved for a gaming license. The only problem was it took forever for the gaming commission to approve him. Bob was beginning to become antsy; he wanted to get out of Harrah's in the worst way; he wanted to start his own business and become a wealthy man.

By chance on my way to the post office, I ran once again into Doug Bushousen, head of Harrah's entertainment. He asked me how things were going and I told him I was doing well. Doug said politely, "Just let me know if I can help."

"Do you know Peter Hurkos?" I asked. "I've always wanted to meet him." Doug replied, "Yes, I do. I'll take care of it in the morning. Don't worry."

The next morning Doug phoned and gave me Peter Hurkos' telephone number. I was stunned.

Imagine what it would be like to finally meet your idol, someone you've greatly admired all your life and watched on television for at least ten years. When I first saw Hurkos on television, I was amazed by his powers. I watched him so intently and began to imitate every move he made. I somehow knew I possessed the same ability that he had.

Meeting him was a chance of a lifetime for me. This dream of mine for so many years was about to become a reality. In my eyes the magnitude of this man and how I felt about him was equivalent to my meeting the President of the United States.

Peter Hurkos was considered by experts to be the foremost Psychic of the century. Born May 21, 1911, in Dordrecht, Holland, he acquired his Psychic "gift" in 1941 after falling from a ladder and suffering a brain injury. He was in a coma for three days at the Zuidwal Hospital. Upon regaining consciousness, he discovered he had developed an ability to pierce the barriers that separate the past, present, and future.

Hurkos gained worldwide recognition as a Psychic detective working on cases involving missing planes, persons, and murder victims. Some of his most famous cases have included The Stone of Scone (London, England); The Boston Strangler Multiple Murders (Boston, Massachusetts) The Missing Thai Silk King, Jim Thompson (Asia); The Ann Arbor Coed Murders (Ann Arbor, Michigan); and The Sharon Tate Murders (Los Angeles, California).

His forte is psychometry, the ability to see past, present, and future associations by touching objects. In 1956 he was brought to the United States by Dr. Andrija Puharich, M.D., to be tested in his Glen Cove, Maine, medical research lab. For two-and-a-half years Hurkos was tested under tightly controlled conditions. The results convinced Dr. Puharich that Hurkos' Psychic abilities were far greater than any he had ever tested; a remarkable 90 percent accuracy.

He was decorated as a war hero by Queen Juliana of the Netherlands (a statue commemorating Hurkos and seven other Dutch underground war heroes is in Rotterdam). He was a consultant to every President of the United States since Eisenhower.

He was an active member of Ronald Reagan's Presidential Task Force. Steven King's movie "The Dead Zone" was modeled after Peter Hurkos. His accomplishments are too numerous to mention.

My association with Peter Hurkos began in the summer of 1981 when Doug gave me Peter's telephone number. I sat by my phone for at least fifteen minutes before I had the courage to place the call. I was scared to death.

I wanted to find out if my gift as a Psychic was genuine. Or was I just plain crazy? I dialed the number slowly. Peter's wife, Stephany, answered the phone. I introduced myself and explained why I was calling.

Stephany was hard on me at first. She asked me to read for her over the phone; I had to prove myself first before I could meet with Peter. She had been in similar situations before where Psychics had asked to speak with Peter to find out if their talents were real. I read for Stephany nonstop for an hour or so on the phone. She said nothing; she just listened. I was definitely being tested.

Stephany was cautious. She felt that I might have read something about Peter in a book. She never commented one way or another about my ability until I reached out with a fact I couldn't possibly have known.

I blurted out that I saw they were going to acquire a seeing-eye dog, and I couldn't figure out why because no one in the family was blind. Stephany immediately put me on hold for a moment.

When she returned to the phone, Stephany said Peter would meet with me on Monday afternoon at 1:30. I was to be at their address in L.A. promptly and the fee for the reading would be $250. As we hung up, I turned to my husband Bob and told him what was going on. I was somewhat stunned. All we had in the bank was $2,000. In addition to the $250 fee, it would cost me $500 to go to

L.A. But this was something I had to do. I finally was going to meet the Great one, Peter Hurkos.

I arrived in L.A. on Monday and I rang the doorbell at the Hurkos residence shortly before 1:30. Stephany invited me in. I was shaking so badly I couldn't remember my own name. Stephany politely introduced herself and tried to calm me down. She sat me down in the living room and told me Peter would be in shortly. Ten minutes passed. I was extremely nervous.

When Peter Hurkos entered the room, his presence was overwhelming. He stood about six feet five inches tall and looked like a giant to me. I was still shaking, but Peter was charming. I began to calm down.

Peter was carrying a box of letters with him. He emptied the box in my lap and asked, "How can I help all these people? They are all crying out for help. Tell me how." I was shocked. He had so much empathy for people.

As he sat down in his chair, he reached out slowly and handed me his ring. Peter wanted me to read for him. I was honored. I told him what I saw. He was pleased. Peter then held my watch and gave me a reading. It was extremely accurate. The "forty-minute reading" that Peter gave me lasted about four hours. By the time it ended, Peter and I were the best of friends.

"So you want me to train you?" he asked in his heavy Dutch accent.

"Yes," I said eagerly.

"Okay, I will train you. But you need a lot of work and whenever I call, you must be available. This may take a while, but I'll train you. Come back in a few weeks and we will begin," he said. "Dayle! One very important thing. You must put down the Tarot cards. You are not a card reader; you are better than that."

I told Peter the cards were my life. Peter explained that he would teach me his way.

He said, "The training will take a long time, so don't be in any hurry, Young Lady. There is so much you must learn if you want to help people."

I was ecstatic! I had admired this man for as long as I could remember and he was actually going to train me. This was more than a dream come true.

Peter Hurkos, the Greatest Psychic in the World. And I was going to be his student.

The testing began in July of 1981. Bob and I flew to L.A. and were welcomed into the Hurkos' home. Peter and Stephany were so gracious to us.

Stephany administered my first tests with the help of her friends and Peter's clients. I knew nothing about any of these people. Stephany is personal manager for many Hollywood stars; these were lifelong friends of hers to whom I gave non-stop readings. Her friends were told to remain silent and Peter's clients were not allowed to comment in any way, shape, or form about my readings.

This was very difficult for me at first. As a Psychic I'm used to my clients responding to my readings. In these test cases, I never knew if I were right or wrong until the next day when Stephany would explain to me whether I had been right or whether I had messed up.

In the evening when we were through with our readings, Peter and I would play a friendly game of backgammon. After a while, however, it would turn out not to be such a friendly game. Peter never liked to lose at anything, and neither did I, for that matter. I noticed Peter would let me win for a while; then, whenever he wanted to catch up on the game, he'd roll seven doubles in a row. It was getting quite aggravating. With those odds there was absolutely no way I could win. So I decided to control the dice with my mind. But that made no difference; Peter's doubles were always higher than my doubles. To make matters worse, he always knew the outcome of the game anyway.

I really don't know why I even bothered to play. Except that there was a challenge in trying to figure out a way to beat him, although I knew deep inside that I could never beat my master at his own game. One evening Peter and I were in a war for doubles. I rolled ten doubles; Peter rolled seven. Our anger was showing. It must have been funny watching two Psychics get mad and try to outdo each other in a simple little game of backgammon.

That same evening, Peter taught Bob how to play a Dutch game of cards. The cards were dealt from a fresh, previously unopened deck. At one point in the game, Peter grew increasingly impatient at Bob, who had been concentrating on his cards for a long time. He wanted Bob to throw a card.

Peter finally shouted, "Bob, throw either the ten of clubs or the ace of spades!"

Startled, Bob quickly looked at his hand. He thought Peter was using a marked deck of cards. Bob was a pit boss at Harrah's casino and was trained to look for marked cards, but this deck wasn't marked. Bob checked for mirrors in the house. He wondered aloud, "How did he know what was in my hand?"

I remember Peter laughed and laughed. He was just using his gift; he was using telepathy. We were all amazed.

Bob was still skeptical of Peter's power of the mind. So as we were eating dinner, Peter asked Bob to pick any fork in the kitchen or go out and buy one. Bob picked a fork and handed it to him. Within moments without ever touching the fork, Peter by pure concentration bent the fork in half. Bob was no longer skeptical.

The next day there were more readings. For my next test I was going to read the wife of a famous general who was a friend of Peters. The general and his wife had given the seeing-eye dog to Peter for his daughter Gloria.

I went into the living room to meet Kitty Bradley, wife of Four-Star General Omar Bradley of World War II fame. Peter told me to read her very thoroughly. I asked Mrs. Bradley for a personal item and she handed me her diamond necklace with four diamond-studded stars representing her husband's rank. I gave her a nonstop reading for about forty-five minutes. At the end of the reading, Kitty commented that everything I had told her was false.

I looked at her in disbelief. I knew what I had told this woman was all true. I shouted, "Lady, you don't need a Psychic. You need a shrink!"

I was furious. I ran into the kitchen where Peter was sitting and screamed at him, "This woman is crazy! I told her the truth and she called me a liar. Besides, she's so cheap she comes to your house in a Rolls Royce and then she checks price tags in the store before she buys you a present. I'm getting out of here. I want to go home to Lake Tahoe. These people in L.A. don't need my help. I want to be among my own people." I stormed into my room and started to pack my bags.

Peter looked in and asked, "What are you doing, Dolly?"

"I'm leaving this place!" I yelled. "All these clients and friends are phony. What I told Kitty was right and she called me a liar. I can't believe this. She must be crazy. I know that when I get these strong feelings I'm right. And no one can tell me differently."

Peter listened to my ranting, then he laughed and laughed.

"Why do you find this so amusing?" I snapped.

"Dolly," he said, "this was just a test. That's all it was." He had told Kitty Bradley to deny everything I told her in the reading. This was set up to get me angry so that my ESP, extra-sensory perception, would increase.

It is a known fact that you do not get a Psychic angry. If you do manage to anger one, for some reason the Psychic's power will increase. Peter and Stephany were trying to see what made me angry; they wanted to know how and when to push my buttons.

Well, it worked. I was so angry that I was livid. It took a while for Peter to calm me down. He then made me go back into the living room to give Kitty another reading. I did so very reluctantly. Considering that my ESP was now at its highest level, the second reading was extremely accurate and Kitty was more than amazed.

I resented what I went through with Kitty, but the testing had to go on. The whole point was to test my accuracy in foretelling future events. If I were to read for important people, the only way to test my accuracy was to test my ability on their friends.

Peter and I had long talks each night. He would explain and put to rest all the fears that were in my mind. I'll admit I didn't understand a lot of things pertaining to ESP. If I don't understand why things are happening, I become more confused. Peter tried to answer every question that was on my mind.

I was beginning to understand the difference between using telepathy and precognition to see the future. When you are telepathic, you read what a person really wants, but that may not be the outcome of their future. When you are precognitive, you see the future as it is.

Peter would yell at me, telling me I was too impatient, that I wanted to know too much too soon, too quickly. He said that I must learn a little at a time. This was very hard for me; I wanted to know it all now.

We also spoke about my relationship with Gene, a relationship that Peter felt was very abusive for me. He told me that in order to be a good Psychic I would have to give up a lot for the sake of helping others. "Your life is not your own. The gift was given to help others."

This was difficult for me to understand. I asked Peter, "Does this mean I have to give up all my dreams and all that I love so much for the sake of the cause?"

Peter looked directly at me and said, "If you don't give this up, meaning Gene, he will be taken from you if he gets in your way of helping others."

I couldn't comprehend Peter's warning. I didn't realize that as a Psychic you are chosen for a reason, whatever that reason may be. Your path is chosen for you to follow. If you do not follow that path, someone else will be chosen to take your place. It seems this is all decided by the higher powers and if I strayed for some reason, this would become a reality.

I tested the higher powers occasionally. I was curious about what Peter had taught me. My goal was to have my cake and eat it, too. Testing, testing, testing.

The things I put myself through to see if I were worthy of this position. For the longest time I tried to be with Gene, but it seemed whenever we tried to be together, a natural disaster would occur.

I trained with the amazing Peter Hurkos for six years. We were together on and off whenever time permitted in between my trips to Lake Tahoe and Hawaii. In time I noticed a pattern; I realized the driving force behind Peter was his wonderful wife Stephany.

Stephany was most amazing. She always protected and guided Peter. She made sure no harm would come to him in any way, shape, or form. She was the buffer zone that everyone had to pass through in order to reach out and touch Peter. It sometimes was a very rough job, but she loved Peter and tried to make sure he was never used or taken for granted. I found her to be sweet, kind, and very venerable. She always cared for everyone else but herself. She was by Peter's side until he died. There are no words in my vocabulary to describe Stephany's special devotion and love, except to say she was a saint in her own right.

Peter and Stephany worked with me endlessly on murder cases as well as on my dealings with people to finesse the ability that I already had. At times it seemed whenever I happened to be at their house, a major crisis would be going on. On one occasion while I was there waiting to be trained, Peter's dog turned up missing. Now, Psychics have a protective mechanism: they can't see the future for themselves, especially if they are emotionally involved. Since it was Peter's dog, he was very involved. It was up to me to figure out who had taken the dog and why. This case was my special assignment that whole weekend. It took me a while, but I figured out the caper and Peter retrieved his dog.

On another occasion Stephany brought home a movie producer. She wanted to know if the gentleman, who was dripping in gold, had enough money to produce a movie about Peter's life. She asked the producer to remove his Rolex watch, handed it to me, and asked me point blank in front of him if he really had the money to produce the movie. Peter stayed in the kitchen, his favorite place, cooking.

I took the watch and held it in my hands. I then looked the man straight in the eye and said, "Stephany, he doesn't have a pot to piss in."

The producer was shocked. As he was led out the door, he shouted, "I don't have the money now but I can get it!"

I heard Peter chuckling in the background. He called out from the kitchen, "You did good, Dolly."

I always watched Peter in awe, hanging on to his every word. I analyzed everything he said, although his heavy accent sometimes made it quite hard for me to do so. Throughout the years of my readings on their friends, clients, and movie stars, he and Stephany always taught me where I was messing up in my readings and how I could get better.

They introduced me to Dr. Andrija Puharich, Peter's teacher. I spent ten days undergoing all sorts of tests with him in North Carolina. At this point Peter was experimenting with crystals. I actually saw him ignite a crystal with just the energy within his hands; sparks were flying out of the crystal. It was most amazing.

Peter also had healing ability. I had bursitis in my left elbow and there were times when I was in terrible pain. One day Peter laid his hands on my elbow and took all the pain away. The bursitis has never come back.

There was the time Peter told me of my mother's death. He said she would be as thin as a rail and he saw her walking in the street, not knowing her own name. Shortly after that, she would die. The time would be approaching soon.

I asked Peter, "If we can see the future, can we change it?"
He didn't know.

Just as Peter had foretold, when the event occurred my mom was wandering the streets in Lake Tahoe. I noticed the aura of death around her. I called my sister in L.A. and we shipped Mom to L.A., where she underwent treatment in a hospital. The doctors pulled her off all medication, which is what had made her ill. Mom is still living today at the age of 82, thanks to Peter making me aware of the future. I found out if you can see the future, sometimes you can change it.

What Peter gave me, no one else in this world could have ever given me. Not only was he a teacher, but a father to me as well. Peter replaced the father I had lost. I was not only a student of the Hurkos family, I was part of the family. I thank them for that.

Peter's daughter Gloria is also amazingly Psychic. She and I took long walks together and I could see myself as a child in her. I could see all the pain she had to endure growing up as a Psychic child. I tried at times to relieve that pain for her, but I also knew she would have to go through it.

In all the years that Peter trained me, I learned so much. I also learned about his lifetime of suffering. He would say at times that if he had a choice he would never have chosen this field. He was made fun of more times than not. There have been such cruel things written about him as well as wonderful things. But the writers who tested and tried him never knew the true greatness of the man.

They never knew how many times he took people in and helped the poor. They never knew how many lives he saved in the course of his life. All they could see was the dollar amount that he charged the public.

One of the funniest stories I remember is about the time Peter was in Las Vegas. Peter never gambled because he thought if he did his gift would be taken away. On this particular day he was fooling around at the craps table and laid $100 on the field. Before he knew it, his $100 had turned into thousands. He didn't want the money; he kept pushing it back and letting it ride on the field. He felt so bad he didn't know what to do. So he finally took the money, $80,000 in all, and bought a fur coat and diamond jewels for his wife. He kept shaking his head and saying, "I don't want the money. It's no good." That's a true story, my friends.

Peter and I trained endlessly up to the time of his death. I took his passing quite hard, but he is still alive in spirit. And I mean that in more ways than one.

PETER HURKOS & DAYLE SCHEAR

## PETER HURKOS
MAY 21, 1911 — JUNE 1, 1988

# MY CRAZY WILD FRIENDS, LIFE WITH RADIO
## CHAPTER 22

I visited with Peter Hurkos on many occasions and he encouraged me to build up my clientele in the Hawaiian Islands. The radio station in Honolulu asked me to come back to the Islands and my business was growing at a very rapid pace. I found myself in somewhat of a dilemma. I needed someone to help me with my business, but Toni was busy attending school and Bob was busy placing his slot machines all around town.

I placed a call to my friend Phil Simpson and asked if he would assist me with my clientele in the Islands. I didn't have to ask Phil twice; he was more than willing. I was ready to go back to the Islands.

I no sooner got off the phone than it rang. It was Barbara, my long-lost friend, calling from L.A. to find out how I was doing. I told her I was preparing to go to the Islands for my upcoming radio shows.

"That's funny," Barbara remarked, "I'm also on my way to Honolulu."

I asked her if she'd mind helping me out with my business and told her about Phil. She replied, "I think it will be fun. Besides, I'd like to stay longer, anyway."

Barbara was special. There was never a dull moment when she was around. She was a comedian by trade and had appeared in many comedy stores in L.A. She was quite attractive and had charisma.

Before I left for the Islands I managed to speak with Gene on several other occasions. I knew we were nearing the end of our relationship. In my heart I wanted him back, but I also knew he would end up with Betty. Yet, I didn't want to give up. I would hang on to him for several more months before my time with him would be at its end.

I was ready to go to the Islands. Phil and I flew into Honolulu together and rented an apartment at Discovery Bay. Phil would help with my clients until Barbara arrived in a week or so. I hooked up with an answering service and was ready to work.

My show steadily gained popularity throughout the Islands. Thanks to radio, everywhere I went people were excited to meet me.

Early one morning I arrived at KIKI radio station, totally unaware of what would happen on that day. Ron Wiley and I were answering the phones as usual; people were calling in with their problems. Ron turned to me on our break and said, "I want you to pump up this commercial with me. The owner, John Parker, is really into this." I agreed without knowing what Ron was referring to.

Ron was promoting AM stereo all across the Islands, letting people know that AM stereo was the wave of the future. The AM stations at that time were virtually dying and listeners were turning to the FM stations. John Parker was nervous about how FM radio might affect his station and had devised this new technique to bring AM back.

Ron made the mistake of asking me while I was on the air for my opinion about AM stereo. I said, "It sounds good, provided you have an AM stereo receiver to receive it." I believe one should always be highly ethical and up front with the people.

Within moments, I heard the front office was trying to get hold of me; John Parker wanted to talk to me personally. I was on the air and the phone lines were jammed with people on hold for well over an hour, and John Parker wanted to speak to me. It dawned on me that I just might be in trouble for what I said about AM stereo.

I turned to Ron and said, "I'm fired. I know it."

Ron tried to reassure me. "Don't be silly. John wouldn't fire you!" However, Ron told me later that AM stereo was an extremely costly project that John was trying to push.

I went home after the show and explained my dilemma to Phil. He said not to worry; I was booked up with readings for well over two months.

Several days later John managed to reach me. On the day of the broadcast he was infuriated when he heard me on his car radio say that one needed an AM stereo to receive the signal. He pulled his car in disgust into a local bowling alley. He placed his quarter into the phone and dialed my number. John felt demoralized. He tried for hours to reach me by phone, but all the lines were busy.

Now he was screaming at me over the phone. "I know you're trying to sabotage my radio station!"

"Pardon me!" I exclaimed. "What do you mean?"

John screamed, "This radio project I've been working on is all too important to me. People believe everything you say."

I couldn't understand why he would be so upset. I said, "John, I didn't do anything wrong. Ron asked me a question and I gave him an honest answer."

I found out later why he was so angry. He was beginning to go into production with the new AM stereos that he was marketing on the island, but he was already indicating to the public that KIKI had the stereos available, which wasn't true. The whole project eventually bombed, anyway; it really had nothing to do with me.

John decided to punish me by keeping me off the air for several weeks. Because of my popularity, he didn't want to fire me. I took the hint; I knew my days were numbered. Although my contract stated that I couldn't work on the island for over a year after leaving KIKI, I ignored it and applied for a job with KKUA radio. They were more than happy to hire me.

John was angry when I left KIKI. I didn't want to leave, but I felt I had no choice. All in all, this turned out to be one of the more intelligent moves I ever made in my career.

Changing radio stations created an overload of work and I joyfully awaited Barbara's arrival.

## WELCOME, BARBARA.

Phil and I picked up Barbara at the airport and drove to our apartment at Discovery Bay. Barbara and Phil became friends immediately. Since Barbara was around to handle my affairs, it was an opportune time for Phil to go golfing every day. This was a really crazy time for all of us.

Our apartment was a comic fiasco. I had rented this one bedroom apartment for $950 a month. Barbara and Phil shared the living room; Phil rented a cot and Barbara had the couch. I acquired the only available bedroom. Our mornings were crazy. Everyone had to wake up early to make the apartment presentable for my clients. Phil shared the one-bathroom with us and we allowed him at least two inches of space. While he was getting ready for his daily round of golf, Barbara and I scurried around to get the apartment ready for clients.

The radio station was promoting me and my business was booming. I sometimes felt like I was the only Psychic in the state of Hawaii. I was given a time slot in the evenings with a deejay named Dave Lancaster.

We worked together twice a week from 7:30 to 9 p.m. We named the show **"ESP & You"** and opened with the song **"EYE IN THE SKY"** by the "Alan Parson's Project." This song became my theme song. Dave and I were extremely popular as a radio team; we became the most-listened-to radio show on the island. His personality was magnetic. We would do some shtick and we were comical as well.

Changes were beginning to take place. I had so many clients who wanted to see me that I extended my stay in the Islands from two months to three. I became so busy I didn't know my own name. I phoned home periodically to speak to Bob. He was also busy; his slot machine business was really taking off. Bob had started with two machines and now had a total of 20 machines placed in local stores. I checked now and then about Gene; he was still with Betty Boops. I decided to stay in the Islands. I was happy there.

Then D-day hit! It was the high season for visitors in Honolulu. Our rent was going to be raised from $950 to $1400 per month. We received a notice from the landlord, the Association of Discovery Bay Apartments, to vacate the premises within 30 days. I was shocked. I didn't know what to do; I had clients booked all over the place and I was out of an apartment.

Barbara and I scanned the paper for rentals, but there wasn't one to be had in all of Waikiki. That day I lay in bed, defeated, not knowing what to do. I decided to take a walk by myself and think my situation through.

By chance I noticed a sign right across the street from Discovery Bay that said "Office for Rent." I inquired within. The rent was $200 a month, but there was a problem; this office had no solid walls, only partitions. Everyone would hear everyone else. However, I had little or no choice; I rented it.

Barbara and I decided to give the office a professional look by decorating it with potted tropical plants and beautiful Hawaiian pictures. We used masking tape on the backs of the pictures so they would stick to the walls.

My clientele was building up again. We had a line around the block in those days and I remember Barbara would wait outside and try out all her newest comedy routines on my waiting clients. That kept them amused until it was their time to see me. Those were the good old days.

One of the funniest incidents I recall was when a general in the military service came in for a reading. Not only could everyone in the office hear our conversation, but also as I was giving the general his reading a strange thing happened. All the pictures that I had so carefully taped to the wall came tumbling down. ALL of them, all at once. The general freaked out; he took this as an omen and promptly left. When Barbara learned what had happened, she laughed hysterically.

Barbara and I got lucky and found an apartment nearby at the Chateau Waikiki. The apartment was about 500 square feet; no room for Phil. Barbara and I had some order in our lives now and Phil decided to move in with a friend.

As we were preparing to move out of Discovery Bay, Barbara became angry at the apartment managers because they were throwing us out. She decided this would be a nice time to get even. Her method was quite unorthodox and ingenious.

I recall that moving day was a Saturday. When I awoke that morning, I saw Barbara in the living room crumbling soda crackers and sprinkling them all over the coffee table. "Barbara," I shouted, "what are you doing?"

"What does it look like I'm doing? I'm feeding the cockroaches." She laughed. "La cucaracha... la cucaracha... la cucaracha!"

She was having so much fun I decided to join in. We knew Hawaii has a major problem with cockroaches the size of steaks and any food left out would attract them by the swarms. The roaches were now dining on the 18th floor of the Discovery Bay apartments. We left the building, singing, "La cucaracha, la cucaracha!"

Barbara was not frightened by cockroaches, but I must admit there were times that I was. Not only do these critters manage to crawl underneath your door while you're sleeping, they also fly and attack you. One enormous roach, at least six inches long, came flying into our new apartment on the 20th floor of Chateau Waikiki. I began to scream while Barbara was on the phone.

"What's the matter?" she yelled.

I shrieked, "I'm being attacked by a 747 cockroach!"

Barbara sprang into action. "Do you have a gun? I'm gonna blow its head off!" She threw a book across the room at the 747. She missed, but the book landed on top of the roach. Barbara jumped on the book to finish off the critter. Do you know, that thing was still alive. We finally gave it a proper funeral; we threw it out of the apartment window and watched it sail twenty stories down.

Before long Barbara decided it was time for her to move back to L.A. We hugged each other and tearfully said our goodbyes. "Barbara, I'm really going to miss you."

Phil decided to help me out for a while till I could find someone to replace Barbara. He said, "Dayle, I have a great idea. Why don't you ask Diane if she'd like to fly out here for a while and help you out?"

That was a good idea. I was a little worried about Diane's multiple sclerosis, but I felt the best gift I could give her was to fly her to Hawaii. If by chance her condition should worsen, at least I would have given her something very special. It was my way of paying her back for all she had given me.

When Diane answered her phone, I said, "It's me. Get your butt on the next plane. I'm swamped and need your help. Barbara deserted me and Phil can't hold down the fort much longer."

Diane was on the next plane to Honolulu.

## WELCOME TO THE ISLANDS, DIANE

I couldn't believe she was here. Diane took Barbara's place, Phil could play golf once again, and I was happy. I decided to give Diane a percentage of my readings so she would have some pocket money. The only problem was that since Diane was on a percentage basis, she would book me solid all day long. One day I did over ten readings and was exhausted. Diane said, "Don't worry. It's good for you."

I introduced Diane to everyone at the radio station and she became my Mystery Lady on the air. We put out some wonderful shows. It was fun for Diane, as well as for me, and she was also becoming well-known. Diane stayed with me for well over a month. We brought a lot of happiness into people's lives and we met many local celebrities.

I was asked to shoot a pilot for one of the local television stations. After shooting the pilot, we were supposed to go out and round up sponsors. Diane and I had no idea how we were going to do this. The opportunity seemed to arise when a friend of ours lined up as possible sponsors the Bank of Hawaii. They were very interested in our TV show, but due to the political nature of a Psychic, they were unable to sponsor us.

Diane and I tried our best. It seemed all we did was work and work. Diane was happy; she was making money and, in her own way, she was helping many people. If for some reason I was unable to see someone, Diane would console them on the phone. We were the perfect team.

My dream about ever being together with Gene was beginning to fade, although we had many conversations on the phone. I was now spending too much time in Hawaii since this was my main source of income. I think the final realization came soon after Gene and I talked on the phone about his coming to the Islands. He wanted to get rid of Betty; he wanted to be with me. I had my reservations about that, but I waited for his arrival with anticipation. Diane really wasn't sure he was coming, and she didn't want to see me get hurt again.

The day finally came when Gene was supposed to be boarding his plane to Honolulu. My phone rang. It was Gene with the excuse he couldn't make it to the Islands because a storm had hit Lake Tahoe and all the roads were closed. I was devastated beyond belief. I knew right then and there that it was over between Gene and me. I no longer wanted to see him ever again, no matter what his excuse was. After that phone conversation, I couldn't help anyone the rest of the day.

It took me many months to recover from Gene, but I stayed in the Islands until I got over him. I went through tremendous pain. I guess I really loved the guy.

Just before Diane was to leave the Islands, I received a very strange call from a lady in panic. She had lost her diamond ring and was demanding to see me. Diane told her I was all booked up and she'd have to wait. The lady refused to wait; she demanded that I see her. She was out of control. I told Diane that it would be all right and I squeezed her in. Her name was Peggy.

## ENTER PEG WILSON

Peggy was a very special lady, so vivacious and full of life, with a personality beyond belief; a strikingly beautiful woman. When she came to me, she was in panic because she had lost her diamond ring. I remember the reading very well. I told her to go home, relax, and have a glass of wine; she would find her ring in the pocket of one of her jackets, and when she did, to let me know.

Meanwhile, Diane had to be heading back to the Mainland. I had tears in my eyes when I dropped her off at the airport. I knew at least she'd have a lifetime of memories. Phil became my assistant once again until I found someone new.

Within a few days Peggy Wilson called to thank me. She had found her diamond ring exactly where I said she would. My reaction to that was, "Damn, I'm good."

Peg explained she had never believed in Psychics before, and only her desperation to find her ring made her turn to one. She happened to hear my show on her car radio and she pulled off the road to take down my number. When I described exactly where she could find her ring, she was blown away. She was now a true believer.

Peg wanted another reading, this time regarding her family. I was more than happy to give her one. I really enjoyed Peg; she was just so full of life. I knew we would be friends.

This time the reading was of a more serious nature. Peg handed me a picture of her husband and wanted to know if they would stay married. I looked long and hard at the picture, paused, and said, "Peg, I'm sorry. He's seeing someone else. I don't feel you have a chance to get him back. However, you must accept this and go on with your life."

Peg was shocked. "Are you sure?"

"I'm very sure," I said. I told Peg she would be moving from her apartment and she'd have to find a new job.

I did have some good news for her. I saw her dating at least twelve men before she'd find the right one, and the man she'd be marrying was connected with a gentleman named Danny. Peg knew of no such person at that time. I told her a friend would introduce her to this man, that he was very nice and wealthy, and she would travel the world with him.

Peg left my place feeling down and disappointed. Within a few weeks she was out of work and her husband left her for another woman. Peg was lost.

When she called me for another reading, I asked her if she'd like to work for me part-time. She accepted. Phil was free at last to play golf once again. I spent almost three months on the island with Peg at my side. We were busy every single day. Whenever we had the chance, we'd lie on the beach or go shopping together. The funny thing was that whenever we went anywhere together, we somehow always lost each other; but I could always find her since she was tall and blond.

Peg was always bringing in new business for me. I remember some of the strange people we attracted. Once she walked into the room where I was preparing for my reading and said in a shocked voice, "Dayle, there's a priest out there." He wanted to confess to me about an evangelist he was seeing. On another occasion Peg introduced me to a rabbi who was getting a divorce. I just couldn't believe it.

One day I was bogged down with readings and had stepped out for a while to clear my head. When I returned, Peg said I had a message from an old schoolmate of mine. I really didn't want to talk to any old schoolmates, but Peg insisted this call was important.

"Well, who is it?" I asked.

Peg said, "Toni Gold." I laid my head on the kitchen table. Seeing my reaction, Peg asked anxiously, "What's wrong? Who's this Toni Gold?"

I told her about how Toni had enticed Bob into her bedroom and ruined my marriage. "I don't understand why she wants to talk to me," I said. Peg just stared at me. I sat on the beach that day, contemplating whether I should call Toni or not and why this was happening to me. I never called her.

Peg became my full-time secretary, private confidante and assistant for many years to come. We were the best of friends; we did everything together. She told me her life story and I told her mine. We were there for each other. I must admit, we were a crazy team.

**It was time for me to be heading back to the Mainland. I had finally caught up with my readings and now I had to straighten out matters at home. I also had to fly to L.A. to continue my training with Peter Hurkos. This would be a short trip, for I had promised the radio station I would return in a few weeks. Peg would hold down the fort for me in Hawaii until I returned. We would stay in contact.**

# THE PAIN OF SAYING GOODBYE
## CHAPTER 23

When I arrived home in Lake Tahoe, my work was cut out for me. I was no longer working for KOWL Radio, since the station was owned by John Parker. I switched to KTHO Radio in Lake Tahoe, which was willing to let me go back and forth to the Islands.

Bob didn't mind my working in Hawaii; he figured when he wasn't busy he would hop a plane and visit me in the Islands. The slot machine business was flourishing and he was begining to prosper; we had more money now than ever before. Our marriage was ironing itself out; yet, in my heart I knew it would only be a matter of time before we would part.

It had been a long time since Gene Ashley and I had spoken. I knew our relationship was over. As I was going through my messages, I noticed that Gene's son Billy was trying to reach me. I dialed the number, expecting Billy to answer; but much to my surprise Gene answered the phone. I hadn't expected this; I was lost for words.

I finally said, "Gene, is that you?"

He recognized my voice immediately. "Dayle! Oh, my god, I haven't heard from you in such a long time. How are you?"

The words caught in my throat and I gasped as I said, "I'm fine, Gene. I'm so sorry for bothering you. I was just returning your son's call and you answered the phone."

"You didn't bother me," he said. "I was just getting ready to move out of my apartment. Betty and I are going to live together."

I paused to gather my thoughts. Gene continued the conversation.

"I can't imagine why my son called you," he said.

"That's okay, Gene, I'm sorry to have bothered you!" I exclaimed.

"Wait!" he shouted. "Don't hang up! Why don't you come down here for an hour or so? There are a few things I'd like to straighten out with you, anyway."

I decided to give the situation with Gene one last try and went to his apartment.

Gene was extremely happy to see me. He pulled out some clippings about my career that he had been saving; he looked at me with pride in my accomplishments. He was very proud that I appeared at Harrah's in Lake Tahoe. When he asked me what I was going to do with the rest of my life, I politely told him I didn't know. I mentioned that my market was building in the Islands of Hawaii and that I was spending more and more time over there.

I asked him, in turn, if he were going to get a divorce and marry Betty. He said, "No!"

I was sitting comfortably on the couch in his living room; Gene walked over and sat down beside me. He put his arms around me and held me ever so tenderly.

"Dayle, I want you to understand something. What I have with Betty is so different than what we had. There are no words to describe the relationship you and I had. You see, there are times in our life when we love someone such as I loved you. In those times you have to decide what is best for the person you love."

Gene looked straight at me and drew out his words carefully and deliberately, as if he'd rehearsed them over and over in his mind.

"I knew I couldn't keep you. I knew I had to set you free. I wanted you to fly; I wanted you to grow; I wanted you to be all that you could be. I knew that as long as you depended on me, I'd be the one to stop you. So I tried to stop myself from loving you.

"When I met Betty, our relationship was comfortable; I was at ease with her. I knew Betty would always be there for me. But I also knew I'd never forget you.

"I knew your destiny was to help hundreds of other people. That was your calling. I guess what I'm trying to tell you is that I never stopped loving you and I never will." As he spoke, his voice began to break.

"I loved you enough to let you go. It took me a long time to come to a decision like this. It ripped me apart inside." He seemed unsure of himself. "I knew I'd always love you. The three years we spent together were the happiest years of my life. It was as if we had spent a lifetime together. I hope someday you can forgive me. I hope you'll understand that sometimes in life when you truly are in love with someone, it's okay to give them up. It may hurt like hell, but I would've done a greater injustice to you if I would have stayed with you."

Gene bent his head down, waiting for me to respond.

I had listened in silence to his long speech, and now it was my turn to speak out.

"Gene, I understand your point of view and I respect that. I know you have stopped drinking, and I'm very proud of you for that. I wish you well with Betty and I hope it works out for you.

"But what I don't understand is I thought that when you love someone you go after them and never let them go, because you just might miss the greatest opportunity of a lifetime. Love doesn't come along that often in one's life. Some people never find it. But you and I had something so special it would take a lifetime for you or me to ever find it again with someone else. Why would you let me go for the sake of becoming the martyr? And, besides, from what I understand, if we don't work this out in this lifetime, we'll have to do it over again in our next lifetime."

Gene smiled and said, "Someday, My Love, you'll understand that I never stopped loving you." He whispered, "Please, Babe, find it in your heart to forgive me."

He inched his way closer to me. He began to unbutton my blouse slowly; he kissed my lips so tenderly and caressed my breasts. As he kissed me, he started to undress himself. I abruptly pulled away from him and began to button up my blouse. He sat on the couch, stripped down to his pants, belt unbuckled, zipper open, and stared at me. "What's wrong, Babe?

"Gene, I'm sorry," I said. I felt nothing. I couldn't respond to him any longer.

"Please, Babe, make love to me just one more time for old times sake," he pleaded.

I was hurting inside. I still loved him, but I couldn't bring myself to make love to him. I finished dressing and reached for my car keys. I glanced at him for a moment, knowing this would be the last time. I stood up and said, "I'm sorry, Gene, but I love you too much to make love to you."

I turned and headed for the door, car keys in hand. I remember leaving him on the couch in a very precarious position. I walked out the door and never looked back. I walked faster and faster till I reached my car. I started the engine, turned on the cassette player, and listened to "Lady" by Kenny Rodgers. That song had so much meaning for me at one time; it was Gene's favorite song to me.

I clutched the steering wheel tightly and sobbed till there was not a tear left. As I drove away slowly, I heard the words to the song in the distance: "Lady, you're my lady; you're the love of my life and I never will let you go, for you're my lady."

I knew it was finally over. I would never see Gene again!

I finally regained my composure. I suddenly felt relieved, knowing that it was over, that I could live my life again

I headed up the hill toward my husband Bob. Now that Gene was out of my life, I was determined to be a good wife to Bob. There was nothing in the way now. Bob was waiting for me at our house. For several weeks I became the perfect wife to him

Everything was going well. The only problems we were having were Bob's slot machines. Every time there was a payoff, we were awakened in the middle of the night and Bob had to run down to make the payoff. It was beginning to get annoying. We didn't have a life of our own; we virtually couldn't go anywhere or do anything together.

The time was growing near for me to return to the Islands. It was time to fulfill the promise I had made to KKUA Radio in Honolulu. Peg, my secretary, was already taking bookings for my arrival in the Islands. She couldn't wait to see me.

**The only hurt and pain I felt was in leaving my dogs behind. I missed them so very much. As for Gene, I would try to strike him from my memory with the help of some of my friends.**

# THE ENTERTAINMENT WORLD; MEETING BLYTHE
## CHAPTER 24

Peg met me at the Honolulu International Airport. She had an infectious laugh every time she was about to greet me. As we hugged each other, she rattled on: "Dayle, everything you told me is beginning to come true. I just can't believe it. You're not going to believe this; I met this young stud by the name of Mike. Oh, my god, I can't wait for you to meet him. He's a surfer, and I met him at the beach. In the last few weeks I don't think we made it out of bed." She sighed.

I finally managed to get a word in edgewise. "Now, remember to take a breath, Peg," I said. "How old is this stud, anyway?"

She replied, "Never mind, Dear. I'm entitled to my fun also."

I smiled. "So what else is new?"

"Well, you have a full schedule. I've booked you solid for at least four weeks. And there are several entertainers on the island that are dying to meet you."

"You don't say," I remarked.

I was suddenly aware of a song playing on the car radio. "Hey, Peg, turn the radio up. Listen to that song; it's unbelievable." As we listened, I became more and more excited.

"Who's that artist, anyway? I've got to meet him. Pull the car over. I'm going to call the radio station and find out who it is."

Peg pulled her car over to the curb near a public phone booth. I actually ran to the phone; I couldn't wait to put my quarter in and call Dave Lancaster at KKUA.

Dave greeted me cheerfully. "Hey, how goes it, Miss Psychic. When did you get in?"

"I just arrived," I said. "Peg picked me up at the airport when I heard that fantastic song on the radio."

"What was it?" he asked.

"I'm not sure. 'Lovers...Friends...' Anyway, that's what I called for. What's the name of the song?" I wanted to know urgently.

"Do you like it, Dayle?"

"I love it."

Dave said, "The song is called 'Lovers and Friends.' It was written by a good friend of mine, Audy Kimura."

"I have to meet this guy," I said. "That song is going to be megafamous."

Dave was willing to make a deal with me. "I'll be glad to introduce you to Audy, provided you don't tell the boss that I played that record on air. I did it from the bottom of my heart. You see, it wasn't written on the record log. I liked it so much, I had to play it. I hope I don't get fired!"

"Don't worry, Dave, you won't get fired," I said. "By the way, 'Lovers and Friends' will be number one on the charts in just a few months and you'll be a hero."

"See you tomorrow, Dayle. It's great to have you back. I think the island people have missed you," he said.

When I got back to the car, Peg asked, "What took you so long?"

We drove to my new apartment in Waikiki. I was becoming a

regular at renting apartments in that area. Peg was eager to go home to her own apartment; she had a hot date with Surfer Mike. Before she left, I filled her in on what had happened with Gene on the Mainland and told her it would take time for me to get over this situation. I also said that Bob would be coming in for a week or so around Valentine's Day.

Bright and early the next morning I awoke extremely refreshed. I would be working the day shift at the station right alongside Dave Lancaster, who was covering for a sick deejay. Peg arrived at my apartment, ready to man the phone lines. She was an extremely efficient assistant; she tended to all my needs and everything she did was well thought out.

When I arrived at the radio station, Dave had a surprise for me. Audy Kimura the singer was waiting there with a friend. I was ecstatic to meet Audy. I kept raving about his new song, "Lovers and Friends."

I gave Audy a reading over the air: **"Audy, you have a very bright future. Your record, 'Lovers And Friends' will hit the top of the charts and so will you. Don't forget to order more albums or you just might run out. My friend, your career has just begun. Don't unpack your bags. You have one of the brightest futures I've ever seen. You'll win many awards and your name will be known to all of Hawaii."** Audy was honored and couldn't thank me enough.

As Audy was leaving, I asked Dave, "Who's that guy with him?"

Dave replied, "That's Blythe Arakawa, Audy's record producer and manager. He's the brains behind Audy's album. From what I gathered, Blythe encouraged Audy to cut the album and Blythe promoted and sponsored him. He really believes in Audy."

**SIX MONTHS LATER, "LOVERS AND FRIENDS" HIT NUMBER ONE ON THE CHARTS IN HAWAII.**

Audy Kimura became a household name and his albums were selling like hot cakes. My prediction had come true. Audy kept running out of albums. It was incredible.

In February I received the invitation while doing my radio show with Dave. It read: **"Dayle Schear, you are hereby requested to attend the 1984 Hoku Awards. Lovers And Friends has been nominated in eight different categories. Please reply."**

I was pleased but stunned; I just couldn't believe this was happening to me. The Hoku Awards was a gala event honoring the best in the recording industry in the Islands. I was positive that Audy would win several awards. I replied I would be happy to attend.

On the night of the awards a limousine pulled up to my apartment building and the chauffeur stepped out to open a door for me. Inside sat Audy and his friends. I noticed Blythe Arakawa in particular, dressed in a tuxedo. I kept staring at him and wondering how this young man could make Audy so famous. Was he a genius or what?

On our way to the Hilton Hotel where the gala event was to take place, Audy commented that, although he was nominated for eight awards, he expected to win only one or two. I said there would be many; not to worry.

I held my breath in anticipation that evening. The competition was stiff. The winners in each category were being announced. Best Song of the Year: "LOVERS AND FRIENDS. "Best New Artist: AUDY KIMURA. Best Album: "AUDY LOOKING FOR THE

GOOD LIFE," BY AUDY KIMURA. And it went on and on. It was the most exhilarating moment in my life to be able to watch a prediction come to life from beginning to end.

A Psychic rarely experiences this. I was able to see the future and, at the same time, participate right along with it. It was a proud moment in my life, to say the least.

The chain of events that led up to the prediction falls along Carl G. Jung's philosophy of synchronicity, the simultaneous occurrence of events that seem to be linked in a significant way: **Dave Lancaster played"Lovers And Friends" without authorization; I happened to hear the record being played and at that exact moment in time called the radio station to find out who the recording artist was; Audy had been waiting to meet me all along; I met Audy Kimura and foretold his great success and many awards to come.**

The odds on this one event happening in time are beyond chance and coincidence.

Audy is an outstanding performer and always will be. He is now recording in Japan and gaining great prominence.

For at least two years after first meeting Audy, I ran into him and his manager Blythe at every function on the island. Blythe and I became very good friends. We often stayed up to the wee hours of the morning talking for hours on end. I realized he was quite talented in helping other people achieve fame.

We began a wonderful friendship. I needed a manager to guide my life. Peg and I were single-handedly working on my career and my popularity was getting out of control. We put in eighteen hours a day; from sunup to sundown Peg and I were on the phone trying to help people. We were exhausted every day.

Long after Peg went home I'd phone Blythe and we'd talk for hours. I told him everything about Gene and Bob. He was very sympathetic. Blythe began to open up to me. He told me how he believed in Audy and his music, that he felt Audy needed a push in the right direction. He sponsored Audy's first album; he gathered friends and family together to invest in the album, and he made it a success.

Blythe's dedication toward Audy and the album left him no room in his life for a woman at this time. He had a girlfriend named Michelle, but he was young and not ready to settle down. He really cared for her, but she wanted more, the more he could not give her. Michelle would follow him everywhere; at times he didn't know how to get rid of her. The album came first to Blythe; he had to see it through, no matter what the price.

I briefly touched upon the possibility of his managing me as well, but it was out of the question; he needed to finish his quest. I understood and didn't press him any further.

Blythe was the most spiritual individual I ever met. He cared more for other people's feelings than he did for his own. My nickname for him was **"YODA."** He was a cute little thing. He was very athletic at one time and coached wrestling. He was also a real estate broker.

Blythe would work three jobs to see that Audy became famous. Never in my life did I ever have anyone like that supporting my work. I was quite envious. I wondered what it felt like to have someone by your side who believed in you, someone who would take the burden off your back.

He was unique, different from anyone I had ever met, and highly intelligent. Blythe carried a lot of the Aloha Spirit around with him. He always saw the beauty in everything. There was a timelessness about him when he spoke. Soon he would become my teacher and my best friend.

In the short time I spent with Blythe, my whole life began to change. My diet changed. The way I looked at people changed. My whole attitude about life was changing. Every day that I spent with him was a new spiritual adventure. He made me more aware of myself. He made me understand the meaning of life and its simplicity.

Blythe believed strongly in ESP and the driving force behind it. His philosophy was one of truth and knowledge. What he taught and what I learned wasn't in any book. I knew I had found my spiritual teacher, one I would follow for many lifetimes to come.

He explained to me that what I was going through with Gene had to be; it was necessary for my growth. Without Gene, I would never have experienced the pain and suffering which made me search within myself for answers. Without Gene, I would have looked for the answers within everyone else. Blythe taught me that the answers were inside of me all along, and that answers were being given to me on all the trips I had taken to the Islands.

He wanted to teach me to live life to the fullest and never to worry about money. He would always say, "If you do what you love, the money will come." This was so opposite of Bob's thinking.

I always felt I was such a lucky person to know him. We spent hours and weeks together as friends. Whenever I was troubled or found myself thinking of Gene, Blythe would always snap me out of my depression and make me smile.

Blythe gave me something no one ever had; he gave me back my life. I was beginning to understand more about my life; I was taking giant steps forward now. I was hungry for knowledge. I began reading every metaphysical book I could get my hands on. I was learning, learning, and contemplating life. There never seemed to be enough hours in the day. All I wanted to do was read. I wanted to understand why this was happening to me. Was there a greater power out there? There had to be more. I wanted to know everything.

What I didn't understand, Blythe would always manage to explain. I spent well over two months on the island, trying to find myself. I was determined not to leave until I found the answers.

My days were full with helping people, lecturing, reading, and spending time with Blythe or Peg. I was beginning to change my way of thinking. I was becoming more in tune with the island people. I realized they were so fragile, they needed my help and guidance.

There is much to be said about the great Aloha Spirit. The people of the Islands are different from any other culture. They are a very giving people. Their land had been taken from them and they have been stripped of all dignity; yet, they reach out from their hearts and give until there is nothing left.

I always wondered why. Blythe explained that the Islands are made up of so many different cultures which learned to live together in peace: Hawaiian, Samoan, Japanese, Chinese, Portugese, Filipino, and so on. Everyone struggles to live there, so they all band together to help one another. I found there were many who had very little to eat, yet they shared with their neighbors.

I realized that the main difference between the Mainland culture and the Hawaiian culture is that a great percentage of Mainlanders always want to know what's in it for them first before giving. In contrast, the Islanders give from their hearts. This, my friends, is the Aloha Spirit, when you give from your heart and not expect anything in return.

We could all take a lesson from the "locals" of Hawaii. Their lives are simple; their wants so small; their needs seldom matter, for they think of others. This was beginning to rub off on me. I wasn't so sure that I ever wanted to leave the Islands.

**There was so much to think about now. Life was changing. I needed to go back to the Mainland for just a few weeks. I had just about made up my mind that maybe it would be better if I moved here and put my dogs in quarantine. There was nothing left for me now on the Mainland. I had to think.**

**Thanks to Blythe, I was just beginning to find myself.**

# CHANGES
# SOMEHOW FRIGHTEN ME
## CHAPTER 25

I was home once again. Bob began to notice that there was something different about me now. This was my cue to talk to him about our life together.

"Bob, there's something I have to say to you. Let's sit for a moment," I said.

"I know I've hurt you in more ways than one. Although you've hurt me just as badly, I don't want to hurt you anymore. I'm sorry about Gene and all the trouble and pain I caused you and his wife Annie. It was a great learning experience for me. No matter what I did to you, you've always been there for me. I respect that, but the truth of the matter is we're just not meant to be.

"It's time I began to stand on my own two feet. It's time for you to go on with your life and meet someone else, to fall in love again and find some happiness. While I was in Hawaii I thought about how poorly I've handled my life. I feel I really messed up everything. I guess if I were to live my life over again, I would change many things. But it's too late now for you and me. I can't go on like this much longer. I want someone who believes in my work; I want someone who's supportive when I'm out there helping people."

I searched Bob's face for some reaction to what I was saying, but there was none.

I continued. "I know you built up your business for both of us. You've always wanted to be a success. But money became your god.

There was never enough money in the world for you to make you happy. I realize you were once poor, but so was I. Money isn't important to me and never has been. I never wanted much: just a home, the love of my animals, food on the table.

"It's time to take a good look at ourselves and realize just what we've done. We let the strangers in. We let the strangers of the world destroy our marriage. You and I were both at fault. There's no turning back; once Humpty Dumpty falls, we can't put him back together again.

"If we stay in this marriage we'll never trust each other. We'll go on and on till we destroy everything good that might be left. I'm sorry. And I'm even more sorry that we've grown apart. I'll always love you and will have fond memories of you. What I'm trying to say is I still love you, but I'm not in love with you anymore."

Bob made no attempt to interrupt me. He simply sat and stared at me with a blank look on his face. He seemed to be in shock.

I told him he could keep the house and everything we had built up for twenty years. "I came into this marriage with nothing and I'm willing to go out with nothing," I said. "However, I'd appreciate a little money for a down payment on a condo in Hawaii so I can live my life in peace. And I won't bother you anymore.

"I feel I have a lot of bad Karma that I've put out in this world. And I've made a decision that it's time I give back some good Karma to the people. I know it's hard for you to understand, Bob, but until I erase all the decay that I've put out in this world, I won't be worth a damn."

Bob finally reacted. "But I still love you. I want us to stay married. We can start over," he said. "Why don't we just go to counseling?" It was as if he hadn't heard a word I said.

I shook my head. "Bob, we don't see things the same way. You resent my career and my helping people. You want me to stay home and be a housewife. I'm not the same little girl you were married to before. I've grown. I can't go backward; I have to go forward."

Bob pleaded, "Please don't leave me. I never left you."

I felt sorry for him. He always wanted me to feel sorry for him. That was how he manipulated me.

Bob tried to convince me that I was making a rash decision. "Please don't get a divorce; let's just be separated for a while. If you want to go back to the Islands, you can. But give me a chance to try to win you back.

I had tears in my eyes. I didn't want to leave my dogs, but I also knew Bob would take good care of them until I decided what I wanted to do with my life.

Within thirty days Bob put our house in Lake Tahoe up for sale. He also gave me the down payment for a condo in Hawaii; he was sure that he and I eventually could live peacefully in the condo forever. I never took another dime from him, even after his slot machine business made him a millionaire within three years.

Everything was changing around me rapidly. KKUA Radio phoned from Honolulu to inform me they were changing their format to all sports, so my position as a Psychic was being eliminated. What timing! I was unemployed.

The news made Bob somewhat happy. However, I didn't let this minor setback bother me. I had made my decision. Come hell or high water, even if poverty should strike, nothing was going to stop me now.

I placed a call to Blythe in Hawaii and explained my situation to him. He said, "Don't worry. I'll try to get you an appearance on the Perry and Price show in Honolulu. Just give me a week or so; I'll get you back to work one way or another."

He added, "By the way, I have to go to Alaska to sell a house for my real estate office." In between helping Audy, Blythe had to earn a living in real estate. He had a sudden thought: "Why don't you stay in Lake Tahoe for a while. Let me see if I can kill two birds with one stone. Send me a marketing package. I know I can get you radio there, anyway."

The possibility of working in Alaska excited me. "Alaska! I've always wanted to go to Alaska. This is wonderful news! I can't wait. I'll send everything out right away. Thanks, Blythe."

Bob had overheard my end of the conversation and he was curious. "What's this about you going to Alaska? Did I hear right?"

"Yes, you did," I replied cheerfully. "Blythe is going to try to get me a job in Alaska."

"Why Alaska?"

"Why not?" I replied.

I waited two weeks for Blythe to call. He wasn't having much luck marketing me in Alaska, but he kept telling me not to give up hope.

I called Peter in L.A. and expressed my concern about the situation to him. Peter told me Blythe would have a tough time without me being there. I should take a plane and go to Alaska. He said I would get a job and make lots of money.

I called Blythe and told him what Peter had said. Blythe didn't hesitate for one moment. "Catch the next plane. I'll pick you up at the airport."

Before I left I consulted with another Psychic. You remember Lauralie. She was the Psychic who told me with amazing accuracy that Gene was seeing someone else. "Don't worry," she said. "Go to Alaska. All will work out." She cautioned me, however, to be aware of a major car accident. She didn't see me hurt, though she saw me spinning out on black ice. I decided I wasn't going to drive; that should ward off any accident.

By the way, every Psychic needs a Psychic.

By now Bob and I had decided that we were separated and each was free to date. But he was still insistent and obsessive about winning me back.

With $1000 in hand, off I went to Alaska. I decided I would come home when the money ran out, but I believed that Blythe would land me a job before then.

## ALASKA OR BUST!

I gazed out the window as the Alaskan Airlines jet touched down on the runway in Anchorage. There was a caribou on the edge of the runway, awaiting my arrival. I was overwhelmed by the beauty of the rugged mountains and towering forests. Alaska was everything I imagined it to be. I could hardly contain my excitement as Blythe greeted me in the terminal.

"I can't believe I'm in Alaska," I said. "It's so beautiful here. It reminds me of Lake Tahoe in the seventies."

Blythe smiled. "You haven't seen anything yet."

We drove to the house that Blythe was selling, in an elite section of Anchorage. It was beautiful, but there wasn't a stick of furniture in it. I asked, "Blythe, why are you living like this?"

He explained, "This house is just temporary, Dayle, until I sell it. All we need are two beds and we can improvise the rest." Oh, well, I had traveled so much I could get used to anything.

I asked him if he had any luck getting me a radio show.

"No, but I'm not giving up," he said. "We've run into a slight problem." Blythe explained that everyone in Alaska was currently focused on the Iditarod, the state's famous dog-sledding race. "I was told that after it's all over I shouldn't have any problem getting you booked on radio. We just have to wait it out for a while."

Two weeks passed. Blythe sold the house and it was now in escrow. I was down to my last $100 with no radio job in sight. Then I received a telephone call from a lady who introduced herself as Mary from **KIMO** Television.

Mary had a local show called **"Good Morning Alaska"** and wanted to interview me. She knew I was a Psychic. I knew I had to give her a reading right then so she would know that I was on the level. Mary was amazed.

"I have fifteen minutes available on Monday," she said. "Would you like to stop by so I can interview you on TV? Maybe you can answer a few questions from our phone lines."

"I'd be delighted," I said. As I hung up the phone, I screamed with excitement. "Blythe, that was **KIMO-TV**. They want to interview me on Monday."

He was pleased but not surprised. "I was hoping they'd call. I stopped in there a few days ago and gave them your marketing package."

I could hardly contain myself. I had never done a television show before. "But, Blythe, I need more than fifteen minutes to prove myself. Oh, well, I'll concentrate. Maybe someone will cancel."

When Monday finally arrived, I was well prepared for my interview. I knew I had to be as accurate as possible to make a hit with the Alaskan audience. At the television station, the producer informed me that someone had canceled and asked if I would mind giving a thirty-minute interview. I smiled as I looked at Blythe knowingly.

I remember being a bit nervous as the interview began. Then a calm came over me. The phones began to light up with incoming calls and I answered question after question. My thirty minutes turned into an hour. This was my first appearance on television and I was on a high.

After the show the whole TV station was buzzing. I was swamped by the staff of KIMO in the lobby. The phones were ringing off their hooks; pandemonium had set in. **Duane Triplett**, general manager of KIMO-TV, approached me and said, "So you're the one who's upset my whole television station. Who are you and where did you come from? Why don't you follow me upstairs. I think I want to talk to you." Blythe and I followed.

We had a long conversation with Duane, who couldn't figure out what I was doing in Alaska. He was more than amazed at the tremendous response I received. He asked me if I would be willing to do a one-hour special for KIMO television in the next few weeks. He wanted to go live. He would set up everything.

I responded, "Sounds great. Let's do it."

As we left the studio, Blythe and I couldn't believe this was happening. We raced home to pick up our messages; there were too many to handle. I was booking people right and left. Whoa, what a rush!

When we finally managed to settle down, I realized we had no furniture. How was I going to do my readings?

"Don't worry," Blythe said. We decided to arrange the house so it would be comfortable for my clients. It took a lot of creative thinking since this $200,000 house was bare to the walls. We pulled a mattress from the bedroom to the fireplace in the family room. Blythe built a table from some cardboard boxes and covered it with a tablecloth. We decorated the house with candles and flowers; it looked like a metaphysical haven.

We were now ready. As my clients entered the house, we led

them through bare rooms to the family room. Everyone sat on the floor next to the fireplace. My clients must have thought I was an eccentric Psychic.

All went well and I was finally earning some money. Before long I became involved in my first unsolved murder case. In April of 1985, a mother whose son had been missing for quite a while came to me, wanting to know what happened. I researched the case diligently and gave my findings to the woman, Barbara Reynolds. I knew her son Paul was dead; I knew she'd find his body in nine months. I was positive the body was in the vicinity of her own backyard. I also knew foul play was involved.

The Paul V. Reynolds case was solved nine months later, in exactly the way I stated it would be.

## LETTER FROM BARBARA REYNOLDS

On Sunday, March 31, 1985 we discovered that our twenty two year old son was missing from our home. We notified our local state police and spent three weeks making inquiries and investigating on our own. On April 20, 1985, I was fortunate enough to contact Psychic Dayle Schear.

Using a picture of my son and a few of his personal items (billfold, truck keys) Dayle told us the following:

**He was no longer alive**
**His body would be found within 9 months very close**
**to home**
**Near water and a little wooden bridge**
**He would be found by a hiker**
**Dayle specified a road by name with emphasis on**
**small airplanes, drainage and junked cars**
**She repeatedly told us to look in our own**
**backyard vicinity**

In the middle of the ninth month of searching, the body was discovered one half mile from our house, a few paces from a drainage ditch with a small foot bridge. He was found by a man walking his dog. The road running by the location of the body is the unpaved seection of the road she named and there are at least three junked cars in the immediate area. A small airfield is located less than one mile away from the same area.

Barbara L. Reynolds
January 8, 1986

The time that Blythe and I spent in Alaska was wonderful. On our days off we took long rides into the country and explored the glaciers. We were becoming more than friends; we were falling in love.

It seems so funny that two people who were running away from past relationships with other people were now running smack into each other. This was the furthest thought from our minds.We had so much in common. We didn't want to leave each other's side. Blythe felt he couldn't do much more for Audy, who was well on his way to becoming a major success. I now became his greatest challenge.

We finally put on our special for KIMO-TV and the show was a wonderful success. I found television to be a unique experience. My TV appearances seemed to burst open the Psychic field in Alaska. I found out that there was a huge underground network of people who were devoting their lives to metaphysics. Before too long we were meeting underground with doctors who were heavily involved with ESP.

Blythe and I spent at least three months in Alaska and met so many wonderful people. We felt very much at home. Away from Michelle and Bob, we found peace and serenity in Alaska.

We explored Alaska whenever we could; there was so much to see. One beautiful spring day we decided to go to the country and rent a hot air balloon. Blythe rented a Dodge Charger for our outing. As we drove through the countryside, the car hit a patch of ice and skidded out of control. We were sliding on black ice, headed into oncoming traffic in the opposite lane. Terrified, I covered my eyes with my hands. I heard the crash and the car shuddered to a halt. I opened my eyes and turned toward Blythe. The door on his side of the car was gone. A truck had managed to avoid a collision with us by swerving away, but the load of snowmobiles the truck was hauling hit the left side of our car and wiped us out.

Blythe put his hand to his leg, then to his head. I could see blood gushing onto the floorboard. I was frightened for him. The people in the truck that hit us took us immediately to a nearby hospital. I checked myself over; there wasn't even a scratch on me. Blythe had to have a few stitches in his left knee. Other than that, he was in top-notch shape. The car, however, was totaled.

I flashed on Lauralie once again. I remembered that she had warned me in Lake Tahoe about the accident. I had tried to prevent it by not driving, but it didn't matter. The accident still occurred. Unbelievable!

We were at least 70 miles away from Anchorage without a car and with no way home. We ended up paying $80 for cabfare home. What a trip! That evening we celebrated our being alive by going out to dinner and a show. The next day we returned the keys to the car rental agency. They were in shock. Fortunately, we had full coverage on our rental car; there is something to be said about insurance. The agency politely gave us a new car.

Well, Blythe had sold his house, I was becoming well-known in Alaska, and the clock on the wall was ticking away. All in all, it turned out to be a very lucrative trip. We had opened up a new market in Alaska and I would return there on many other occasions.

Blythe had to head back to Honolulu. I promised him I'd join him in a week or so. Leaving Alaska was very difficult for both of us; we had fallen in love.

When I reluctantly returned to Lake Tahoe, I found it more difficult than ever before to cope with my marriage and Bob. Blythe and I were in love. I began to pack my bags for Hawaii. I explained to Bob that I was going to buy a condo in the Islands; I was tired of renting. He was all for it. He was dating other women and didn't seem to mind my leaving for the Islands once again. He said he might join me in a few weeks.

I tried to convince Bob that our marriage was over. I wanted him to go on with his life without me. But the more I mentioned this, the more he pursued me. I knew I would soon be heading for a divorce.

I called Blythe and asked him to look around for a condo in the Waikiki area. He said he had his eye on something very special.

**I couldn't wait to get back to the Islands. I really missed him.**

# TELEVISION FAME AT LAST!
## CHAPTER 26

Blythe had wonderful news for me when I returned to the Islands. He had scheduled an appearance for me on THE PERRY AND PRICE RADIO SHOW. Perry and Price are the number one radio team in the state of Hawaii. Blythe was so excited. He felt this show could make me famous in the Islands.

And that wasn't all . He had also found me an apartment in the Waikiki area that was for sale at a very reasonable price. What a welcome home to the Islands! When I saw the apartment, I fell in love with it; it was just what I wanted. It was fully furnished and only $89,000. The owner was willing to hold the paper on a five-year note and I could move in right away. I bought it.

It's funny how life sometimes works. One small change in our lives can turn into a lifetime of bright new changes.

I began moving into my new apartment. I phoned Peg, my dear friend and assistant, to find out what she was doing. She came running over with all kinds of decorating ideas for the apartment, which she loved. We spent hours catching up on each other's life. I filled her in on all my exciting experiences in Alaska.

Peg asked, "What are you going to do for a car?"

"I guess it's time I buy one," I replied.

Later that day I bought a brand new car, a Honda Prelude, as I recall. I picked up Peg at her apartment and we went for a drive around the island. We had a ball.

Peg loved the car. She asked, "How much are the payments for this baby?"

I said, "About $289 per month."

"What!" She threw a fit. "Dayle, you're out of work! Why are you buying this car?"

Peg was right. I could have my car sent from the Mainland, and I really didn't need the pressure of making the payments. Why was I buying this car? "Peg, it's too late. I already bought the car. What should I do?"

"I don't know. Maybe you can sleep on it and come up with a solution."

I slept on it. At around 6:30 a.m., I called Peg. "I'm sorry I woke you, but I just couldn't sleep. We have to return this car."

That woke Peg up. "What? How are you going to do that?"

"I have an idea," I said. "Peg, we'll go down to the car dealership in a few hours and I want you to pretend you're my mother. This has to be convincing, you understand."

"I'm listening!" She was fully awake now.

"We're going to tell the car dealership that when my husband found out I bought this car without his permission, he went CRAZY!" So Peg and I went to the dealership and laid the story on them. After much wailing and many tears on our part, the dealership took back the car and tore up my contract.

We drove home in silence in Peg's car. I finally said, "I can't believe they took back a whole car. I've heard of department stores taking back items, but I've never heard of a car dealership taking a car back."

Peg and I looked at each other and smiled. "This is one for the books," she said.

I then took her advice and called Bob to ship my car to the Islands for me.

Peg and I were crazy together. Her sex life was getting HOT! It was everything that I had predicted for her, and more. When Peg entered my life, she was a torn and broken-hearted woman. She had been married for thirty wonderful years and fell to pieces when her husband left her for another woman. I tried to make her understand that she was a wonderful person and these things sometimes happen. I reassured her about her future.

No sooner had two months passed than Peg met the man of her dreams. Recently divorced himself, Moe was introduced to her at a party by a fellow named Danny. Moe was quite the man. He lived in New York and traveled the world. He and Peg started dating and began a whirlwind romance. Whenever Moe was in Hawaii, he wined and dined her.

Peg's only problem was trying to give up all her other lovers. She had been hit hard by the mid-life crisis and she wasn't ready to settle down yet. But Moe was slowly winning her heart. Peg traveled all over the Far East with Moe. She was beginning to fall deeper and deeper in love with this wonderful "Teddy Bear."

As for Blythe and me, we were growing closer and closer. He was sweet and kind; he'd give the shirt off his back to anyone that he cared about. Blythe began to move several of his shirts into my apartment. I think we were living together. We had so many wonderful and romantic times together. He never ceased to surprise me with something special.

But I still had to contend with Bob. No matter how hard I tried I couldn't seem to convince him that I wasn't going back to him. Even though he had a steady girlfriend named Stephanie, he still wanted me back. He sometimes made my life miserable with his persistence. The time finally came for me to insist on a divorce. When Bob realized I definitely wasn't going back to him, he consented to an uncontested divorce. Our marriage was ultimately over.

Meanwhile, Blythe came home with the wonderful news that I was scheduled for the Perry and Price radio show in a week. I couldn't wait.

The show turned out magnificently. There were many local celebrities in the audience, and as a Psychic I was 100 percent accurate. After the radio show, new and wonderful things began to happen to me. Perry and Price asked me to become a regular guest on their show once a month. My bookings were increasing and I wasn't worried about earning a living anymore.

A gentleman who happened to be in the studio audience the day I was on the radio show approached me about appearing on a local television show. He was Randy Brandt, producer of "The Hawaiian Moving Company," an extremely popular and much acclaimed TV show hosted by Michael W. Perry, of Perry and Price. My segment was filmed live at my next appearance on the radio show. The exposure caused my popularity to soar in the Islands more than ever before. Bookings were coming in by record numbers.

Next, a producer from KGMB-TV asked me to do a local one-hour special for the station. I was scared and excited all at once. I couldn't believe the sequence of events that was occurring, but I knew that it was meant to be. My career was being launched and television would be my next medium.

My one-hour special would be called "YOUR FUTURE with Psychic Dayle Schear" and my co-host would be Michael Perry. Blythe and I learned all about television production from the personnel at KGMB. In turn, we wanted to teach the producers how a Psychic really works. Most importantly, I wanted to bring some credibility to the field.

"YOUR FUTURE" was a HUGE success. The people of Hawaii were more than ready for such a show and the ratings were extremely high. I asked the station's program director if he would like to produce more shows about ESP. He said he'd discuss it with Lee Enterprises, which owns KGMB, and get back to me. In the meantime, I decided to change the name of the show to "ESP & YOU." Not only was the name catchy, but it also already had a following on radio from my appearances with Dave Lancaster.

As it turned out, the station did not have the budget to sponsor more shows. I was extremely disappointed, but not discouraged. I asked how much it would cost to produce the show myself. When I heard the figures, I nearly died. The cost was well over $10,000 per show.

It didn't matter to me; I was determined to make myself a success and willing to take the risk. Sometimes in life if you don't take the risk you never will amount to anything. At least that was my motto. To quote Shirley MacLaine: "If you want to get to the fruit of the tree, you have to go out on the limb."

Besides, I loved the thrill of the uphill battle and took pride in accomplishing a number of "firsts" in my field. I was the first female Psychic to appear at Harrah's in Lake Tahoe. The first female

Psychic to appear on Reno. The first Psychic to have a TV show in Alaska, and so on.

I liked the idea of being an innovator of my time. I guess that's why I respected Shirley MacLaine. She definitely went "Out on the Limb." I realize now that my greatest fear as a child was being made fun of. Yet, I've clearly put myself into situations to be made fun of over and over again, all because I believe in ESP and metaphysical knowledge.

I've exposed myself to ridicule purposely to learn. Ironically, what I've learned the most is to have a THICK SKIN. On a more serious note, I learned that my purpose in life is to help people, no matter what the price.

Television gave me the opportunity to educate and enlighten the public. I wanted to let the world know that there was something else out there besides what they could see. I wanted people to open their minds and their hearts to ESP.

My television shows were extremely important to me. I wasn't only selling myself, I was selling a belief. It was a blessing in disguise that the TV station didn't have the funds to back me. It became up to me to put together my own TV show exactly the way I wanted it to be. I owned the show; I had full control, so I could do whatever I wanted to do.

Even though there wasn't much money left over, I always had enough to produce another show. "ESP & YOU" took off in the Islands like a bat out of hell; there was no stopping me now. The people wanted more and more. My only problem was I couldn't give the people as much as they wanted due to lack of funds.

In order to recoup some of the monies spent and to subsidize more shows, I worked at least eighteen hours a day helping people and put on a private show at the Ala Moana Hotel. All the effort paid off; "ESP & YOU" and Dayle Schear became as popular as good old apple pie.

On one of my TV shows, we opened the phone lines and Hawaiian Telephone Company tabulated 210,687 caller attempts into our show during a one-hour period. Our ratings were sky high, but Hawaiian Telephone was not pleased with me. I heard through the grapevine that we were very close to downing all of Waikiki's phone lines.

To this day I enjoy doing television in the Islands. I doubt I'll ever give up my TV show, "ESP & YOU." We try to produce at least two shows a year. My biggest dream is to go national with "ESP & YOU," live from the Islands of Hawaii. And also from Lake Tahoe.

Well, Blythe was right. The Perry and Price Show was my stepping stone to fame in the Islands. Television became second nature to me; I loved every minute of it. I'll never forget the response to one show that I produced. The number of calls logged by my answering service in the course of a week totaled 6,000. Unbelievable!

Peg, my secretary, went crazy handling all the messages. She would start at 8:00 in the morning and leave at 10:00 at night. The next day she'd ring me on the intercom and say, "I'm ready to work. Beam me up, Scotty."

Those were the days. I would lecture at local schools and even managed to put together an Outer Islands tour. More than anything else, I loved my work and I loved helping people.

Blythe was my magical lucky piece. Everything we did together turned out wonderful. There was never a mountain too high to conquer.

On one occasion Blythe booked me on an American Hawaii Cruise out of Honolulu. I was so excited. It would be my first appearance on a cruise ship. I was to perform two days only and the rest would be leisure sailing time with calls at each neighbor island and free meals. I hired Dave Lancaster to co-host my show and took plenty of Dramamine seasick pills with me. I was ready to give everyone a great performance.

I didn't realize that while I was aboard the ship my extra sensory perception increased tenfold. I guess the negative ions were at work. When a Psychic is surrounded by water, so the theory goes, ESP increases. The power within me became unmeasurable.

As I called people from the audience on stage with me, I began to see things about them I didn't want to see. I saw people having affairs and others hiding out. When the ship's captain asked for a reading, I told him that he was very disorganized and carried little pieces of paper in his left pants pocket. He was amazed and showed the audience the little pieces of paper on which he wrote notes.

I realized I wasn't the entertaining Psychic that everyone thought I would be. I couldn't help myself. As a consequence, my ship-board career ended when the cruise ended; I was never called back again. The ship's entertainment director told me that they were not prepared for a Psychic who was as accurate as I was; they would have preferred someone more light-hearted.

**FAME, FAME, FAME WAS MY LOT.** Everything Blythe and I touched seemed to turn to gold. Every day was a new adventure. Offers were coming in from all over the United States, most of which I turned down. I wanted to stay in the Islands; I loved Hawaii and her people.

I decided to take the big step of moving my two beautiful German Shepherds from Lake Tahoe to Oahu. Although it was heartbreaking to know they would have to be quarantined for four months, according to Hawaii's laws, I needed my dogs to be with me. Blythe and I planned a trip to Lake Tahoe to arrange for my dogs to come to the Islands.

When we arrived in Lake Tahoe, I happened to watch a television show called "A.M. San Francisco." For some strange reason I called the TV station to inquire about any opening slots for guests. Much to my surprise, a guest had cancelled, the show needed a replacement right away, and I was asked to appear on the show. Blythe and I drove down to the Bay Area and were put up at the posh Fairmont Hotel by the TV station.

I appeared on "A.M. San Francisco" and the viewers in the Bay Area loved me. We were another overnight success. I was asked to appear at least once a month for a year. I decided to delay my trip back to the Islands and pursue this turn in my career first.

Blythe and I moved to the Bay Area with the dogs. We found a cute little house in Pacifica with a huge backyard for the dogs. Eventually, however, I had to return to Hawaii; I had been away too long.

I asked my ex-husband Bob to watch my dogs while Blythe and I returned to the Islands. The house in Lake Tahoe was still on the market with no buyers in sight. If I were to bring the dogs home to Hawaii, I needed to buy a house there right away.

Blythe the real estate broker found the perfect house for me in

Hawaii Kai. There was one problem: I didn't have the down payment. I didn't know what to do, but miracles do happen. Within 24 hours Bob called with news of a buyer for our Lake Tahoe house; we were going into escrow. I now had the down payment for the house in Hawaii Kai and I was now able to bring my dogs from the Mainland to the Islands.

Blythe went back to the Mainland and transported our furniture from San Francisco and my dogs from Lake Tahoe to the Islands. Having my dogs with me was pure heaven. The dogs were treated wonderfully during their four-months-long quarantine. Quite frankly, it seemed I was the one in quarantine, not my dogs. I was able to get work permits for them to appear on my show and they were let out of the shelter periodically. I had it all: my house, my dogs, and Blythe at my side. I was becoming extremely famous in the Islands, to boot.

## PSYCHIC DETECTIVE WORK

Now I was to embark on something new. I was being called in on missing persons cases, not by the police but by the families involved. Since the Honolulu Police Department did not readily use Psychics in its investigations, the families themselves were asking me for help. When the police, perhaps because of their case overloads, were unable to supply answers, concerned families turned to me for the answers. I was getting case after case on the island. Some I could talk about, and others I couldn't.

### Roxanne Tandal Missing

**Roxanne Tandal** was missing for two weeks and the Honolulu Police Department had no clues whatsoever as to where she might be found. It was then the family came to see me. Blythe gave the family a specific time to meet me at my home and asked them to bring along Roxanne's unwashed clothing, pictures, and jewelry.

The next day the Tandals arrived at my home with maps of the Honolulu area. Time was of the essence now. If she were alive, we would try to find her. I sat at my dining room table and slowly placed all the pictures on the table. I always keep a pad and pencil right next to me in case I get impressions. I held onto a picture of Roxanne in one hand and her jewelry in the other. We opened up a map of the Honolulu area and placed her picture on it. I let the pencil guide me and information on how to locate the body was given spiritually.

**Transcript of the tape from the Tandal Case:**

ROXANNE TANDAL IS NOT ALIVE. SHE WAS MURDERED. ROXANNE KNEW WHO HER MURDERER WAS. THERE WAS A BRUTAL FIGHT AND ARGUMENT, LEADING HER TO BE HIT WITH AN OBJECT. SHE WAS THEN PROPPED UP IN A CAR, MADE TO LOOK LIKE SHE WAS STILL ALIVE, WHEN IN FACT SHE HAD BEEN MURDERED. ROXANNE WAS WRAPPED UP IN A BLANKET NOT TOO FAR FROM WHERE SHE LIVED. IT SEEMS TO ME I SEE A SHRIMP FARM NEARBY. THIS SEEMS TO BE A MARKER OF SOME SORT. I SEE AN OLD AIR STRIP NEAR-BY, ONE WHERE PLANES COULD LAND AT ONE TIME OR ANOTHER. KAHUKU AIRPORT, IF THERE IS SUCH A PLACE. SHE IS OFF A DIRT ROAD WRAPPED IN A BLANKET NO MORE THAN TEN FEET FROM THIS ROAD. IF YOU TAKE ALL THE MARKERS INTO CONSIDERATION, YOU SHOULD

BE ABLE TO FIND THE BODY.

I then proceeded to mark the untouched map and I gave explicit directions as to where the body would be found and in what position it would be lying. I then described the person with whom she was involved and described her murderer to the family, down to the color of the shirt he was wearing. I found out later how accurate I was. I asked the Tandal family to form a search party to cover the three-mile radius from the shrimp farm to where the Kahuku airport used to be. Her body would lie within this area, off a dirt road, on the left-hand side.

The very next day seventy people, family and friends, searched the area I had specified. They found Roxanne Tandal's body exactly where and how I stated it would be.

I don't know how this ability of mine works, but it surely is a gift. I just wanted her soul to rest in peace. Through my findings on this case, I believe that this was a love triangle. The murder was not done intentionally, only out of anger. However, within six months a man was arrested and charged with the murder of Roxannne Tandal.

The next day Perry and Price got wind of the story. It was blasted all over the radio and television. An interview took place through the Honolulu Star Bulletin; however, the story never ran. I heard several days later from the reporter covering the story that she had been told by her editor to kill it; it would never make print. When I asked why, I found out that someone from the Honolulu Police Department had spoken to the editor and simply said, **"I WOULDN'T PRINT THAT IF I WERE YOU."** Oh, well, the worth of a Psychic is not always credited.

Several months later the father of Roxanne Tandal approached me and said, "You're the one who found my daughter. I can't thank you enough." He had tears in his eyes.

## Diane Suzuki Missing

Then there was the case of **Diane Suzuki**, a pretty young dance instructor who was missing one afternoon in broad daylight. I was called in by a member of the family a few days after she was missing. My findings as a Psychic in this case were that Diane was no longer alive from Day One; she was murdered and buried somewhere on the island.

A picture in hand of Diane Suzuki led me to the dance studio where she had been seen last. I, in turn, found her jewel pendant with the initial D and a small diamond attached to it on the dance studio floor, even though the police had searched that area thoroughly for well over five hours that same afternoon.

Five years later I was asked to take a lie detector test by the Honolulu Police Department after new evidence in the case was presented. I more than passed the test.

If it hadn't been for Michael Perry and Larry Price of KSSK Radio, I would never have received one ounce of credit in the case. I thank them.

Due to the inconclusiveness of the case at this time, read all about Diane Suzuki and the conclusion, and about many other cases in my next book, **THE PSYCHIC WITHIN**.

**Fame, fame, fame was my lot. It was too much to handle at times. Time was marching on. My personal life was beginning to come together, and so was my business life. I had been officially divorced from Bob for several months. Blythe and I were looking forward to getting married soon.**

# MARRIAGE, MARRIAGE EVERYWHERE
## CHAPTER 27

Blythe and I spent five years building up my business in the Islands. He was born and raised in Hawaii and knew the market. With the dogs and Blythe by my side, I was happy. Everything was going the way it should in my life and we were beginning to settle down. My fame was well under control and I was producing at least two shows a year in the Islands, not counting reruns.

Blythe and I had known each other for well over six years before we decided to get married. We were quietly married on December 11, 1988, in a small wedding attended by our families and a few friends. We wanted it that way. Blythe and I planned to honeymoon on the Neighbor Islands, but we both came down with colds. We postponed our honeymoon until our first wedding anniversary came around.

I wanted to surprise Blythe for our honeymoon-anniversary. I thought it would be wonderful to tour all the Hawaiian Islands by cruise ship. I immediately called my travel agent in November to make the arrangements.

The cost was $1,100 for a five-day trip on the American Hawaii Cruise ship. The agent asked if I'd like to buy insurance for the trip, just in case it rained. I thought about it for a moment, then decided to get the insurance.

When I reached home, I was so excited. I explained to Blythe all about our trip on American Hawaii Cruise and that I even bought insurance just in case something unforeseen should happen.

Blythe looked me straight in the eye and said, "No matter what, Dayle, we're going on this trip. I think you should cancel the insurance." He knew I had pulled out of past trips unexpectedly. I debated the point, but Blythe was emphatic. I called the travel agency and asked them to cancel the $200 insurance; they put through the order.

Two days later when I picked up my tickets, I noticed that the insurance had not been canceled. I asked the agency again to cancel the insurance. However, my tickets still read that I was insured. They say three times is a charm. I said to Blythe, "The universe is trying to tell us something. I keep canceling the insurance for this trip and my tickets keep coming back insured. What should I do?".

Blythe told me to cancel it again. At this point I was quite hesitant, but I tried again and the insurance was finally canceled just before our trip. We started preparing for our wonderful cruise. Then it began to pour; a storm was approaching the Islands. I had a bad feeling about this one, but I packed my bags anyway. We had our friends come over to watch the dogs and off we went to the cruise ship.

We boarded the American Hawaii Cruise ship about 7 o'clock in the evening; the ship was due to sail at 10 p.m.. The rains were beginning to let up as we were shown to our cabins. I felt somewhat queasy. We unpacked our bags then we made our way to the ship's dining room for dinner.

During dinner I had this very strange feeling come over me. I wanted off the ship. I knew there was danger ahead. I picked at my food and checked my watch nervously. I never had to say a word to Blythe. I just looked in his direction and he knew what I was thinking.

**"Dayle, I'm not leaving this ship until I finish my $550 DINNER!"** He was quite firm about that.

I was panicking now. I had to get off the ship at all costs. I watched as Blythe devoured his $550 dinner. What a wonderful husband he is. How many husbands would listen to their CRAZY wives and go along with leaving a cruise ship?

We returned to our cabin and I started packing nervously. I then called the purser and explained that I was leaving the ship; I wanted to go home. The purser tried to change my mind, giving me every reason why I should stay on board the ship. When I realized I was getting absolutely nowhere, I decided to tell her the truth.

**"Look,"** I said, **"I'm a Noted psychic on the island and this ship is in danger. I really don't want to ride out 60-foot waves and be rained on for my honeymoon. So either you let me off this ship or I'll create a scene."**

The purser decided to let me off the ship. She promised us that she would call the higher-ups within the week and reschedule our trip for a later date. I was relieved. Blythe and I took a cab home and explained the situation to our surprised house sitter.

The next day it rained cats, dogs, and you-name-it; there was no let up in sight. I realized I had left my tape recorder in a drawer in our ship's cabin. I called the office of the American Hawaii Cruise and explained that I had forgotten my tape recorder on board. The fellow I was talking to sounded very agitated.

"Unfortunately, there's no way to contact the ship at this point," he said. "They're experiencing rough seas. As a matter of fact, they're unable to dock at the island of Kauai. You'll have to call us back at a later date." He slammed the phone down.

I relayed the message to Blythe. It continued to rain for at least five days. My prediction was right. I was extremely happy that I had decided to leave the ship.

Several days later I retrieved my tape recorder from The American Hawaii Cruise Ship office. I asked about the trip. I was told, confidentially, that I had made the right decision. It was one of the roughest sailings they had ever experienced. The waves hit well over 50 to 70 feet, and several people were hospitalized.

**AMERICAN HAWAII CRUISE NEVER MADE GOOD ON THEIR PROMISE TO GIVE US ANOTHER TRIP. THEY EVEN REFUSED TO GIVE US ONE OF THEIR EMPTY CABINS DURING THEIR OFF-SEASON. WE WERE OUTRAGED. OH, WELL, WHAT GOES AROUND COMES AROUND.**

Blythe and I eventually flew to the Big Island of Hawaii to visit the volcano and we ended up having a wonderful trip. Those were the days.

The next person to marry was Peg, my best friend and secretary. She married Moe and soon after moved to New York. Moe traveled the world and took Peg with him everywhere he went. Peg would come back to the Islands at least twice a year. I missed her terribly, but I was happy for her since I had predicted these events all along. I knew she would be happy with Moe and she would be well taken care of.

Life was moving on for Blythe and me. We had spent many wonderful years in the Islands. I realized, though, that I was beginning to get into somewhat of a rut. We were working so hard and putting in so many hours, we never had time to enjoy life anymore. Times were changing for the island people as well. The Japanese were beginning to swarm over the Islands; prices of houses were rising; the islanders were unable to live in their own land. I felt a great need to move on with my life.

# TIMES WERE CHANGING
## CHAPTER 28

Major changes were occurring in the Islands in 1989. The Japanese nationals were slowly buying up Honolulu and the rest of Hawaii. At first many locals were selling out to these rich buyers from Japan. Everyone wanted the good life, to make a huge killing in the real estate market. Slowly but steadily, the prices of homes were doubling and tripling. In the beginning everyone was happy. Wild stories circulated throughout the Islands.

One story tells it all. A couple were sunbathing on Waikiki beach. A Japanese gentleman walked up to them and asked if they knew of anyone who had a condo with an ocean view for sale in Waikiki. The couple said they had a condo with an ocean view but they weren't planning to sell it. The Japanese gentleman offered them $700,000 cash for the unit. Needless to say, they sold out. Wouldn't you?

For two years we heard similar stories, most of them true, about unbelievable offers for real estate. The residents of up-scale Kahala were the first to sell out. Other islanders followed suit; people were selling and moving to Las Vegas, Oregon, and Washington. You see, the problem we faced was that once we sold to the Japanese, there was very little left that we could afford to buy on the island. Prices of all the other houses had skyrocketed.

The mass exodus had begun. Thousands of local people were

now leaving the Islands. I counseled people for well over a year before I, myself, began to awaken. I felt their pain deep within my heart. Some people were homeless; others left the Islands; and those who stayed were taxed to death. The Japanese, on the other hand, were cleaning up with their golf courses and homes. They time-shared a lot of their properties to Japanese citizens.

The times were definitely changing. I needed a vacation, a change of pace. I was beginning to feel the burn-out. I asked Blythe if we could take a trip to Lake Tahoe in the near future. It had been five long years since I had been back. I wanted so desperately to see the snow once again. There is something about Lake Tahoe that always draws me back to her. The same warm feeling from years past was sweeping over me once again.

Something was happening to me, something I couldn't explain. I wanted to give everything up; I wanted to start over. I had this overwhelming desire to be left alone with my thoughts and to write a book.

My friends thought I was crazy. Give everything up that I worked so hard for? Richard Grimm, the general manager at KGMB, wanted to know why I wanted to be poor. "Give it up, Dayle," he said. "Do you have a screw loose or something?" But no matter how often people questioned my sanity, I knew I was being drawn away from the city once more.

I began watching movies such as "Baby Boom" with Diane Keaton. I could see in the movie how happy Diane Keaton's character was when she gave up everything and moved to the country. Tears began to roll down my cheeks. Something was definitely coming over me, and this time it was out of my control.

My desire to look at mountain cabins was beginning to engulf me once more. I had sent away for "The Tahoe Tribune," a small local town paper, and I was now scrutinizing the real estate listings in it. I circled the houses in the paper, carefully selecting the ones that would fit my budget. There it was, the house of my dreams!

**House for sale, $145,000. Mountian view, fireplace, 3 bedrooms, 2 full baths, 1300 SQ. feet, double car garage. Recently remodled. On one-half acre close to main road and ski area.**

This was it; I had a gut feeling about this one. I found out from my realtor in Lake tahoe that the house was approximately two blocks from where I once lived with Bob. I knew the area well. This would be perfect for my retirement, a perfect place to write my book in the future. Meanwhile, we'd have to rent it out in order to pay the mortgage. We made an offer on the house, sight unseen. It was accepted immediately. We were the proud owners of a mountain dream house. I was ecstatic; I couldn't wait to see it.

Blythe and I finally took our vacation to Lake Tahoe on May 29, 1991, to see what we had bought. I wasn't the least bit disappointed. I loved the house so much I didn't want to rent it out. Blythe insisted renting it would be the only way we could afford the payments.

I was having so much fun decorating the house and preparing it for renters, when I saw something outside that made me suddenly stop what I was doing. It was snowing! Snowing in Lake Tahoe in May? I couldn't believe it. I was mesmerized. As I stared out the window, watching the snow, with the fireplace going, my thoughts began to drift and race at an incredible speed.

**Years of fighting traffic, staring at cement cities. You**

**finally wake up one day and realize that life is passing you by.
Something inside of you begins to stir. It's time to make a move.
Give it all up; start over; see where the road will lead you.**

This voice inside of me grew louder as I watched the snow fall
in its silence.

**I FLASHED UPON HAWAII, FLASHED UPON ALL
THE READINGS I HAD GIVEN TO MY PEOPLE.**

Somehow I knew starting over wouldn't matter. I knew that I
needed the peace and serenity of the clear blue mountain land. The
time had come to shed all the craziness in my life and find out what
I was truly missing. It happens to all of us; one day you awake and
say: "What am I doing to myself? Why am I living in the city? There
must be a simpler way of doing things. I don't need all the toys
anymore; enough is enough."

Then the voice inside of me said, "The transformation is about
to begin."

Some people say it's not the place, it's the person within. I beg
to differ. Hawaii was truly the place in my life, but slowly over the
years a transformation took over. The cement got bigger; high rises
sprang up; the cost of living went skyward. My readings with the
people of the Islands were getting deeper. I wanted them to have a
better way of life. I was tired of hearing about the locals working
three jobs just to survive; tired of seeing adult children living with
their parents, unable to afford a home of their own.

In all my readings I encouraged my clients to move to a better
place. I said, "Go to an outer island. Go to Nevada, Oregon, or
Washington, where you'll finally be able to feed yourself and have
money in your pocket." I wanted them to be prosperous, not to

merely survive. Reading after reading, it was the same. There was a mass exodus out of the Islands.

I finally looked at myself and said, "You must live as you preach. It's time for you, Dayle, to move on. Times are changing." With that very limited thought I bounced right back into the center of my being. My thoughts returned to Lake Tahoe, and I was once again looking out the window at the falling snow.

I looked at Blythe and said, "I want to write my book. Can we find a way to move here for a while? I'll never give up Hawaii completely; I'll still do my shows and see my people. But I need that special place in my heart to come back to."

Blythe replied, "We'll try to find a way."

That one thought began to manifest itself into reality. The phone rang; it was my real estate broker Jim on the line. "Dayle, would you happen to be in the market for another house?"

I was floored by his question. "Another house!"

Jim explained, "You see, a house just came on the market. It's only two blocks away from where you just bought your house. It has everything you can imagine." I couldn't believe my ears. "Let me just show it to you."

I was game. Maybe the universe heard my prayer. When Jim drove us to the house, I was afraid to walk in. I knew this would definitely be the house of my dreams.

The house was 2,600 square feet on two acres, with a hot tub, fireplace, panoramic lake view and more. The most special feature of this house was that it had only one level. A one-level house in Lake Tahoe? This was a dream in itself.

I asked Jim the price. It was $300,000. There went my dream. It was out of the question; we couldn't afford a house like this. I told Jim I'd think about it.

I couldn't sleep that night. That house was everything I ever wanted. How was I going to purchase it? The other obstacle was the owner. He was hurting financially and needed to close escrow within three weeks. Great, another call for a miracle. But I kept believing that the house soon would be mine. I didn't know how; but if you believe, wonderful things can happen.

Blythe and I were headed back to the Islands. I took several pictures of the house and kept them in my purse. On our flight home, I drifted off once again. That little voice inside of me started to speak again.

**It's time to change, it's time to grow; you can feel the pains upon you. Part of you wants to go. Where does it hurt? You don't know. You are in the midst of change. You are in the midst of growth. But few understand the calling. Most turn their backs and keep on going. How many people out there have the guts to change? Most people go about their business and hope that their feelings will subside.**

**Then one day you'll awake and ask yourself: Where did my life go; how many days will it take for me to awake and see the true meaning of life?**

**In all my life I have had very few regrets. I've followed my inner feelings, taken the risk, taken the chance. I've rolled with the punches. The most important thing I've learned from life is to follow the spiritual signs and you'll always be on the right path.**

You'll always know deep within if you should stay or you should go. Whether it may be leaving someone or changing your job or moving, you'll always know deep inside of you. You may not want to listen, but you have had the answer all along. Open up your heart, open up your soul; the answer lies deep within you.

I awoke as the plane was landing in Honolulu. At that moment I made up my mind. I was going to sell our house, move to Lake Tahoe, and write my book, something I've always wanted to do. Blythe was happy that I finally made a decision. I didn't know how it would come about, but I was going to trust in the universe.

# MARION & STANLEY, THIS IS FOR YOU
## CHAPTER 29

We were back home in Hawaii, but all I could think about was Lake Tahoe. The more I thought, the more I began to manifest my dream. For nearly two weeks all I did was float around in my pool, looking at the picture I had taken of the house we wanted to buy in Lake Tahoe.

Everyone, including my husband, thought I was losing my mind again. I guess this was my way of figuring out how I could purchase my dream house. I truly believe that when I want something badly enough, I can make it happen. That explains why I was floating around the pool, conjuring up my dream. It seems simple enough to me, anyway.

My mind was certainly not on my work. I even began to manifest people coming to my home, and instead of me giving them readings, they were giving me readings. I was drawing Psychic people into my home. This always seems to happen when I'm troubled. Whenever I'm in need of help, someone always appears.

This time wasn't any different from the rest. A pleasant young lady, who introduced herself as B.J., came to see me for a reading. She happened to be a Channeler, **one who gives you information through a higher self or spirit.** After I gave her a thorough reading, she said, "By the way, I have some information for you, information you're not going to believe."

I said, "B.J., there's very little that I don't believe anymore. Go on, hit me with it." She did.

"Dayle, you are going to move to the Mainland in a few months," she said. "You will sell your house and write a book for the world to see. This will make you very famous."

I replied, "You must have been reading my mind. What you're doing is not channeling; it's called telepathy, reading the mind of a person." In spite of my doubts, I was amazed that she knew I would be moving.

"No, Dayle, you'll have to believe me. What I see will truly come to pass." She spoke with conviction.

I asked her how it will all come about. B.J. answered, "There will be a couple, a man and a woman, who will show a great interest in you. They will want to help your career. Make no mistake about it, they will come into your life." I wanted to believe what she was telling me; but I was just a little hesitant, for I had seen so many Psychics before who were more wrong than right.

As B.J. was leaving, she turned around and smiled. "Let me know when this happens. You'll hear news of this in two weeks."

Two weeks passed and I was still floating around my pool, trying to manifest this house that I wanted. Suddenly, I had the answer. I knew how I was going to get my house in Lake Tahoe. Excited, I jumped out of the pool and ran for the phone.

I called a friend of mine, Marion, who was not only a long-time client but also a very remarkable lady. She had a heart of gold and was always sticking her neck out to help others. "Hi, Marion, this is Dayle. I have a question to ask you. I want to sell my house in Hawaii Kai. Would you know if any one of your friends is in the market for buying a home?"

Marion was surprised at my question and had questions of her own. "Why do you want to sell your house and where are you going to live?"

I replied, "I have to get away from here. I want to write my book. I need some peace and quiet."

Marion felt badly about my leaving; several other friends were moving out of the area and she would miss some wonderful friendships. I explained my situation regarding the house and the owner's need to close within thirty days. I told her that if I didn't purchase the house within that time frame the price would increase by $30,000. Timing was a major factor.

Marion said she'd check with some of her friends and get back to me as soon as possible. About a week later she and her husband Stanley came to my house to discuss the matter with me. They asked me how much money I could come up with and I told them that all I had was a home equity loan. They had a great idea, a plan.

I never expected such a unique plan. Marion and Stan suggested we pool our money and co-own both my house in Hawaii Kai and the house in Lake Tahoe. I could pull some money from my home equity loan on the Hawaii Kai house and they would give me the rest of the money for a down payment on the house in Lake Tahoe. That way we could close escrow on time. I felt in my heart that this was a great idea. I was willing to risk it all and put my house on the line for the sake of writing this book, without knowing if I would fail or succeed.

Marion and Stanley were willing to help with no strings attached. The one promise I made to them was that I would write my book, and that promise had to be kept. That's all they wanted. This was too good to be true, but miracles certainly do happen. Because of them, my dream was about to materialize.

All the money was deposited into an account and dispersed in time; the house in Lake Tahoe was ours. I can't thank Marion and

Stan enough for being there when I needed help so desperately. Without them I don't know what I would have done. Without them this book would have just remained a dream.

How do you thank people for giving you a new life? The best way I can think of is to become successful, to justify their faith in you. Surely, words are not enough. I'm determined to live up to their standards. Hopefully, one day I'll be in the position to help others.

Marion and Stan are Dream Makers. They always remember when they were once poor how someone came along and believed in them and made their dreams come true. From that day on they decided to help others when they were in the position to do so. I hope to follow in their footsteps. I highly respect these people and truly know the goodness in their hearts. To give of oneself without expecting anything in return is truly a wonderful gift.

THANK YOU, MARION AND STANLEY,
FROM THE BOTTOM OF MY HEART.
THANK YOU FOR MAKING MY DREAM COME TRUE.
"DARE TO BE DIFFERENT"
IS DEDICATED IN PART TO THE BOTH OF YOU.

Well, B.J. the Channeler was right; I had my dream home in Lake Tahoe. Blythe and I decided to make a few changes in the house, so we took a quick trip back to the lake. We met with Bob Dore, our contractor, and gave him the responsibility of remodeling our house to make it perfect. Back in Hawaii, we planned our move to Lake Tahoe for October, 1991.

As I was packing my bags, I started flashing back. **I flashed back in time. I began thinking at a very rapid pace. I thought of all the people with whom I had been connected in the past**

**and of how my life had changed. I was no longer that person I used to be, the one having affairs and disrupting other people's lives. I was different, more spiritual and more caring. my life had surely changed.**

I thought of **Bob Schear,** the man I was married to for 21 years of my life. I thanked him for letting me go and giving me the space to grow. I forgave him for the affair he had with Toni Gold. I realized he was young and naive, and we both learned our lessons in life.

I thought of **Toni Gold** and felt sorry for her. I hoped that someday she would find the love she had been looking for all those years.

I thought of **Jerry Nisker.** I thanked him for introducing me to Bob and for losing the bet.

I thought of **Diane Ash.** What a wonderful friend she was to me. The love that I have for her even now will never dissipate. She gave so much to everyone but herself.

I thought of **Gerry Turner,** my very special love. Without him I would have never grown up. He was so special.

I thought of **Dana.** What wonderful times we had.

I thought of **Phil and Esther Simpson.** Those were the best years of my life. It's so wonderful to have true friendships.

I thought of **Toni York.** What a joy she was to have around. She brings life to everyone she touches.

I thought of **Gene Ashley,** my love. He taught me how to love myself. He taught me the Indian way, never to show how one really feels.

I thought of **Regis Connally.** What a wonderful, CRAZY guy. Without him my life would have been different.

I thought of **Annie Ashley.** I hoped she could find it in her heart to forgive me for all the hell I put her through. If the year were now, that never would have happened.

I thought of **Betty Inn-White** and thanked her, for she is now living one of my parallel lives.

I thought of my teacher, the great **Peter Hurkos, and Stephany and Gloria Hurkos.** Without his tender love and care, I would have been lost. He is still alive in spirit.

I thought of **Barbara** and all the fun times we had. She brings comedy into everyone's life that she touches. She has such a fine quality.

I thought of **Peg Wilson.** Such a great friend. Even today she teaches me how to love life.

I thought of my husband **Blythe Arakawa (YODA),** my teacher, my friend, the love of my life. Without him I would be nothing.

I thought of the **People of the Islands of Hawaii.** Without their Aloha Spirit I would have never changed and become the person I am now. I thank them.

I thought of **Lake Tahoe.** What fond memories she has given me. I hope they never end.

I thought of **Mom and Dad.** Without them I would have never been given this gift to help others.

I thought of **Marion and Stanley.** What could I say to them? They gave from the heart until there was nothing more to give.

**I thought of all the rest of the PLAYERS who contributed every little thing without realizing it. Every contribution enlightened me and helped me become a better person.**

**I began to snap back to reality as I was packing my last book to take to Lake Tahoe. My dream of ten years, to write my book, was now becoming a reality. I knew in my heart I would come back to the Islands many times, for Hawaii is where my roots are. This is where a part of me belongs. There will be many more shows to come in the Islands, and certainly many more books to write.**

# LAKE TAHOE,
# A WRITER'S DREAM
## CHAPTER 30

We finally made it to Lake Tahoe. Blythe, the dogs, and I. **I had given it ALL UP!** As I sat at my desk writing my book, I gazed out the window at the snow falling ever so gently. I realized this was my homecoming back to nature, back to the woods where my roots began. It is a place so special that time could stand still.

I used to wonder what drew me to the mountains; I wonder no more. I thank God that I have eyes to see the beauty that is before me, a beauty that is so unexplainable that I can only touch upon this with the words that I write.

As I awake upon the snow-covered hills so early in the morning, the mountains look ever-changing as the snow falls from the heavens. The sky has its patches of blue. The crisp coldness of the wind doesn't feel truly cold because, all at once, a new person begins to emerge. The child within, the child that lay dormant for so many years, begins to stir. That child wants to play again. My dogs run beside me, chasing and catching wanton snowballs. Snowmen fill themselves with laughter. Everyone around me suddenly looks five years old. This, my friends, is truly living.

I was back in the country. It was October 26, 1991. The ritual sounds were heard wildly across the mountains from the frosted tree tops to the flatlands of Carson and Reno: "Pray for snow, pray for snow." The radio stations were blasting their sounds with joy of the coming new season. Winter had arrived. Slowly, but surely, as you turned the radio dial, they were shouting their Indian war dance, pray for the Indian warrior to shed the beautiful white snow upon us to end the longest drought in the history of Lake Tahoe. And there it came, the trees were becoming flocked. The powder was falling steadily well into the night. The old-timers of Lake Tahoe had predicted this all along.

As I sit within my house nestled within the mountains, overlooking the beautiful pine trees, a foot of snow is on the ground. There is a slight gentle breeze blowing, a sure sign of more winter to come. No neighbors to fight with, two acres of our own. To my right is Lake Tahoe, almost 75 miles around and almost 1,600 feet deep. The panoramic view of the lake and mountains is breathtaking, overwhelming and peaceful. Now there are patches of blue in the sky and the air is clear, crisp and wonderful.

Tahoe is just as beautiful as it was in the 1970's. But this time it's different for me; I'm older and wiser. This time I won't make the mistakes I've made in the past. I can look at this land with love from the Indians and appreciate every breath I take.

I had made a 360-degree turn, right back to where all my fame had started. This time, though, it was different. This time I was writing about my life. The pain of being a writer. I embarked on this task thinking that somehow it would be so easy to do. I found out the hard way that it would take every ounce of my being to write the **HORROR** stories of my life. I thought many times that I would give up, but something inside of me kept saying.....

**"IT'S OKAY TO BARE YOUR SOUL, FOR AS YOU SHED YOUR IMAGE YOU WILL BE HELPING THOUSANDS OF OTHER PEOPLE."**

With that unlimited thought, I continued writing my book, **DARE TO BE DIFFERENT!** This book bares the truth of my soul and more. As I struggled to finish it, I thought I would never write another word again.

**Lake Tahoe, is truly a writer's dream.**
**This Time It's Forever!**

## THE END
Or maybe it's just the beginning?

LOOK FOR MY NEXT BOOK
# THE PSYCHIC WITHIN
IN THE FUTURE!

# Ordering Information

# Psychic Dayle Schear

## BOOKS

**Dare To Be Different** (Soft cover) ................$18.95

**Dare To Be Different** (Hard cover)) .............$24.95

**The Psychic Within**   Soon to be released
(Read all about missing people, psychic detective work
and how ESP works.)

## VIDEO

**Tarot Video** (For Beginners) ........................$24.95
(Includes Tarot Book)
**Tarot Book** ....................................................$6.00
(A simple step-by-step guide to reading the Tarot cards)

Shipping & Handling........................................$3.50
     (Plus $2 for each additional item)

Check, money order, Visa & Master card accepted.

Phone Orders Call **1-800-538-8209, 1-702-588-5108**

# TO ORDER

Name _____

Address _____

City_____State _____ Zip _____

Phone  (____) _____

Visa/ Master Card # _____ Exp date _____

☐  Please add me on your **Mailing List**

☐  Please call me for the new release of **The Psychic Within**

| | QTY | $Amount |
|---|---|---|
| **Dare To Be Different** (Soft Cover)  $18.95 | | |
| **Dare To Be Different** (Hard Cover)  $24.95 | | |
| **Tarot Video** (For Beginners)  $24.95 | | |
| **Tarot Book**  $ 6.00 | | |
| | | |
| | | |
| Shipping And Handling | | $3.50 |
| Plus $2 For Each Additional Item | | |
| Plus Tax From Your State | | |
| **TOTAL** | | |

Allow 2-3 weeks for delivery

Mail order to:  **ESP & ME, INC.**
**P. O. BOX 172**
**ZEPHYR COVE, NEVADA 89448**

Phone Orders Call **1-800-538-8209, 1-702-588-5108**